SAGE was founded in 1965 by Sara Miller McCune to support the dissemination of usable knowledge by publishing innovative and high-quality research and teaching content. Today, we publish over 900 journals, including those of more than 400 learned societies, more than 800 new books per year, and a growing range of library products including archives, data, case studies, reports, and video. SAGE remains majority-owned by our founder, and after Sara's lifetime will become owned by a charitable trust that secures our continued independence.

Los Angeles | London | New Delhi | Singapore | Washington DC | Melbourne

INTERNATIONALIZATION
OF HIGHER EDUCATION
IN INDIA

INTERNATIONALIZATION OF HIGHER EDUCATION IN INDIA

VIDYA RAJIV YERAVDEKAR
GAURI TIWARI

SAGE

Los Angeles | London | New Delhi
Singapore | Washington DC | Melbourne

First published in 2017 by

SAGE Publications India Pvt Ltd
B1/I-1 Mohan Cooperative Industrial Area
Mathura Road, New Delhi 110 044, India
www.sagepub.in

SAGE Publications Inc
2455 Teller Road
Thousand Oaks, California 91320, USA

SAGE Publications Ltd
1 Oliver's Yard, 55 City Road
London EC1Y 1SP, United Kingdom

SAGE Publications Asia-Pacific Pte Ltd
3 Church Street
#10-04 Samsung Hub
Singapore 049483

Published by Vivek Mehra for SAGE Publications India Pvt Ltd, typeset in 10.5/13 pt Times New Roman by Fidus Design Pvt. Ltd Sector 31-D Chandigarh and printed at Chaman Enterprises, New Delhi.

Library of Congress Cataloging-in-Publication Data Available

ISBN: 978-93-860-4216-3 (HB)

The SAGE Team: Shambhu Sahu, Neha Sharma, Kumar Indra Mishra and Ritu Chopra

To my father Dr S. B. Mujumdar,
Founder and President, Symbiosis, and
Chancellor of Symbiosis International University,
for having dedicated his life to foreign students
who come to India to pursue higher education

— **Vidya Rajiv Yeravdekar**

Bulk Sales

SAGE India offers special discounts
for purchase of books in bulk.
We also make available special imprints
and excerpts from our books on demand.

For orders and enquiries, write to us at

Marketing Department
SAGE Publications India Pvt Ltd
B1/I-1, Mohan Cooperative Industrial Area
Mathura Road, Post Bag 7
New Delhi 110044, India

E-mail us at **marketing@sagepub.in**

Get to know more about SAGE

Be invited to SAGE events, get on our mailing list.
Write today to **marketing@sagepub.in**

This book is also available as an e-book.

Contents

List of Tables

List of Figures

List of Abbreviations

AB	Accreditation Board
ACDPAE	Australian Committee for Directors and Principals in Advanced Education
AHELO	Assessment of Higher Education Learning Outcomes
AICTE	All India Council for Technical Education
AIIMS	All India Institute of Medical Sciences
AISHE	All India Survey on Higher Education
AIU	Association of Indian Universities
ANQAHE	Arab Network for Quality Assurance in Higher Education
APEX	Accelerated Programme for Excellence
APQN	Asia-Pacific Quality Network
ARWU	Academic Ranking of World Universities
AUSAPI	Association of US Academic Programs in India
AVCC	Australian Vice Chancellor's Committee
BCI	Bar Council of India
BRICK	Brazil, Russia, India, China, Korea
CABE	Central Advisory Board of Education
CBHE	Cross Border Higher Education
CCH	Central Council of Homeopathy
CCIM	Central Council for Indian Medicine
CIE	Consortium for International Education
CIPHE	Centre for International Partnerships in Higher Education
COL	Commonwealth of Learning

COPIE	Committee for the Promotion of Indian Education Abroad
CSIR	Council of Scientific and Industrial Research
CSR	Corporate Social Responsibility
CTE	CASE Trust for Education
CU	Central Universities
DAAD	Deutscher Akademischer Austauschdienst
DBT	Department of Biotechnology
DCI	Dental Council of India
DEA	Department of Economic Affairs
DIAC	Dubai International Academic City
DIPP	Department of Industrial Policy and Promotion
DIT	Department of Information Technology
DKV	Dubai Knowledge Village
DST	Department of Science & Technology
ECR	Education Commission Report
EDB	Singapore Economic Development Board
EHEA	European Higher Education Area
ENQA	European Association for Quality Assurance in Higher Education
EQAR	European Quality Assurance Register
EQUIS	European Quality Improvement System
ERP	Education Commission Report
ESOS	Education Services for Overseas Students
FDI	Foreign Direct Investment
FICCI	Federation of Indian Chamber of Commerce and Industry
GATS	General Agreement on Trade in Services
GER	Gross Enrollment Ratio
GIQAC	Global Initiative for Quality Assurance Capacity
GNI	Gross National Income
HEI	Higher Education Institutions
IaH	Internationalization at home
IAPP	International Academic Partnership Program
IAU	International Association of Universities
IAVU	Indo-Africa Virtual University

ICAR	Indian Council for Agricultural Research
ICCR	Indian Council for Cultural Relations
ICRISAT	International Crops Research Institute of the Semi-Arid Tropics
ICSEE	International Committee for the Study of Educational Exchange
ICSSR	Indian Council for Social Science Research
IEC	International Education Cell
IEQA	Institutional Eligibility for Quality Assessment
IFEZ	Incheon Free Economic Zone
IGNOU	Indira Gandhi National Open University
IIE	Institute of International Education
IIEP	International Institute for Educational Planning
IIM	Indian Institute of Management
IISc	Indian Institute of Science
IISER	Indian Institute of Science Education and Research
IIT	Indian Institute of Technology
INC	Indian Nursing Council
INQAAHE	International Network for Quality Assurance Agencies in Higher Education
ISCED	International Standard Classification of Education
ITEC	Indian Technical and Economic Cooperation
IUB	InterUniversity Board
IUCEE	Indo-US Collaboration for Engineering Education
IUSSTF	Indo-US Science and Technology Forum
KAEC	King Abdullah Economic City
KMS	Knowledge Management System
KLEC	Kuala Lumpur Education City
LERU	League of European Research Universities
MCI	Medical Council of India
MDG	Millennium Development Goals
MEA	Ministry of External Affairs
MHRD	Ministry of Human Resource and Development

MIT	Massachusetts Institute of Technology
MIT OCW	MIT OpenCourseWare
MOHE	Ministry of Higher Education
MOOC	Massive Open Online Course
NAAC	National Assessment and Accreditation Council
NAFSA	National Association for Foreign Study Affairs
NASSCOM	National Association of Software and Services Companies
NBA	National Board of Accreditation
NCHER	National Council for Higher Education and Research
NCTE	National Council for Teacher Education
NEP	New Education Policy
NET	National Eligibility Test
NIEPA	National Institute for Educational Planning and Administration
NIRF	National Institutional Ranking Framework
NKC	National Knowledge Commission
NPE	National Policy on Education
NPTEL	National Programme on Technology Enhanced Learning
NUEPA	National University for Educational Planning and Administration
OBHE	Observatory on Borderless Higher Education
OCI	Overseas Citizenship of India
ODA	Official Development Assistance
OECD	Organisation for Economic Co-operation and Development
OER	Open Education Resources
OSKI	Obama–Singh Knowledge Initiative
PCI	Pharmacy Council of India
PIHEAD	Promotion of Indian Higher Education Abroad
PIO	Persons of Indian Origin
PPP	Public–Private Partnerships
PTR	Pupil–Teacher Ratio
QS	Quacquarelli Symonds

RIACES	RedIberoamericana para el Aseguramiento de la Calidad en la Educaión Superior (Red Iberoamerican Network for Quality Assessment and Assurancein Higher Education)
RMSA	Rashtriya Madhyamik Shiksha Abhiyan
RUSA	Rashtriya Uchchatar Shiksha Abhiyan
SAARC	South Asian Association for Regional Cooperation
SAP	Study Abroad Programs
SAR	South Asian Region
SCDL	Symbiosis Centre for Distance Learning
SCIE	Symbiosis Center for International Education
SIP	Study India Program
SIU	Symbiosis International University
SNPE	Statement on the National Policy on Education
SSA	Sarva Shiksha Abhiyan
STEM	Science, Technology, Engineering, and Medicine
SUNY	State University of New York
SWAYAM	Study Webs of Active-learning for Young Aspiring Minds
THES	Times Higher Education
TPRM	Trade Policy Review Mechanism
UGC	University Grants Commission
UIS	UNESCO Institute of Statistics
UKCOSA	United Kingdom Council for Overseas Student Affairs
UKEIRI	UK–India Education and Research Initiative
UMIOR	University Mobility in the Indian Ocean Region
UNDP	United Nations Development Program
UNESCO	United Nations Educational, Scientific and Cultural Organization
UNESCO-CEPES	Centre Européen pour l'Enseignement Supérieur

USIEF	United States–India Educational Foundation
USIHEC	US–India Higher Education Cooperation
VASAT	Virtual Academy for the Semi-Arid Tropics
WCU	World Class Universities
WTO	World Trade Organization
WUN	Worldwide Universities Network

Foreword

The higher education landscape and its international dimensions are changing as a result of economic, political, social/cultural, and academic developments. *Internationalization of Higher Education in India*, by Vidya Rajiv Yeravdekar and Gauri Tiwari, is a timely book as it positions India in this changing landscape, a country and its higher education sector little known for its internationalization, and in search of finding its own place and approach in this process.

We can argue that universities have always been global in that they have always had some form of international dimension, either in the concept of universal knowledge or in the movement of students and scholars. However, the international dimension of higher education has changed dramatically over the centuries into the forms, dimensions, and approaches that we see today. These range from the mobility of and competition for students, teachers, and scholars, research cooperation, knowledge transfer and capacity building, export of academic systems and cultures, internationalization of the curriculum and learning outcomes, cross-border delivery of programs, projects and institutions, and virtual mobility and collaborative online international learning.

From the second half of the 1990s onward, there has been a gradual but increasingly visible shift from political to economic rationales for internationalization, even though there is a continued rhetoric around the need to better understand different cultures and their languages. International student recruitment, employability of graduates for the global labor market, attracting global talent for the knowledge economy, cross-border delivery of education, and capacity building have become important pillars of the internationalization of higher education over the past decade. The emergence of national and global for-profit higher education conglomerates, franchise operations, articulation programs, branch campuses, and educational hubs, and more recently, virtual learning and massive online open courses (MOOCs) are clear expressions of this development.

Internationalization is driven by a dynamic and constantly evolving combination of political, economic, socio-cultural, and academic rationales that will take on different forms and dimensions both in the different regions and countries and in the institutions and their programs. There is not one universally applicable model. Regional and national differences are varied and constantly evolving, and the same is true within the institutions themselves (public/private, research/applied sciences, comprehensive/specialized, etc.).

However, as the international dimension of higher education gains more attention and recognition, people tend to use it in the way that best suits their purpose and this has led to many myths and misconceptions concerning internationalization of higher education. Indeed, it is important to highlight the fundamental point that internationalization is not an end in itself but a means to enhance the quality of teaching, research, and the service role of higher education in the society.

Understanding and Enacting Internationalization

The most commonly accepted definition of internationalization is "the process of integrating an international, intercultural, or global dimension into the purpose, functions or delivery of postsecondary education."[1] However, there is also increasing acknowledgment of the complexity of the concept and its relationship to globalization and regionalization, and the role of higher education in these two processes. Internationalization has become a broad umbrella term that covers many dimensions, components, approaches, and activities. It includes credit and degree mobility for students, academic exchange and the search for global talent, curriculum development and learning outcomes, and franchise operations and branch campuses, for both cooperation and competition.

In the broad definition of what internationalization is, or should be, there are two key components in the internationalization policies and programs of higher education that are constantly evolving and becoming increasingly intertwined.[2] One is *internationalization abroad*, understood as all forms of education across borders: mobility of people, projects, programs, and providers. The other is *internationalization at home*, which is more curriculum-oriented and focuses on activities that develop international or global understanding and intercultural skills. However, internationalization abroad can also be curriculum related and develop international or global understanding and intercultural skills, so there are limits to such a distinction.

We know more about internationalization abroad than about internationalization at home. The authors of this book correctly point to the need to place more attention into the later. Internationalization is unfortunately perceived mainly as mobility of students, of academics, of programs, and of universities. But one has to be aware that the very large majority of students and academics will not be mobile, at least, not as part of their study or academic career. An exclusive focus on the mobility would imply an elitist approach to internationalization as it serves only the small groups which are willing and be able to be mobile. The authors of this book correctly point that, when they state in their introduction, "internationalization does not have to be an elitist proposition. It can be for all of us who partake in the higher education process."

This focus on all students and academics is reflected in the current approach to the internationalization, for instance, in a study for the European Parliament on *Internationalization of Higher Education*,[3] which I had the pleasure and honor to lead. The drive to internationalize is a key preoccupation in higher education today as a means to face the competitive pressures of the new environment. Nevertheless, what and how to internationalize, which balance of activities and approaches to use, and which stakeholders to involve are questions that institutions often struggle to answer. What is apparent, however, is that an ad hoc approach to internationalization will not produce an appropriate response.

In general, we still witness much rhetoric around internationalization of higher education that does not always match reality on the ground. Competitive pressures of globalization may have led to a greater convergence of aspirations, but this has not always led to a translation into actions. In an attempt to shift the focus towards a concept of internationalization that could have wider reach and create greater impact, the European Parliament study, based on a Delphi Panel exercise, set out to revise Jane Knight's generally accepted definition in a way that it could guide and inspire higher education institutions (HEIs) in their efforts for internationalization. The exercise came up with the following revised definition with additions or alterations highlighted in bold. Internationalization of higher education is "the **intentional** process of integrating an international, intercultural or global dimension into the purpose, functions **and** delivery of post-secondary education, in order to enhance the quality of education and research for all students and staff, and to make a meaningful contribution to society."

The revised definition seeks to make three key points:

1. It indicates that the process is a planned and purposeful one, which creates a framework for future direction and is designed to strengthen and enhance HEI performance and quality. An intentional process is one of consideration, decision, and action.

2. It reflects increased awareness that internationalization of higher education needs to be more inclusive and less elitist and that the "abroad" component as an integral part of an internationalized curriculum for all students. It also includes staff since Internationalization of higher education is critically dependent on active engagement and wholehearted commitment of all HEI members who, through their various academic and management functions, will be at "the coalface of delivery."

3. It re-emphasizes that Internationalization of higher education is not a goal in itself, but a means to enhance quality within and beyond the institution and for that reason, it should not focus solely on economic rationales.

It is in this emerging landscape of internationalization of higher education, broader, more diverse, and more challenging, that the relevance of the book *Internationalization of Higher Education in India* has to be placed. As Elspeth Jones and I have stated,

In the current global-knowledge society, the concept of internationalization of higher education has itself become globalized, demanding further consideration of its impact on policy and practice as more countries and types of institution around the world engage in the process. Internationalization should no longer be considered in terms of a westernized, largely Anglo-Saxon, and predominantly English-speaking paradigm.[4]

India is a key political and economic player, and its higher education sector is in a process of modernization and internationalization as the authors well describe. This book not only provides insight on the process of internationalization in higher education for its national audience, but also is an important contribution to the understanding of higher education in India and its internationalization efforts for an international audience.

Dr Hans de Wit

Professor and Director, Centre for International Higher Education, Lynch School of Education, Boston College

Founding member and past president, European Association for International Education (EAIE)

Founding Editor, *Journal of Studies in International Education* (SAGE)

Notes

1. Knight, J. (2008). *Higher education in turmoil: The changing world of internationalization.* Rotterdam: Sense Publishers.
2. Knight, *Higher education in turmoil.*
3. De Wit, H., Hunter, F., Egron-Polak, E., & Howard, L. (Eds). (2015). *Internationalisation of higher education. A study for the European Parliament.* Brussels: European Parliament, Directorate-General for Internal Policies Policy Department B: Structural And Cohesion Policies
4. Jones, E., & de Wit, H. (2012). Globalization of internationalization: Thematic and regional reflections on a traditional concept. AUDEM: *The International Journal of Higher Education and Democracy, 3*(3), 35–54.

Preface

It is my pleasure to present this book to you. In it are culminated my insights on the subject of internationalization, especially as it pertains to Indian higher education. It is a great privilege of mine to have been associated with the Indian higher education system for the better part of my life. This engagement has been both, close and multifarious. It has brought me an understanding of the system from the viewpoints of practically all stakeholders. I hope to have distilled into this book some of my observations and experiences.

Few institutions in India would be so naïve as to dismiss internationalization in the present times. Internationalization is a catchphrase found everywhere in the higher education and labor market circles. It is frequently touted as an institutional mission by higher education institutions and as an indispensable element in career-preparedness skills. Why then has it not earned the status of a sub-specialty in higher education studies or found place in policy deliberations at the national and supra-institutional levels? Perhaps a key reason for this is that, although internationalization of higher education in India is but the projection of a global phenomenon on a smaller backdrop, the recent forward leaps have occurred predominantly in private institutions in a fashion that is unchanneled, self-generative, and disengaged with the public policy on higher education.

I think we, the educationists, must address the subject more pointedly. It is about time that we move past relegating the discussions to round table conferences that do little more than spout platitudes. Much of what comes out as findings and recommendations is the elaboration of shopworn laments that outline the many ways in which the higher education system in the country is bogged down and that it is a situation that we would have had improved. Although internationalization features frequently as one of the areas that is addressed in the public policy on higher education, it is not placed "front and center" but comes across as an afterthought. More commonly is seen the absence of debates that outline concrete issues such as less-than-satisfactory numbers of inbound international students, lack of directives to regulate international joint programs, missing directories that catalog academic exchanges in institutions, and no government-backed incentives to attract top-ranking foreign institutions to speak of. For a higher education system the size of the Indian system, it is regrettable that such core issues remain a fogbound corner. This shortfall has continued to imperil not just the higher education system in India, but the country's footing on the wider grounds of human resource capabilities.

I believe that research must be the wellspring of policies, directives, and action at all levels—legislative, executive, and institutional. It is just not possible to arrive at concrete problems and their solutions in the absence of information from close afield. We have a track record of fruitless conferences and ensuing statements to prove that policy-making that does not take into account how internationalization operates at the level of the base of the pyramid will not go the distance. Although internationalization of higher education is increasingly becoming a highly dynamic variable, it does not find voice in many government areas with which it is intertwined, such as the Ministry of External Affairs, the Ministry of Overseas Indian Affairs, the Ministry of Commerce, and the Ministry of Human Resource Development. It is for this reason that the few times when it does make presence in reports, it is only as an aside, for example, the Five Year Plan recommendations in the past and the National Knowledge Commission report. The problem is further compounded by the case that the University Grants Commission has not been channeled to work complementarily with the Association of Indian Universities to monitor international student mobility and other related phenomena; inconsistencies are frequently found in the number of inbound international students and the number of undertakings within the category of international academic exchanges. The lack of ground work possessed of ample academic caliber is certainly one of the root causes of why we have not moved much further from square one. Nevertheless, in a reversal of trend, the present Prime Minister Mr Narendra Modi has undertaken trailblazing initiatives to put India on the global map. Internationalization of higher education must be seen in this larger context.

Using this book as a medium, I hope to establish a dialog with all those who have an investment in higher education and those who see internationalization as a way forward.

The subject of internationalization of higher education, in particular, holds a great deal of significance for me. I was born into the academic life. My father Dr S. B. Mujumdar, a professor of botany, is first and foremost an academic and my mother, a postgraduate in zoology, standing by his side, is a committed member of the higher education community. Together, they have established an organization called Symbiosis for the welfare of international students coming to study in Pune.

To me, the higher education circle has always been an extended family—I can't think of it otherwise. It must have been the fact of my being from Pune that I was drawn to the subject of internationalization. Pune, as is common knowledge, is at the forefront of internationalization—the most prominent evidence of which is that it has traditionally been the city to draw the most international students. These students, coming mostly from African and Asian countries, were my window onto the world of international education. I grew up relating to them as peers and playmates, not as foreign faces. It is through the lens of this close and abiding relationship with international students that I first came to see internationalization of higher education.

It was my inspired choice to settle on higher education as my lasting vocation after my specialization in medicine and several years of rewarding practice in the field in India and abroad. Although higher education leadership and management account for most of my time at work, internationalization, as specialism, is my preferred area of academic research and advocacy. It is the subject of my doctoral dissertation and many academic and journalistic efforts. I hope to continue to make attempts to bring this area to the fore of academic discourse as well as policy deliberations. It is my firm belief that internationalization of higher education is the way to bring the Indian higher education system from periphery to the center, cast India as knowledge economy, scale the global value chain, and prepare global citizens.

I hope that you will find the book an informative and insightful source of knowledge on the subject of internationalization of the Indian higher education system. If the book succeeds in kindling in you an inspiration to join in the cause of internationalization, then I would have done all that I had set out to accomplish.

Vidya Rajiv Yeravdekar
Pune, April 2016

Acknowledgments

Although this book has taken form over the last several years, the inspiration had come much earlier—as early as several decades ago, when I joined in the world of higher education. Much of the substance has emerged out of my personal and professional association with the Indian higher education system.

The subject of internationalization of higher education is one that holds special significance to me on several levels. An inspiration always has to have a context. In my case, the motivation comes from my ties to the city of Pune. Pune, the "Oxford of the East," is home to me. It is also my good fortune to have been born into the academic life. My father Dr S. B. Mujumdar is an academic and an educationist. My mother Mrs Sanjeevani Mujumdar, a never-failing source of motivation to the family, is also an active member of Pune's higher education community. Symbiosis is the emblem of my parents' commitment to the cause of internationalization of higher education. I was sensitized to the challenges faced by the international student community in Pune as a young person, who grew up taking in the presence of students from neighboring countries right in my household.

Thus, I express my deepest gratitude to the city of Pune and to my parents for instilling in me sensitivity to the importance of internationalization as part of the ethos of global citizenship—*Vasudhaiva Kutumbakam*.

The natural progression from then on would be the organization of Symbiosis and all its members. Symbiosis is an institution in its own right, renowned for inspiriting the Indian higher education system to champion the causes of the welfare of international students and international collaborations in higher education. My engagement with Symbiosis has given me a unique vantage point from which to acquire close understanding of the challenges, the competition, and the rewards that come with internationalization. There is something to be said for the knowledge that comes with being "on the field" day in and day out. Symbiosis has given me the opportunity to *practise* internationalization at the organizational level.

My gratitude is also due to the Indian Government and all the affiliated bodies that have allowed me insight into the Indian higher education system. It is my privilege, indeed, that I have been a member of the Central Advisory Board of Education, the University Grants Commission, and the Indian Council of Cultural Relations among other Government of India bodies related to higher education. I have had the most wonderful opportunities to bring my insights into the charting of public policy and steering the course of higher education in the country.

I would like to acknowledge the role of my research associate Gauri Tiwari, who has been a valuable resource to me, especially in her assistance with the language side of things. I have to thank her for ensuring correctness of grammar and style in the text as well as for bringing eloquence to prose.

Last but not the least, I thank the editorial team at SAGE. It has been a pleasure associating with the SAGE team. I am grateful to Mr Shambhu Sahu, in particular, who has extended utmost positive regard and support since I began working on the book.

Vidya Rajiv Yeravdekar

With the greatest admiration and regard, I thank Dr Vidya Rajiv Yeravdekar for being my academic mentor. Dr Yeravdekar has been my singular source of encouragement in many endeavors academic and professional. She is further thanked for being my role model for women empowerment and for leadership in international education. I am grateful to Mr Shambhu Sahu for his unwavering support and guidance through the publication process.

Gauri Tiwari

Introduction

The present is an opportune time to bring internationalization from the back quarters to the center stage. Although many initiatives on higher education have addressed internationalization in the past, it was almost always done as an addendum.

It is a welcome development that the momentum has gathered force. The New Education Policy, the plan for which is being discussed in advance of final decisions being taken, includes internationalization as an item of priority. It is my privilege, indeed, to have been invited to contribute to the deliberations, and I hope that when the Policy is presented to the nation, it will not disappoint those, such as me, who consider internationalization to be the driver of India's development across all realms, not just higher education.

Initiatives must be armed with some authority to exert corrective enforcement. Absent this, they are likely to be limited to educative reviews that take stock of the situation and propose counteractive recommendations. The initiatives related to internationalization, as happens often with those related to other agenda items in higher education, are conceptualized and gestated without the authority that would hold under scrutiny findings and counsels with the view to effectively influence government bodies and hold them to account as they implement policies.

There is much to be desired in the initiatives on internationalization in India, many of which are referred to in the book. These working groups sit atop a slow-moving circuitry, which consists of consultative experts in higher education. Often, these members function in committees as both reviewers and reviewees, combining, as they do, the roles of arbitrator and solicitor in the same organizational persona.

The outcome includes reports that detail findings and recommendations along the lines of "soft law" methods—recommendations, guidelines, and directions to set up more advisory committees. As if these were not enough, the squeeze on funds and the shirking of private participants seal a bleak prognosis.

The inquiries are usually framed against the backdrop of one or more of the terms of reference that include low inbound international student mobility, student exchanges, scholarships for international students, and developing "world-class" infrastructure.

Although challenges related to these issues persist, there are many secondary concerns within the umbrella term of internationalization that have assumed significance but do not figure in the course of such inquiries: poor convertibility of discipline-specific knowledge into career preparedness skills, inability to produce sufficiently large workforce that is globally competent, lack of interdisciplinary approach to learning, the paradox of large number of unemployable graduates, institutional non-presence in global rankings, abysmally low output of research in international publications, lack of institutional benchmarking pointers at the national level, and, above all, modernization of curriculum—the core of the teaching–learning process.

If one were to review the reports, one would find that the term internationalization is used to denote student mobility and its attendant issues—a reductionist approach, which equates internationalization with student mobility. This view has fallen from favour in the developed world and some countries that are not yet there, such as China.

To liken student mobility with internationalization would be to make the latter concept extraneous to the Indian higher education system, merely a "nice to have" advantage.

It began with the concept of internationalization itself. Cross-border student mobility has been shorthand for internationalization in North America and Europe since the period immediately following the Second World War, the era of the advent of the United Nations. Student mobility, promoted by the Erasmus program in Europe and Study Abroad programs in the United States, has been the hallmark of internationalization for the longest time indeed.

Student mobility, to state the obvious, requires heavy capital investment at the end of the institutions unless there is access to generous scholarship programs, such as those administered by the Erasmus program. Then again, such scholarship programs, small in number, can only be for a miniscule segment of the student population—the best and the brightest. Thus, either way we look at it, student mobility promotes selectiveness and elitism, going against the ethos of egalitarianism in higher education or in the lexicon of higher education studies—massification.

That student mobility drove the burden of internationalization single-handedly is not surprising given the era in which it was incepted—one when technology in communication was not developed sufficiently to allow for the exchange of information without the physical movement of the participant.

Further, this was the era when international education, as was the case with international relations, operated on the guiding idea that international entities are divided along a line that separated "us" from "them." The enrollment of the overwhelming majority of colonial India's internationally outbound student population in British universities and, later, in the Cold War era, the unproportionally large number of academic exchanges between India and the erstwhile USSR are cases in point.

Thus, we note that internationalization has evolved substantively over the last several decades and, consequently, there needs to be a change in how we apply internationalization on the field—classrooms, campuses, and government think-tank chambers.

I think an important point that I make in the book and one that may be of value to educationists in India is that internationalization does not have to be an elitist proposition. It can be for all of us who partake in the higher education process. As opposed to how it has been presented in the reports on Five Year Plans and those on the "World-class Universities" project by the Ministry of Human Resource Development, internationalization can be of benefit to the entire populace that makes up the higher education cohort.

Many BRICK countries (Brazil, Russia, India, China, and Korea) have employed internationalization in their higher education systems to move up the global value chain. As a section in the book details,

China has achieved some degree of success in doing this; Brazil is another instance. An important point here is that these countries are not in the Anglophone world; indeed, they have managed to optimize internationalization without the use of the English language, the *lingua franca* of international education.

I hope to drive home the point that internationalization can be practiced without massive investments, and that there are countless ways in which to do this. As much as we can identify one with the other, the two are not tied together.

Nor is internationalization only for those on the "pinnacle of excellence" at the IITs (Indian Institute of Technology) and the IIMs (Indian Institute of Management), to use Altbach's oft-quoted expression. We, the educationists in India, must make commitment to uphold the ideal of massification of higher education—to make international education accessible to those on the base of the pyramid.

The first chapter of this book gives an introduction to some salient characteristics of the Indian higher education system. The chronological evolution of the system is an important aspect because the historical roots have shaped the system to a very large extent. It explains many similarities of the system in India to those in countries that were formerly colonized by the British. To be sure, there are important lessons to be learnt from the successes and failures that mark the systems in these countries.

The London model of affiliation, a remnant of the British system of higher education, has continued without any revision as a hallmark of the Indian system. An operational framework which worked well to meet the unique requirements of the colonists' rule and suited the structure of institutions in the country, is now an impediment and squarely accounts for many systemic failures, such as the poor performance of state universities.

Herein lies the importance of studying the governance and the regulatory structure of the system, including the framework of quality assurance management. Internationalization of higher education takes place in an operational framework which is unyielding and slow to change. This structure, encumbered with obdurate bureaucratic institutions and processes, is criticized by researchers as being outdated and unresponsive to modern advances in higher education.

It is the regulatory structures indeed that accounts for the lack of initiative and dynamism. In the specific case of internationalization, the regulatory structure obstructs progress in more ways than one: keeping out of private participants from decision-making processes, legislative backlogs, uncoordinated partnering between regulatory bodies, and undifferentiated apportionment of funds are some issues that have been discussed in the book.

The last reference to differentiation alludes to a concern that is possibly the most important of them all. Efforts in the service of internationalization can only deliver results in a system that is differentiated well, both vertically and horizontally.

In other words, efforts towards internationalization yield the best results in a system that is stratified along the lines of differentiating properties that categorize institutions based on their selective orientation, that is, research, professional–vocational training, teaching institutions, and so on. Another pathway to systemic differentiation would be the one based on performance: to selectively invest in those institutions that are predetermined as "elitist" (as in their intake). As discussed elsewhere, the Chinese system preferentially invests in research universities that work towards generating internationally competitive research output.

Further, institutions that can be expected to generate positive outcomes related to internationalization are those that practice stratification based on selective areas of expertise and focus. An instance of this would be purposely individuating centers and divisions within the organization along the lines of strength in a particular area.

As important as the matter is, differentiation is neither practiced as a functional strategy and nor does it feature in critiques on Indian higher education. Internationalization is yet another instance where models are copied from high-performing institutions in the United States and the United Kingdom without factoring in the consideration that the Indian system is as yet undifferentiated.

The imitation of this referential model, in the absence of stratification, is neither achievable and, more importantly, nor advantageous to us in India. In a developing country, the higher education system must serve, above all, the developmental goals. Higher education is a key instrument of nation building and, in a country such as India, the goal of internationalization must work with and not against the immediate socio-economic realities. The Indian Government's goal of "access, equity, and excellence" reflects accurately the gaps that afflict the system.

An important argument that is raised repeatedly in the book is that only such internationalization will serve as the one that helps the Indian system to move in the direction of massification and differentiation. The internationalization model practiced in "world-class universities" targets a university system that is geared towards high post-graduate enrollment, benefits from extravagant endorsements and government funding, and, most importantly, operates in an *ecosystem* that is conducive to internationalization through extra-institutional supportive factors.

After an introduction to the salient characteristics of the system, the text moves to the second chapter, which goes over the theoretical descriptions of internationalization and globalization. The chapter includes discussions on elements and benchmarking pointers of successful internationalization. An important yet frequently overlooked aspect of internationalization is the economics approach; the second chapter covers this.

The third chapter overviews the dynamics of cross-border student mobility in the international student market. The chapter details the author's fresh perspectives on levels that denote the distinctive patterns in the evolution of cross-border higher education the world over. The chronological turn of events follows events and ideologies that lie beyond the scope of higher education studies—the two most important ones being political patronage and colonial legacy. The factors that influence cross-border student mobility in the present times are those that could collectively be called "market principles."

Cross-border mobility comes with some perils that pose an even greater obstacle to developing countries such as India—countries that have traditionally been "sending" countries. It is important to ascertain that international education does not become a guise under which countries of the "North" propagate socio-economic imperialism. The absence of international bodies that might oversee regulations and guidelines to steer collaborations is a continuing deficit—one that leaves much room for double-dealing and trickery.

What could be even more treacherous is the "Trojan Horse" [institutions] (Altbach, 2008), to borrow Altbach's expression. This is a grave concern indeed, and one that Indian educationists must heed. There are scores of institutions in the United States, the United Kingdom, and Australia that are actively scouting potentially profitable territories in Asian countries, the country possibly on the top of the list is India. It is important to identify possible threats to national self-determination and long-term developmental goals.

Then there are challenges related to the lack of "world-class" talent and infrastructure at our end in India and the resulting lack of enthusiasm at the end of "world-class" institutions in partnering with Indian institutions. Thus, there are concerns on both sides of the weighbridge, but either way we look at it, the balance of observational evidence indicates cautious judgment in identifying and forging partnerships with foreign institutions.

The fact of the matter is that cross-border higher education is an article of trade and investment across the globe, and, based on the recent reports from the Institution of International Education (IIE), it is one that generates millions of dollars for the traditionally strong "host" countries. Market-driven considerations bring some positive strains into international education too. For instance, the diversification of quality assurance management in higher education and the urgency that the concept of quality assurance has assumed institutionally and nationally follow-on from the commoditization of international education. This explains why quality assurance plays out so differently now than how it did in the past. The trends in the favor of self-evaluation (by means of benchmarking against institutional goals), evaluation against peer-performance (for example, to have the institution compete in global academic rankings), and "student satisfaction" are demonstrative examples.

Branch campuses and education hubs have captured the imagination of educationists the world over. This is another area that confirms the hypothesis that the lack of practice and precedence necessitates that much more caution. This was a wave that swept over the Middle East and South-East Asia precipitously, only to bring the sobering reality of shutdowns later. A section of the chapter delves deeply into this dynamics and presents a note of forewarning and recommendations on the matter to Indian educationists.

The fourth chapter presents an overview of regulatory stipulations in respect of internationalization, including a brief mention of legislative and extra-legislative reformative action related to internationalization. The working groups have shown minimal success and, as has been discussed previously, there are predictable reasons that explain why outcomes are so limited. The chapter also goes into the common regulatory loopholes that allow institutions, both Indian and foreign, to "slip through the cracks."

An important aspect of the regulatory structure is its "obstructionist" stance in respect to private participants. This, along with the success of private institutions in internationalization, presents an interesting paradox: it speaks to the dynamism and resourcefulness of private institutions in the face of the burden of having to generate funds and complying with stringent regulatory guidelines.

The chapter also presents a brief overview of the opportunities that might be of particular interest to foreign providers.

The fifth chapter presents internationalization of higher education in India in a relational context. It does so by examining India's performance in relation to other countries. The chapter utilizes three frameworks for this evaluation: global rankings, the concept of "world-class" universities, and the comparative performance of India and neighboring countries with regard to internationalization. The discussions suggest that India must develop its own ethos of excellence in internationalization. It would be unwise to borrow properties from the developing world and apply them to the Indian landscape in higher education. The burdensome reality of a long colonial past and the present challenges that come with being a developing country cannot be dismissed in favor of the competitive spirit. Cross-border higher education is not a level playing field; rather, it is a zero-sum game—one's gain is another's loss. The matrices that pass for indicators of internationalization are, more often than not, those that befit the concept of elitist universities in the United States and the United Kingdom. At the heart of the inequality is the difference in funding, including funding from external sources as well as exorbitant tuition fees.

The flip side of the competition would be India's performance with those countries that share common variables—geographic location, colonial history, and developing country status. The chapter presents an overview of the performance of some of India's neighbors in respect of internationalization. Regulatory framework emerges to be the weak link in the chain. There are important lessons to be learnt, and the chapter touches upon some of them.

The sixth chapter is all about global student mobility patterns and some salient characteristics of inbound and outbound student mobility in India. The skewed ratio between inbound and outbound mobility is startling, indeed. There is much to be desired in the manner in which the regulatory bodies promote mobility. To begin with, we, in India, do not have a definitive description of who an international student is. At times, we follow the UNESCO definition and, at other times, the one set out by the IIE. Muddying the waters even more is the question pertaining to distance education students or those enrolled in "off-campus" programs.

In the spirit of egalitarianism and, in keeping with modernization (or diversification) of providers, it is suggested that we widen the horizons and not make too much of the length of the program and whether it is "on-campus" or not. Student mobility is not the only marker of cross-border higher education. Student mobility is projected to growingly share space with modes that are not quite so "bricks and mortar," to include unconventional modes such as Massive Open Online Courses (MOOC). It is to be hoped that as policies on internationalization become streamlined, the data on international students will better represent the actual presentation.

In addition to the skewed ratio between inbound and outbound students in India, there are other disproportionalities as well. International students in India come from a few identifiable sources in terms of geography, aspects related to ethnocultural origins, the level of the program of enrollment, and sponsorships. Thus, this group is not as diverse as one might hope for it to be.

International students are not distributed regionally in a homogenous fashion in India either. It is demonstrated that international students in India are drawn to just a handful of cities and institutions.

It is suggested that the Indian Government initiate strategies to increase the catchment area of international students and develop more regional hubs in the country.

The chapter discusses some popular vehicles of academic mobility within cross-border higher education in India, such as Study India Program. It also goes over the emerging pathways in distance education.

The seventh chapter discusses the concept of national "soft power" in relation to the internationalization of higher education. It applies the concept, as explained by Joseph Nye, to the Indian landscape, especially in light of the country's contributions to cross-border student mobility in the neighborhood.

Central to the discussion is the argument that higher education systems in Asian and African developing countries suffer from systemic lapses. India's contribution to capacity-building through higher education, especially in neighboring countries, greatly influences India's soft power. An important point to bear in mind is that such a contribution can prove to be more valuable than financial aid, which is the traditional mode of bilateral assistance. Higher education enhances the human resource base, which is self-generative and sets into motion a chain reaction of a range of developmental cycles that are replenishable. This is why capacity-building of the human capital base through higher education is encouraged by the United Nations as the preferred delivery method of international aid exchanges.

India has contributed to international education from the ancient times, and the recent initiatives by the Indian Government in this regard are indeed a throwback to the time when India enjoyed a headship role in much of Asia and Africa. The chapter mentions some such initiatives—one of them being the Pan African E-network Project, a shining example of the Indian Government's initiatives related to "South-South cooperation."

The last chapter presents concrete and specific recommendations to improve inbound student mobility in India. These recommendations are divided into those that are institutional and others that are policy-oriented.

The chapter concludes the discussion by identifying and tying together strains in the book that are particularly important to the subject.

Reference

Altbach, P. (2008, July 15). Beware of the Trojan horse. *The Hindu*. Retrieved from http://www.hindu.com/2008/07/15/stories/2008071555180800.htm

1

The Indian Higher Education System

Introduction

Higher education or tertiary education refers to learning that takes place at the postsecondary level. The Indian higher education system has been an object of much deliberation in the last few decades. The discussions are generally underpinned by three distinct strains of thought; above all, the significance of the Indian higher education system in view of a large number of comprising institutions as well as the mass of populace that it covers. Further, the role of higher education in meeting the developmental needs of the country and the impact of globalization on the Indian higher education system are also important thematic considerations.

The higher education system has gained unprecedented focus over the last few decades in the backdrop of India's emergence on the global economic scene. The Indian higher education system is the third largest in the world. In spite of this, the gross enrollment ratio (GER) has remained low. In 2014–15, GER was only 23.6 and total enrollment was 33.3 million (calculated for those in the 18–23 years of age group; AISHE, 2015, p. i).

The modernization of Indian higher education, in the sense of espousing drift towards internationalization and other global advances in pedagogy, can be traced to the earlier half of the 1990s—the era that heralded economic liberalization. A cursory survey of the maturing of higher education system reveals that the idea of the knowledge economy has gained increasing thrust and it has, in turn, propelled higher education to the fore. The Planning Commission, through its Five Year Plans, and the Ministry of Human Resource Development (MHRD) have made rousing proclamations to better the systemic challenges that beset the system. These afflictions are, as a matter of fact, symptomatic of problems that are entrenched even deeper. The sheer mass and diversity of the population , regional disparities, and insufficient resources amount to unrelenting problems that are, at least, as pressing as the ones related to higher education. A core concern in the discussion is the utter inadequacy of public expenditure on education in general and higher education in particular.

It is also remarkable that deliberative research on the subject of higher education is not nearly enough and the scantiness of data comes across as an obtrusive insufficiency. It would not be an overstatement to maintain that factual information and evaluative synthesis thereof must form the wellspring of policy on higher education. The strategy must stem from the ground up in order to ensure that it does not fail those it is meant to serve.

Indian Government's pronouncements about its aim of recasting the country as "knowledge economy" and making a mark on the global economic scene rest heavily on enhancing human capital by expanding the skill base. The "new growth theory," which is central to any reference to the "knowledge economy" construct, highlights the contribution of knowledge in driving economic growth. Thus, technology, research and development, education, and training are not merely catch phrases but the very pivots on which economies swivel. This line of reasoning no longer allows education to continue in the background as an instrument of the larger "public good," but drives it to the fore as an item of high priority. Higher education has long been an area of forsaking in the country, and it is about time policymakers worked out an effective reformative action.

The "knowledge economy" construct is an outcrop of globalization, and, in the particular context of higher education, the construct is intertwined with internationalization. Internationalization of higher education, in the present times, refers to the concept within the context of the exigencies in higher education that result from globalization—"massification," "tertiarization," and "privatization."

Thus, this reference stands in contrast to the idea of internationalization, as it was taken to mean, let us say, 50 years ago. The context of globalization makes internationalization of higher education an imperative, not a matter of discretion. It is widely believed that higher education systems across the world will continue to grow interconnected and increasingly become "sum of parts." It also implies, in the language of internationalization, that cross-border higher education will be a zero-sum game—one man's gain being another's loss. The competition is estimated to expand in terms of the scale—it will continue to become consolidated and level up from national to supranational to international. This interconnectedness, for its part, will necessitate that higher education be methodized and the instruments of benchmarking and comparative information be standardized.

Is the Indian higher education system prepared to meet the challenges that the above-mentioned competition entails?

The system is encumbered with countless issues that go with the facts of a long history of colonization, of belonging to a developing country, and of having to serve the needs of one of the largest higher education cohorts.

On the upside, India has to its credit the reputation of being the first country in the world to practice internationalization of higher education. Ancient Indians, people who greatly valued the generation and dissemination of education, pioneered the idea of internationalization of higher education. The ancient universities at Nalanda and Taxila are shining examples of the value that Indians placed on higher education and its internationalization. More importantly, to them, this value system was not driven by the profits that abound in the "global student marketplace" but by the ideal of *vasudhaiva kutumbakam*—the world is one family.

In India, internationalization is characterized by some peculiar features in the present times—a massive imbalance between inbound and outbound international students, disproportionally large intake of international students from neighboring countries, regional and institutional pockets of inbound international students, and the headship role of private participants in driving internationalization forward.

As will be discussed in the following paragraphs, internation-alization of the Indian higher education system, as it has evolved in the past few decades, has been an osmotic phenomenon. It has followed on from certain inherent forces, not from deliberate public policy. Furthermore, the inflow of inbound international students, such as it is, is best seen as the result of the aggregate of contributions of a handful of institutions, most of which are privately managed. Of importance is the consideration that these institutions are not recipients of incentives, financial or otherwise, from the Indian government, but are driven by institutional dynamism and initiative. Apart from these self-generative institutions, there is not much to write home about.

Some initiatives have been carried out in the recent past by the Government of India agencies, and these projects have yielded satisfactory outcomes—the Pan-African e-network project is one such example. Yet, these efforts are not nearly enough. For one, many public organizations that should come together and work com-plementarily do not do so. The workings of Association of Indian Universities (AIU), University Grants Commission (UGC), Ministry of Human Resource and Development (MHRD), and Ministry of External Affairs (MEA)—the apex organizations—are not opti-mally collaborative and channeled. An illustrative instance is the variance in the number of inbound international students, which, among other things, is a result of the lack of a unanimous definition of international student.

The Indian Government must rise to the occasion. International-ization is not merely a platitude to be spouted in public pronounce-ments. It is the lever of "knowledge economy." If it hopes to optimize human resource capabilities and scale the global value chain, the Indian Government has no choice but to bring internationalization of higher education into the heart of public policy.

Evolution of Higher Education in India

The Indian subcontinent boasts a truly magnificent cultural heritage. The extensive documented history proves that the history of higher education goes as far back as 5 BC in Taxila (Greek rendering). The university in Nalanda in 5 AD was also a monumental milestone. At its zenith, the university attracted scholars and students from as far away as Tibet, China, Greece, and Persia. It is also notable that it is one of the first residential universities. The tradition of higher education was modeled after the traditions of Hindu *gurukuls* (residential schools in South Asia. Before Independence, they were the primary educational institutions. The tradition of *gurukuls* was followed by Hindus, Buddhists, Jains, and Sikhs) and Buddhist *viharas* (Sanskrit and Pali term for a Buddhist monastery). The medieval period in the country's history is not particularly remarkable, except that the Islamic scholarship tradition of madrassa was introduced. The period of British colonial rule in India was marked by a higher education policy that was expressly expedient and politic. It is scarcely a surprise that the curriculum was based on the British model and the medium of instruction was English. The first amongst such colleges was set up in 1818 near Calcutta. By 1857, two more central universities were set up in Bombay and Madras, and a total of 27 colleges were affiliated to them. By the time India gained Independence in 1947, a total of 19 universities had been established. During this time, the weight of colonialism loomed heavy on the higher education system. It was manifestly deserted and decoupled with the socio-economic landscape of the country. In tandem, the economy was predominantly agrarian and the industrial sector was limited to the areas that were directly linked to natural resources such as mining. The period that immediately followed Independence was marked by a number of working groups to examine the state of higher education in the country. Of these, the University Education Commission in 1948–49 stands out as the most noteworthy. The group was chaired by Dr S. Radhakrishnan, and its report is widely considered to be the foremost in terms of comprehensiveness, insight, and vision.

A landmark finding of the report was that even at that time secondary education in the country was worryingly malfunctioning and that the manner in which it complemented university education was flawed. The vast majority of its recommendations were related to the expansion of the university system and ways in which it could be better adjoined to secondary education. It was counseled that school education add up to 12 years and include intermediate education also. This was to be followed by three years of post-secondary education. In order to propel higher education into the national agenda, the report proposed that education be placed in the concurrent list. Also remarkable is the Commission's advocacy of regional languages as the media of instruction. Whereas, the report of the Commission was extensively deliberated, not very many of its recommendations were implemented. Of those that were put into effect, the setting up of UGC is very significant. Guided by the British model of its namesake, the central government established UGC in 1956. The Commission was set up primarily for the coordination, determination, and monitoring of standards and quality of teaching, examination as well as research. It is also responsible for disbursal of grants to higher education institutions. UGC enjoys nationwide jurisdiction. It exercises direct control over universities established through Acts of Parliament and state legislatures, and deemed universities. The Commission's control over affiliating colleges comes about as a result of its authority over universities.

The Government of India, alerted to the disquieting condition of secondary education by the Commission of 1948–49, appointed an investigative group headed by Dr Mudaliar in 1952 to examine the concern. The group recommended numerous reforms, and some of those were incorporated in successive Five Year Plans. The Government's policy on higher education was characterized by Nehru's socialist leanings, coming perhaps from the sway of the erstwhile Soviet Union. The guiding idea herein was to promote industrialization through central planning; thus, the state invested heavily in higher education in techno-engineering. The rewards of this investment did not come right away as it took years for institutions such as IIT to build capacity and generate the expected outcome of highly specialized workforce. Nonetheless, the seeds were sowed, and the significance of specialized technical training was driven home.

The establishment of the first IIT in 1950 in Kharagpur, West Bengal, through a special Act, by all accounts, is a monumental achievement. The IITs stand out as zenith of distinction the world over; their inimitableness lies in that they stand in defiance of all the usual challenges that plague the Indian higher education system (see Altbach & Salmi, 2011). The IITs are a true gift to the Indian

---

Box 1.1. The IITs: "Pinnacles of Excellence in a Sea of Mediocrity"

The IITs prove that purposeful public policy in higher education can achieve the most amazing feats. The IITs are widely considered to be more selective than most US Ivy League schools. In 2005, The Times Higher Education Supplement ranked the IITs as globally third best engineering school after Massachusetts Institute of Technology (MIT) and the University of California, Berkeley.

These institutions speak to the forethought and ingeniousness of their planners. It is particularly noteworthy that at a time when internationalization of higher education was hardly the catch phrase it is today, the IITs were established through far-reaching collaboration with foreign governments and institutions and international organizations. The first IIT, modeled after MIT, was established in 1951 in Kharagpur, West Bengal, with support from UNESCO. The second IIT was established in Mumbai in 1958 with the assistance of erstwhile Soviet Union and UNESCO. The third IIT was set up in 1959 in Chennai with a support from Germany. The IIT Kanpur was established next, assisted by a consortium of US universities. Afterwards, the IIT Delhi, aided by the British Government, was established in 1961.

Source: Altbach as cited in Pathak and Kanwar (2012) and Salmi (2009)

higher education system as illustrated in Box 1.1. The IITs are also remarkable for their indisputable international standing—they are internationally competitive and fashioned with inspiration and assistance from international universities. The IIM, set up a decade later, followed the IITs' tradition of academic excellence, and both boast a steadfast tradition of international repute.

This period was a scene of prolific activity and initiatives on many other counts, including the formulation of the Scientific Policy Resolution in 1958 and the setting up of notable agencies such as All India Council of Secondary Education, the National Institute of Basic Education, the National Council for the Education of Women, the National Council of Educational Research and Training, and the National Institute for Educational Planning and Administration (NIEPA).

In order to address the concern that the rapid expansion of higher education system was not accompanied by improvement in the overall quality of education, the government established the Education Commission in 1964 headed by Professor D. S. Kothari. The Education Commission Report (ECR) is frequently compared with the outcome of the Radhakrishnan Committee in respect of the range and profundity of its survey of the system. In emphasizing the pressing need for qualitative improvement, the Commission reported that higher education in the country was not brought into line with national development. To remedy this, it was suggested that institutional expansion be regulated by planning at the state and local levels.

The ECR, as with the Radhakrishnan Committee report, succeeded in rousing policy debates and deliberations across the country and continues to be regarded as a formative reference on the subject of the Indian higher education system. In furtherance of the recommendations of the report, a Parliamentary Committee was instituted in 1967 to review the findings and recommendations of the ECR. The outcomes of the ECR and the Parliamentary Committee of 1967 accounted for the Statement on the National Policy on Education (SNPE) in 1968. The SNPE delivered an extensive set of recommendations, which was received only half-heartedly by the Government.

The 1970s saw the initiation of privately managed higher education institutions in India. The case that public higher education system fell short in meeting the needs of the populace is counted as the key trigger that set off privatization of higher education in India. The Government, steered by its policy of welfare and positive affirmation, provided financial assistance to a large number of private institutions or grant-in-aid institutions, as they came to be called. Once the trend picked up, there was no looking back—by 1980 there were 132 universities and 4,738 such colleges, accounting for a third of all colleges in the country.

The 1970s and 1980s stand out as eras of socio-democratic policy, which translated into the Government taking upon itself a protectionist stance. There was not much to write home about on the higher education front. Unlike the preceding era, higher education was not an area of high priority, and public investments were not as impressive as in the Nehruvian period. In this, India did not align itself with the Asian Tigers—the stronger economies to the east of India—which took deliberate steps to integrate with the West. The tendency of being insular ran parallel in the higher education realm too. Whereas countries like Brazil, Japan, the UK, and the US moved away from the traditional mold of curriculum in favor of technical and professional education earlier on, India rose to the possibilities much later. It is also commonly maintained that the decade of the 1980s marked the beginning of a long drawn out period of the Government's disinclination with higher education—diminishing funds and increasing private participation are possible explanations for this development.

In chronicling the maturation of higher education in the country, the "42nd Amendment to the Constitution" in 1976 is an important milestone. Up until then, education was the responsibility of the states, whereas the Center was given the function of coordination and determination of standards as per Entry 66 of the Union List of the Constitution of India. Through Entry 25 in the Concurrent list of the Constitution of India in 1976, the Center was also given the responsibility, along with the states, for all levels of education. Whereas the role of the state remained largely unchanged, the Center assumed greater responsibility of policy-making and disbursement of funds related to education. A decade later, the National Policy on Education (1986) was revisited and a subsequent committee headed by Acharya Ramamurthy was constituted to review the Policy in 1990. The Policy was extensively critiqued across the country, and after much deliberation, it was endorsed with some modifications in 1992. Possibly, the most important contribution of the policy was in emphasizing the role of higher education in strengthening the skill base of the manpower. The policy also asserted that higher education be utilized as an instrument of socio-economic transformation and equal opportunities. This was also a period that saw the precipitous expansion of private institutions and the accompanying concern that supervision of regulations and quality assurance were becoming increasingly unmanageable. It was in this backdrop that the National Assessment and Accreditation Council (NAAC) and the National Board of Accreditation (NBA) were set up in 1994.

The founding of the National Knowledge Commission (NKC) in 2005 emerges as a true leap forward in modernization of higher education in the country. The Commission functioned by way of an advisory body to the Prime Minister of India on higher education and related issues. The Commission was driven by the overarching goal of transforming India into a knowledge economy. It is widely lauded for its prolific output of reports and recommendations during a brief term of three and a half years. It is also significant that a number of its proposals were put into effect or are being implemented at both the central and state levels.

The Higher Education and Research Committee (the committee to advise on renovation and rejuvenation of higher education in India) headed by Professor Yashpal was constituted by the central government of India in 2009 to evaluate the higher education system and suggest reformative action. The Yashpal Committee Report, as it is popularly called, is considered quite radical in its approach for revamping the higher education system. The recommendations that emerged from the Report counseled in the favor of abolishing UGC and several other statutory bodies in order to fuse them into an overarching entity called National Council for Higher Education and Research (NCHER). The Indian Government received these recommendations favorably and drafted the NCHER Bill, which is yet to see the light of day. It is noteworthy that recommendations from the Committee report were utilized to frame the Higher Education and Research Bill in 2011 by the MHRD. Similarly, the Foreign Educational Institution (Regulation of Entry and Operation) Bill 2010 was passed in the Cabinet but remains stalled in the Parliament. It relates to regulations that govern the entry and operations of foreign educational institutions in India. The New Education Policy, the plan for which is being discussed in 2015–16, marks a welcome development and it is notable that the initial consultative discussions place internationalization at the center of the deliberations.

In reflecting on the developments in the Indian higher education system over the last decade, it emerges that the single most prominent strain is the bourgeoning of multiplicity of education modes and providers. Among the more prominent ones are distance education (correspondence and online), self-financing programs in public institutions, foreign providers and collaborators, and the non-university sector. At present, widespread discussions suggest that in forecasting the future, it would be safe to surmise that MOOCs will have the most definite impact on higher education in the country.

Governance and Regulatory Framework

Higher education in India, as complicated as it is, works itself out at a number of levels and through many channels. The federal structure of the Indian Government and the country's long colonial past are instrumental in casting its organizational structure. True to the spirit of India's centralized cooperative federalism, the higher education system is a shared responsibility of both central and state governments with the balance of power, especially financial power, tilted in favor of the Center.

The Center manages the higher education system through a complex interplay of the MHRD, UGC, and coordinating councils. The MHRD also collaborates with the Planning Commission in framing policies and disbursement of funds. The determination of guidelines that govern higher education institutions is the constitutional obligation of the central government, as is the coordination of public policies across the board. The UGC is, in actuality, the Center's conduit for exercising its policies and fund allocation. The fact that UGC is armed with some autonomy keeps the Center from abusing its power over purse strings to interfere excessively and also from taking decision with vested party-political motives. The UGC is unarguably the Center's chief funding agency; save for nearly 42 technical institutions, which are funded directly by the central government, all others are funded through UGC. The central government is also responsible for declaring educational institutions as "deemed-to-be university" on the recommendations of UGC.

State governments along with professional councils, state councils, and affiliating universities are the chief partakers in higher education at the state level. States are responsible for the establishment of state universities and colleges, and provision of planned grants for development and non-planned grants for the maintenance of universities and colleges. The functioning of the machinery that mans higher education at the state level has been an object of widespread criticism. Whereas the Center has a distinctly defined apparatus comprising of the UGC at the helm followed by professional councils and other statutory bodies, the state functions through departments and directorates related to education, which are often bureaucratic and lack the self-determination to bring about change.

The interface between the state and the Center is a matter of great importance since much depends on the communication of ideas and information between the two entities. The inclusion of education on the concurrent list has been contributory in the evening out of cross-interaction at the twin levels. The concurrent status of education has gone a long way in establishing Center's hegemony in matters of the public policy. A number of bodies help coordinate policies and processes from the top down. Of these, the Central Advisory Board of Education (CABE) and UGC are at the very helm of affairs.

The CABE is primarily a high-level advisory body. It reviews educational policies and their outcomes at the central and state levels, and makes recommendations to the government on reformative action. Similarly, UGC, also an apex national body, is responsible for determination and maintenance of standards in teaching, examination, and research. It is also entrusted with the very important task of allocation of grants. The UGC commands national jurisdiction over the entire range of institutions—central and state universities, deemed universities, and so on. It works in coordination with statutory councils such as the All India Council of Technical Education (AICTE) for the coordination and planning of educational policies. The statutory professional councils function at the central and state levels and are responsible for recognition of courses, promotion of professional institutions, and provision of grants to undergraduate programs and various awards. The 13 professional councils at the national level include the following:

- All India Council of Technical Education (AICTE)
- Medical Council of India (MCI)
- Indian Council for Agricultural Research (ICAR)
- National Council for Teacher Education (NCTE)
- Dental Council of India (DCI)
- Pharmacy Council of India (PCI)
- Indian Nursing Council (INC)
- Bar Council of India (BCI)
- Central Council of Homeopathy (CCH)
- Central Council for Indian Medicine (CCIM)
- Council of Architecture

- Distance Education Council
- Rehabilitation Council

The statutory councils can be categorized into two groups. First, those that enjoys both funding and regulatory powers relating to education, such as AICTE and NCTE. The other group includes councils with regulatory powers relating to education arising mainly from the need to maintain minimum standards in respective professions, such as BCI and PCI.

The regulatory framework that guides quality assurance comprises of three bodies: NAAC set up by UGC in 1994 to accredit institutions of higher education, NBA established by AICTE in 1994 to accredit programs in engineering and related areas, and the Accreditation Board (AB) established by ICAR in 1996 that accredits agriculture institutions (see Figure 1.1).

It emerges that the regulatory framework that oversees the higher education system is complex indeed. The countless numbers of organizations and the varying levels at which they function often

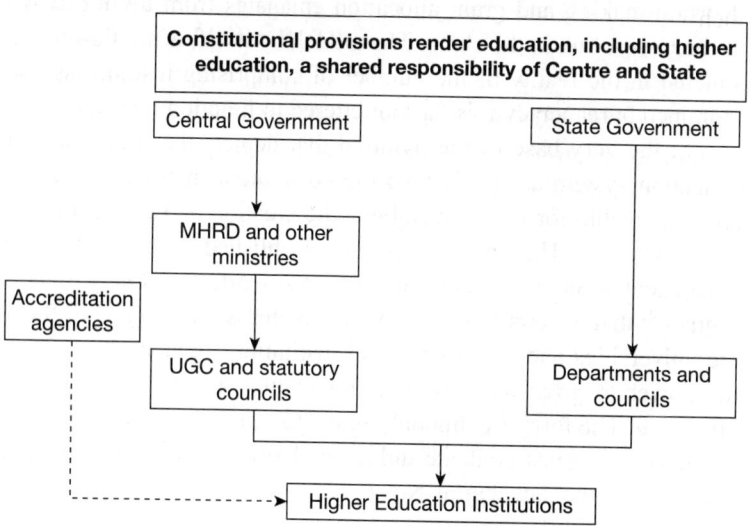

Figure 1.1 The Regulatory Framework in Indian Higher Education System
Source: EY-FICCI (2009).

result in one body being superimposed by the other and ensuing disputes related to jurisdiction and conflicts of interest. Time and again, the end result is that the wheels that move higher education are encumbered with the thickets of bureaucracy. By the time one reaches the end of line—affiliating colleges—self-governance is dwindled to very little. Regrettably, the ones who are the most familiar with the operational challenges at hand are armed with little power to make a difference.

Key Characteristics of the Indian Higher Education System

Organizational Outline

Possibly the most important causative factor in institutional modeling is the affiliating structure of the Indian higher education system. The present configuration of the system is derived from the "London model" of institutional affiliation owing to the country's colonial past. The affiliating model is decidedly a top-down mechanism, where decision making and grant allocation emanates from the top down to the lowest link in the chain. The model, by itself, is not flawed but situated in the reality of the number of comprising institutions and ingrained bureaucracy it is far too fettered to function optimally.

At the very base of the pyramid that depicts the Indian higher education system are positioned the constituent institutions, which are responsible for the deliverable—the creation and dissemination of knowledge. The institutions are established through Acts of Parliament or State legislation and form an assortment of very diverse segments that are conjoined in intricate patterns. The largest of these are universities and university-level institutions, which alone enjoy the power to grant degrees. The universities are either unitary or affiliating. The former commonly refers to stand-alone organizations that have strong postgraduate and research orientations in identifiable disciplines—the Jawaharlal Nehru University comes to mind as a prominent example.

Typically, an affiliating university is identified by a nodal center to which multiple institutions are affiliated. Whereas research is not as big a focus as it is with the unitary universities, it is carried out at the postgraduate level by organizations that are often referred to as schools and departments, which also manage postgraduate teaching and examinations. Undergraduate and, to a smaller extent, postgraduate level academics is worked out through affiliating colleges, which may be located close to the central campus or spread across districts. The affiliating colleges operate in accordance with the jurisdiction of the university.

At par with universities are university-level institutions, of which there are two kinds—deemed universities and "institutions of national importance." The central government is responsible for conferring the status of deemed-to-be-universities on institutions that have proven track-record of excellence in specific disciplines and streams, such as the Symbiosis International University, Birla Institute of Technology and Science, and Manipal University. Institutions of national importance, such as the IITs are recognized by Acts of Parliament.

The lowest denomination in this composition is the whole gamut of colleges, the vast majority of which are affiliated to universities and enjoy little power with respect to self-governance. In this case, the internal management is supervised by the governing body, which is composed of representatives from a number of parties that hold stake in the college, including the university and state government. In all the matters related to financial and educational policies, the university holds utmost sway. Most importantly, the university determines the guidelines and standards that colleges are to abide by. It is the prerogative and responsibility of the university to monitor processes and outcomes of colleges, ensure compliance, and take corrective measures if there be a need. It is noteworthy that the university enjoys absolute power over examination, curriculum, and grant of degree. Given that the affiliating structure is derived from India's colonial past, it is only reasonable that its fruitfulness be revisited periodically. The consideration is even more relatable in the present milieu, which is marked by unprecedented dynamism and expansion with respect to higher education providers.

A recently taken corrective step to tackle the challenge of the affiliating structure, among other issues, is the granting of autonomy to select colleges. According to the UGC website, in May 2015, there were 526 autonomous colleges in the country (UGC, n.d.). The concept of granting autonomy to colleges has been discussed for many years in the past. The National Policy on Education (1986–92) formulated the objectives for autonomous colleges. Highlighting the importance of autonomous colleges, the UGC document on the X Plan profile of higher education stated the following:

> The only safe and better way to improve the quality of undergraduate education is to delink most of the colleges from the affiliating structure. Colleges with academic and operative freedom are doing better and have more credibility. The financial support to such colleges boosts the concept of autonomy.

"Autonomy" is the functional status given to a college by UGC by extending greater self-governance for the purpose of assisting the college in achieving academic excellence. The idea is to enable colleges to award degrees on behalf of the university by providing more academic and operational freedom. Autonomous colleges that have completed three terms can confer the degree under their title along with the seal of the parent university. Examples of autonomous colleges include "College of Engineering" and "Symbiosis College of Arts and Commerce" (affiliated to University of Pune).

The relative freedom enjoyed by autonomous colleges applies to areas such as courses of study, syllabi, elective courses, reservation policies, methods of assessment, conduct of examinations, notification of results, instructional technology, and community programs and activities.

The Commission offers extensive assistance to autonomous colleges, including assistance in areas such as financial assistance, training of faculty members, redesigning of curriculum, examination reforms, infrastructural support, and fees (such as NAAC accreditation fee). The Commission's commitment to the promotion of autonomous colleges can be judged by the case that the UGC Standing Advisory Committee on Autonomous Colleges mandated in 2013 that at least 10 percent of all eligible colleges in the country were to be conferred with autonomy by the end of XII Plan. Moreover, under the Rashtriya Uchchatar Shiksha Abhiyan (RUSA), autonomous colleges desirous of converting themselves into universities were to be provided with funding up to ₹550 million each.

The status of autonomy is an impressive brand-building instrument for the institution. Above all, it reflects the capability of self-governance and the potential for excellence in education.

Furthermore, the concept of autonomous colleges is a strong counterforce that can be utilized in remedying the persistence of overburdened and unmanageably large universities. It is often envisaged that a cluster can be developed around an autonomous college, which could later evolve into a university in its own time and through its own course.

The push towards autonomous colleges speaks to the larger thrust towards liberalization of higher education. The UGC XI plan document that outlined the advent of grant of autonomy to colleges (that are affiliated to universities) marked a new era in advancement and modernization of higher education.

In developing autonomous colleges, it is hoped that these institutions will usher in innovative advances in pedagogy, research, and operational efficiency, as a result of being delinked from cumbersome regulatory and institutional structures that weigh down other institutions.

The underlying assumption is that autonomous colleges have enough merit that they can customize curriculum and other academic processes in order to increase the demand-responsiveness and competitiveness aspects of institutions. This relative freedom to make decisions to design institutional procedures and practices is a step towards the direction of "educational entrepreneurship."

The provisions of RUSA also merit note in the discussion on public policy steps to liberalize and democratize the higher education system. The RUSA is a commendable policy initiative, designed to bring about reformative change in the Indian higher education system. Launched in 2013 by MHRD, the centrally sponsored scheme aims at providing strategic funding to higher educational institutions throughout the country.

The RUSA was initiated as follow-on to several successful innovative educational policy reform projects, notably Sarva Shiksha Abhiyan (SSA; 2001) and Rashtriya Madhyamik Shiksha Abhiyan

(RMSA; 2009). It is relatable that UGC is directed to take steps to evaluate the state of higher education periodically and to take up corrective steps if there be a need; the Commission is provided with funds to support it in carrying out these projects.

The deliberations that led to the RUSA project centered on the issue of challenges faced by state universities, which, though large in number, grapple with limited resources, outdated and unhelpful regulatory and institutional structures, and poor performance.

Although the RUSA project aims at achieving overall development of all higher education institutions, the top priority is to increase the gross enrollment ratio to 32 percent by the end of the XII Plan in 2017. Some of the other key goals are as follows:

1. To improve the overall quality of existing state institutions by ensuring that all institutions conform to the prescribed norms and standards and adopt accreditation as a mandatory quality assurance framework
2. To bring about transformative reforms in the state of higher education system by creating a facilitating institutional structure for planning and monitoring at the state level, promoting autonomy in state universities, and improving governance in institutions
3. To ensure academic and examination reforms
4. To enable advancement of high-potential institutions into world-class research universities
5. To create growth opportunities for affiliated colleges
6. To improve capacity-building by ensuring availability of high-caliber faculty members
7. To expand the institutional base by creating additional capacity in existing institutions and establishing new institutions
8. To correct regional imbalances in access to higher education by facilitating access to high-quality institutions in urban, semi-urban, and rural areas
9. To improve equity in higher education by providing adequate opportunities to underprivileged groups

An important feature of the RUSA goals is to offer encouragement to autonomous colleges. Among other concerns, it is thought that doing so will go a long way in overcoming the burden that is placed on affiliated colleges, especially those that are affiliated to state universities.

A long-term goal is to encourage high-potential autonomous colleges to develop into universities. It is also planned that "college cluster universities" will be launched by clustering many colleges. Another innovative plan includes setting up "model colleges" to be mentored by "parent" institution. It is commendable that some provisions of this scheme are designed to encourage accountability by offering performance-based funding.

It emerges that *sensu lato*, the most easily identifiable trend in the Indian higher education system has been one of *massification*—moving from elite to mass. Higher education systems have been classified on the basis of enrollments as elite, mass, and universal. A higher education system is elite when the GER ratio is less than 15 percent. It is mass when the corresponding figure is between 15 and 50 percent, and universal when it is more than or equal to 50 percent (Trow, 1973, cited in Agarwal, 2006). In India, the most prominent indicator of "massification" is the increase in the demographic base with access to higher education. Encouragingly, this development has occurred across all parameters—total numbers, regional distribution, and so on. This advance has also democratized higher education in the sense that higher education is increasingly within the grasp of demographic groups that had no access to it hitherto.

Enrollment and Institutional Trends

To maintain that the rate of growth in enrollment and institutional headcount in India has been phenomenal would not be an overstatement. Additionally, the upturn has occurred across almost all parameters. Encouragingly, the last few years have witnessed the most growth (see Table 1.1).

In the year 2011–12, the total number of universities and colleges stood at 659 and 33,023, respectively (EY-FICCI, 2012, p. 8). In 2013–14, there were 712 universities, 36,671 colleges, and 11,445 "Stand Alone Institutions" (MHRD, 2014, p. 3). In 2014–15, there were 757 universities, 38,056 colleges, and 11,922 "Stand Alone Institutions" (AISHE, 2015, p. i). Similarly, the gross enrollment ratio for higher education, which was 17.9 percent in 2011–12 (EY-FICCI, 2012, p. 8) rose to 23.0 percent in 2013–14,

Table 1.1
Growth of Higher Education in India (1950 to 2013)

Indicator (Number of)	1950–51	2013–14	Fold Increase
Universities (tens)	3.2	75	23.4
Colleges (thousands)	0.7	39.7	57
Enrollment (lakhs)	3.97	237.65	60
Teaching staff (lakhs)	0.24	10.5	43.7

Source: Adapted from UGC Annual report 2013–14.

and 23.6 percent in 2014–2015 (AISHE, 2015, p. 4).[1] Further, the total enrollment in higher education, which was 25.9 million in 2011–12 (EY-FICCI, 2012, p. 8), rose to 33.3 million in 2014–15 (AISHE, 2015, p. i).

According to AISHE (2015, p. i), the institutions are categorized and enumerated thusly:

1. There are a total of 267 "Privately Managed Universities."
2. There are 43 "Central Universities."
3. There are one "Central" and 13 "State Open Universities."
4. There are 69 "Institutes of National Importance."
5. There are 316 "State Public Universities."
6. There are 5 "Institute under State Legislature Act."
7. There are 37 "Deemed Universities."
8. There are 6 "Other Universities."

The AISHE (2015, p. i) further reports that 76 percent of the institutions are "privately managed," 61 percent are "private unaided," and 15 percent are "private aided."

As will be discussed later in depth, learning modalities that do not fall into the traditional "bricks and mortar" category are projected to expand both in number and in diversity in respect of instructional delivery. As is the case with nontraditional providers, there has been a surge in newer modes of education delivery. Of these, distance education is undoubtedly the most prominent. Therefore, it is important that research on enrollment keep record of enrollment trends in distance education. The AISHE (2015, p. ii) notes that, in the year 2014–15, distance enrollment constituted 11.7 percent of the total enrollment in higher education, and 46 percent of this group comprised women.

In respect of traditional institutions, the AISHE (2015) report, which presents the most recent publicly available information on higher education statistics, notes that "about 80% students are enrolled in Undergraduate level Programme. [sic] 112,812 students are enrolled in Ph.D. [sic] that is about 0.34% of the total student enrolment" (p. ii). In other words, "of the total 3,32,72,722 students, a vast majority of 2,65,76,140 students are enrolled in Under graduate . . . 11.45% students are enrolled in Post-Graduation which is approximately 38.1 lakh students" (p. 2). The relative enrollment at the level of diploma is 6.75 percent and at the levels of "PhD," "PG Diploma," "MPhil," "Certificate," and "Integrated" programs are all under 1 percent.

As for the male–female ratio in higher education, it is in the favor of men at all levels, except for MPhil programs. Yet, the difference in relative enrollment is not remarkable in any category. The GER for male population at the national level is 24.5 percent and 22.7 percent for women.

It is commendable that AISHE (2015) undertook the initiative of collecting and presenting data on the profile of teaching staff in higher education in India. According to AISHE (2015, p. ii), the total number of teachers within the higher education system in India is 1,418,389. Of this, more than half (61%) are men. Further, the pupil teacher ratio (PTR) is 24 (24 pupils for one teacher).

It emerges that the country has succeeded in thrusting higher education forward. All areas have recorded growth; furthermore, newer providers of higher education and modes of delivery have emerged steadily to change the landscape of higher education in the country. The subject of private participants in higher education is an important one and merits detailed discussion; it has been analyzed subsequently. It would not be far-fetched to surmise that the future holds promise of change for the better.

Policy on Higher Education

The Five Year Plans, which are the responsibility of the Planning Commission of India, are good indicators of the direction that the economy is slated to take in the succeeding five years. Speaking specifically, Five Year Plans outline the thrust areas for all sectors of the national economy. Encouragingly, a cursory look at recent Five Year Plans reveals that higher education is increasingly being impelled into the center (EY-FICCI, 2012).

Sixth Five Year Plan (1980–85): the main emphasis was quality improvement, which pivoted on two action plans:

1. Improvement of standards and regulation of admission this is not an independent clause, so ca not end with terminal punctuation
2. Restructuring of courses for practical orientation and greater relevance

Seventh Five Year Plan (1985–1990): the focus was on research and academic development through the following action plans:

1. Creation of research facilities and centers of excellence
2. Encouragement of academic mobility and cross-fertilization of ideas
3. Restructuring courses offered at first degree level to increase employability

Eighth Five Year Plan (1992–97): the key agenda was allocation of funding for developing new departments/courses through the following action plans:

1. Strengthening of existing postgraduate departments in terms of laboratories, workshops and library services
2. Opening of new specialized courses and departments and doing away with outdated ones

Ninth Five Year Plan (1997–2002): the key objective was adapting to social and economic changes through the following action plans:

1. Encouraging relevant courses with a professional focus to enable career development
2. Addressing the education needs of under-represented social groups
3. Generating revenue through increased university-industry linkages

Tenth Five Year Plan (2002–07): the primary aim was to improve the quality and relevance of higher education through the following action plans:

1. Strengthening of research institutions as well as open and distance education system
2. Knowledge and use of new information and communication technology
3. Focus on quality, evaluation and accreditation of higher education

Eleventh Five Year Plan (2007–12): the thrust area was promotion of inclusive growth of higher education through the following action plans:

1. Expanding HEIs to eliminate regional imbalances
2. Making higher education accessible to all socio-economic strata of the society
3. Improving quality of education by promoting research, quality assurance systems and faculty and infrastructure development

It is commendable that policymakers are now cognizant of the changing expression of higher education in the country. The public policy is reflective of the recognition that the peripheral in higher education is increasingly closing in towards the center. Thus, hitherto outlying delivery modes, streams/disciplines, providers, and so on are inching inwardly and being taken into greater consideration. This realization is tied to the understanding that the demands on higher education system are exacting, and alternative course of action is the only way forward.

The Tripartite Challenge of "Access, Equity, and Quality" Within the Context of Limited Public Expenditure

The sheer mass of populace that the higher education system in India serves, combined with the country's emerging presence in the global economy, presents a very forceful case for thrusting the whole higher education sector as a top agenda item in national policy-making and allocating sufficient funds.

Although all sectors in India have witnessed squeeze in public expenditure, the one in higher education has received the worst hit (Mitra, 2013; Rani, 2002, cited in Mitra, 2015). The high importance that the Indian Government accords to enhancing accessibility within the base of the higher education cohort in the country necessitates that the Government consider increasing public expenditure on higher education.

Perhaps the most persuasive argument for increasing public expenditure in higher education is that higher education is the least accessed by those in the "lower income group" (Mitra, 2015, p. 86). This is so because the opportunity cost of undertaking higher education rises when one considers all the factors that are involved in the decision-making processes in the lower income group. This argument, by itself, serves to build empirical ground for increasing public spending. More importantly, this line of reasoning negates the popular notion that the strengthening of the private sector is sufficient reason to slack off on public expenditure. Indeed, the Indian Government must invest more in coming up with schemes such as differentiated fees structure for the lower income group to increase and sustain enrollment amongst students in the marginalized socio-economic brackets.

The expenditure on higher education in absolute and relative terms remains low, as is demonstrated in the data presented below:

In the Twelfth Five Year Plan (2012–17), the "Gross Budgetary Support" for the MHRD was ₹4,537.28 billion—of this the share earmarked for the Department of School and Secondary Education accounts was 75.6 percent and for the Department of Higher Education 24.4 percent. Further, the plan for the budget announced by the Indian Government for the year 2016–17 allocated a total of ₹689.68 billion for the education sector as a whole (*The Indian Express*, 2016).

Table 1.2 depicts the "plan" and "non-plan" expenditure on the department of higher education for the years 2014–15, 2015–16, and 2016–17.

Table 1.2
Expenditure for the Department of Higher Education in 2014–15, 2015–16, and 2016–17

(In crores of ₹)

MINISTRY/DEPARTMENT	TOTAL EXPENDITURE OF MINISTRIES/DEPARTMENTS											
	Actuals 2014–15			Budget 2015–16			Revised 2015–16			Budget 2016–17		
	Plan	Non-Plan	Total	Plan	Non-Plan	Total	Plan	Non-Plan	Total	Plan	Non-Plan	Total
Higher Education	12,157.86	10,577.73	22,735.59	14,700.26	11,000.00	25,700.26	13,373.00	1,0971.00	24,344.00	15,245.00	12340.00	27,585.00

Source: Ministry of Finance. (n.d.).

Although it is held by many that the allocation for the education sector in the 2016–17 budget is not nearly enough, many provisions that were outlined along with the announcements related to allocations have been received positively by educationists. The creation of a Higher Education Funding Agency (HEFA) for redressal of grievances related to educational loans is one such example. Other commendable provisions include the opening of 62 more Navodaya Vidyalayalaya schools, allocation of ₹17 billion for setting up 1,500 multiskill training institutes, the launch of Pradhan Mantri Kaushal Vikas Yojna (a skill training scheme), and the initiation of the "Digital Literacy Scheme" (*The Indian Express*, 2016).

It must be pointed out that public expenditure on education as apportionment has increased slowly but steadily over the last several decades, as can be deduced from Table 1.3.

According to the most recent World Bank data, India has not scored high on the variety of indicators that represent the share of Government's total expenditure on education, and on higher education as a subset within education (World Bank, n.d.a; World Bank n.d.b).

In India, the expenditure on education as percent of total government expenditure in 2012 (the most recent year for which data is cited for India) was 14.2 (World Bank, n.d.a), and the Government expenditure on education as percent of GDP 3.9 (World Bank n.d.b).

Education, in India, has continued to be the weak link in the chain that makes up the sum total of the UN's Human Development Index. The United Nations Human Development Report 2015, which ranks countries based on where they stand on the list of "Human Development Index," ranked India 130 on a list of 188 countries. On this list, many countries that do not meet the criteria from "developed economies" fared better than India—Russia, Brazil, China, and South Africa are some of them (*The Indian Express*, 2016).

The growth of the Indian higher education system within the context of insufficient funds, as impressive as it is, has taken place in the absence of equal opportunities and excellence. Therefore, there is much to be concerned about even if there is an upturn in the graph that depicts the evolution of higher education since Independence. This is because expansion has been unplanned and unchanneled; more accurately, growth has occurred in response to a

Table 1.3

Public Expenditure on Education in India

Year	Educational Expenditure as % of Public Expenditure	Educational Expenditure as % of GDP
1951–52	7.92	0.64
1960–61	11.99	1.48
1970–71	10.16	2.11
1980–81	10.67	2.98
1990–91	13.37	3.84
2000–01	14.42	4.28
2008–09	13.63	3.77

Source: UGC (2012).

compelling need to educate the teeming millions and not as a result of public policy.

Of all the challenges, the one about access looms the largest. Simply put, it refers to the large mass of higher education demographic that goes without accessing higher education. Of the utmost concern is the low GER figure. At 23.0 percent in 2013–14 (AISHE, 2015, p. 4) and 25 percent based on the World Bank criteria, it was much lower than many developed and emerging economies (see Table 1.4).

The problem of equity denotes the underrepresentation of certain demographic groups in the higher education system. In India, this presents a formidable challenge across a number of variables— gender, socio-cultural groups, and the urban–rural divide. The GER varies greatly across a number of dimensions. In terms of regional distribution, the disparity is astounding: whereas Chandigarh has recorded GER values higher than 50 between 2012 and 2015, Dadra and Nagar Haveli and Daman and Diu have scored below 10 for the same period (AISHE, 2015, p. 9). It was noted that social denominations also scored unevenly. Against the national GER of 23.6 percent, GER for "scheduled castes" population was 18.5 percent and for "scheduled tribes" 13.3 percent (AISHE, 2015, p. 4). In the discussion on the distribution across the gender divide, it was not surprising to note that GER figures were skewed in the favor

Table 1.4
Gross Enrollment Ratio at Tertiary Level[2] in 2013 (%)

Country	Ratio
Republic of Korea	98
United States	89
Turkey	79
Hong Kong	67
Israel	67
France	60
Germany	60
United Kingdom	60
France	60
Iran	58
Thailand	51
China	30
India	**25**

Source: World Bank (n.d.c).

of men—women constitute only 46 percent of the total enrollment (AISHE, 2015, p. 4).

The concern with respect to quality refers to the subpar standard of education across a number of parameters, such as contribution to skill-development, job-preparedness, and research. Among the shortfalls, the lack of innovation in curriculum and pedagogical practices count as the most widespread. One of the most conspicuous challenges relates to the figures that depict representation of teaching staff across higher education institutions in the country. There persists a shortage of faculty members—the student–teacher ratio is 24:1—and there are 64 women teachers for every 100 men teachers (AISHE, 2015, p. 5).

Research, which depicts the pinnacle of academic excellence, has been an area of abysmal performance for the country. India has persistently lagged behind in the volume of research publications, which is considered a fair indication of research output. Given that research is the most significant indicator in academic rankings, it is no surprise that global rankings have eluded India. According to the QS World University Rankings 2015, only two Indian institutions made it within the top 200—Indian Institute of Science (IISc) Bengaluru and IIT Delhi (Sinha, 2015).

The disengagement between economy and higher education has been the subject of a number of high-level working groups. It has been widely contended that the Indian higher education system does not result in a large enough skilled workforce. The concern about low employability takes on an even greater importance in the backdrop of India's emergence as knowledge economy. The EY-FICCI 2012 report on higher education cited National Association of Software and Services (NASSCOM)—McKinsey Report (2005)—which stated that merely 25 percent technical and 10 percent nontechnical graduates are actually employable. To state the obvious, these graduates will find it difficult to obtain employment. If they do find jobs, it will fall to the employer to invest in further training to fill the skill gap.

Emergence of Private Partakers in Higher Education

"The only real, substantial answer is enhancing private participation . . . [It] can improve supply, build capacity, create excellence, reduce large foreign exchange spending . . . and make India a global education hub" (*Outlook Business*, 2008).

Privatization of higher education is a very prominently emerging global phenomenon. It is widely regarded to be the fastest growing sector in higher education across the globe. It is also considered to be the result of what is commonly referred to as "massification" of higher education. Higher education, as with any other realm that represents human activity, has undergone a continual transformation. The very nature of demand for higher education has transmuted so much that it is a far cry from what it was towards the end of the Second World War all across the globe. A number of factors are responsible for this. First, it would not be an overstatement to hold that state expenditure in higher education has borne the axe the world over. The state's incapacity to cope with the teeming millions who are added into the higher education demographic is at the heart of rapid escalation of private partakers in higher education. Second, the correlation between higher education and employment has increasingly been strengthened. Generally speaking, private institutions are more responsive to the demands of their patrons and better acquainted with projections and trends in higher education. Last, an increase in the size of middle- and upper-middle classes with more disposable income has allowed for non-public alternatives to emerge. As things stand today, private higher education is a mainstream, and not a marginal, sector.

In the Indian context, private institutions are those that are established and managed by non-governmental organizations and are self-financing for the most part. The advancement of private higher education in India has been driven by a very compelling demand in the higher education demographic, rather than deliberated public policy. The germination of the private sector in India can be tracked down to the 1970's when the Indian higher education system was confronted with dispossession of funds. Looking for a stopgap arrangement, more than anything else, several states allowed admittance of "self-financing" colleges that catered to the rising demand for professional education, which denotes education that is geared towards dispensing job training and vocational instruction. As the name signifies, these colleges do not receive any financial assistance from the government and count primarily on tuition to cover their expenses. The 1980s also heralded a new era in Indian higher education—the concept of employability and skill formation were beginning to be linked to higher education in an unprecedentedly emphatic manner. Given that the peninsular states were at the forefront of economic development, it is no surprise that the advent of higher education in the country occurred there. The northern states took a long time in catching up, much later in the mid-1990s. In the year 2002, India had nearly 4,400 professional colleges of which about 3,150—upwards of 70 percent—were in the private sector (Powar and Bhalla, 2005, cited in Powar, 2012). This growth has continued unabated. In the year 2012, the total number of diploma granting institutions stood at 12,748 of which 9,541 were in the private sector. More importantly, the private sector has recorded growth at the broadest level: in the year 2012, as many as 64 percent of higher education institutions were in the private sector. This growth was reflected in other parameters as well—59 percent of student enrollment in higher education was in the private sector. The trend is also mirrored in the choice of programs and courses—while general education accounts for the majority of enrollment, professional courses (such as engineering and medicine) have witnessed higher growth. The compound annual growth rate for general education between 2007 and 2012 was 5.6 percent and the corresponding figure for professional courses was an impressive 20.6 percent. The most recent information, provided by AISHE (2015), notes that in the year 2014–15, 76 percent "colleges" were privately managed.

Given that the fee for such courses is significantly higher than general courses—as much as upwards of ten times—the majority of expenditure on higher education is accrued in professional programs and courses. The growth of professional education in the private sector, as encouraging as it is, must be viewed in the backdrop of knowledge that growth of professional institutions in the public sector has been sluggish.

The Indian Government's position on private participants has been frequently criticized as one that is out of step with the maturation of higher education in India and elsewhere. The concern with respect to excessive centralization merits note in the discussion. The federal structure of the system, especially in the wake of the "42nd Amendment to the Constitution" (1976), generates its own complexities. Few would disagree that it makes the policies suscept-ible to political vagaries and self-interests. In matters of disputes over higher education policies, the Center supersedes state to the extent of contradiction. For instance, in cases of conflicts between center and state legislation, the provisions of center legislation are *ultra vires* to the extent of the variance.

In the Indian situation, the discussion is incomplete without noting the Government's proclaimed thrust on propelling higher education as the key vehicle for recasting the county as knowledge economy. Dahlman and Utz (2005) define the knowledge economy as "an economy that creates, disseminates, and uses knowledge . . . to enhance its growth and development . . . any economy [that] harnesses and uses new and existing knowledge to improve the productivity of agriculture, industry, and services and increase overall welfare." (p. 2). The World Bank researchers highlight the role of higher education in enabling knowledge economy by creating "a sustained cadre of knowledge workers" (p. 8). In discussing the significance of skill development and training in the Indian context, the authors recommend, "Raising the quality of all higher education institutions, not just a few world-class ones (such as the IITs)" (p. 11).

In the next few decades, India is speculated to have the world's largest set of young people. Whereas the correlation between higher education and nation building is indisputable, the working-age population can be an asset only if their potential employability is brought to fruition. Conversely, if the state does not harness the endowment, this demographic group can turn out to be a heavy economic and social millstone. With the singular purpose of modeling recommendations and means to tap into this reservoir, the government founded the NKC in 2005. The Commission aims to provide a channel to harness the country's vast human capital, more specifically the demographic dividends that accrue from the working age population. The decision to set up the Commission suggests the Government's cognizance of the importance of developing the appropriate paradigm in which to invest in intellectual capital by developing the skill set of the population and encouraging research, innovation, and entrepreneurship (see Box 1.2).

Box 1.2. National Knowledge Commission: A Giant Leap Forward

NKC was constituted in 2005 to operate within a time frame of three years. As a high-level advisory body to the former Prime Minister of India, NKC was given a mandate to guide policy and direct reforms, focusing on certain key areas such as education, science and technology, agriculture, industry, e-governance, and so on. Easy access to knowledge, creation and preservation of knowledge systems, dissemination of knowledge, and better knowledge services were core concerns of the Commission. In its endeavor to transform the knowledge landscape of the country, NKC has submitted around 300 recommendations on 27 focus areas during its three and a half years term. While the term of the NKC has come to an end, the implementation of NKC's recommendations is currently underway at central and state levels.

Source: The National Knowledge Commission (Govt. of India)
http://knowledgecommissionarchive.nic.in/ (accessed on April 6, 2016).

It is important to take note of the concern that no development scheme is complete without plans that address inclusion and welfare of all the beneficiaries. The idea of a knowledge economy is bogus without egalitarianism and welfare priorities. It is also imperative not to get carried away by pockets of excellence in higher education—IITs and IIMs, for instance. The sobering fact of the matter is that there is a latent ongoing crisis in higher education. This paucity is only compounded with a corresponding shortfall in the quality of higher education. Thus, we infer that if the higher education system in India is to benefit the economy, it has to be revamped systemically so it can reach as wide a base as possible without watering down the merit.

The quest for finding a solution to the systemic challenges in higher education begins with the acknowledgment that not all answers necessarily lie with the Indian Government. To begin with, meager public investments in higher education presage undesirable outcomes. A vast majority of public allocation is used up in the maintenance of facility and payment of salaries. It leaves very little for investing in innovation and research in education and pedagogy. The fact of the matter is that even faculty salary structure, as indicated by the Sixth Pay Commission, falls abysmally short in attracting talent to the higher education sector. Internationally competitive higher education requires adequately paid professoriate since this group of academics is a part of global labor market. An international survey revealed that India was at the bottom of a group of 15 countries in academic salaries (Rumbley et al., 2008 cited in Altbach, 2009). Further, the growing disparity in the salaries of academe and industry in India is responsible for the shortage of internationally competitive faculty members at premier institutions such as the IITs and the IIM's (Neelakantan, 2007 & Bradshaw, 2007, cited in Salmi, 2009). Gupta and Gupta (2012), citing MHRD report, estimate this figure to be in the range of nearly one-third of faculty positions for aforementioned premier institutions as well as central universities. Additionally, the absence of tenure system detracts from the lucrativeness of teaching as a career choice (Altbach, 2009).

For this reason alone, it is important to open the system to competition from non-governmental sector and allow enough transparency that the "best man wins." This will not only allow surplus capital to be invested back into the sector, but also draw in enterprise and talent. It is not enough that "checks and balances" are in place to hold existing institutions answerable; a responsible system must also provide education and training that is qualitatively competitive and peer driven. None of that would be possible until the policymakers decide to remodel a rulebook that was drafted over 25 years ago (in fact, the original version of National Policy on Education was drafted in 1968).

The scale of shortfalls in the system is disquieting indeed. India's gross enrolment ratio of 23.6 percent (AISHE, 2015) is much lower than that of many developing countries. This is only compounded by an even glaring underperformance with regard to quality. It cannot be overstated that the government by itself is not equipped to take on the challenge. Public investment backed by public–private partnerships is a more realistic route. Marking a break from its long-standing stance of "obstructionism" with respect to private institutions, the Indian Government stated in the "Economic Survey of 2010–11"—a flagship annual document authored by the Ministry of Finance— that public–private partnership is the route to establishing global education hubs in the country (*Business Standard*, 2011).

Indeed, it is the dynamism of the private sector that has allowed it to spawn and capture forte segments in higher education. This has pushed the sector to the fore, even in the face of "over-regulatory" government fiats and missing policy direction. This is in stark contrast to the scenario in neighboring countries to the southeast, especially Singapore, Malaysia, and Thailand. In view of the consideration that private sector is no longer an outlying phenomenon but one that is securely grounded in the mainstream, it falls to the policymakers to sketch out policy which will shepherd the private higher education such that as it moves forward. It also addresses the systemic challenges of access, equity, and quality.

The Quality Assurance Concerns

The concept of quality in higher education has assumed the center stage in India, as it has done in other countries. A lot of it is attributable to globalization, and the consequent thrust on attaining international competitiveness and homogeneity. Broadly speaking, this has to be one of the most transformative forces in higher education. Internationalization of higher education has altered the very goalposts which depict excellence and quality in higher education. In India, the phenomenon of "massification" has brought added exigency to the question of quality assurance. It has also rendered the line of attack "over-regulatory," as has been discussed earlier.

It is important to be heedful of the limitations of such an approach: regulatory frameworks must work to optimize the promise of excellence in an institution rather than appoint a charter built out of checklists. To set the question down baldly, does the regulatory apparatus in Indian higher education system reduce quality assurance to accreditation? This is a broader thematic concern that inquires whether the concept of quality assurance is in keeping with the emerging subthemes of attaining equivalence as higher education gets "massified," newer models of performance appraisal in education, in leadership, management of higher education, and so on. It is ever so important in the changing global context to ascertain that public policy on quality assurance breaks away from its *idée fixe* of ensuring minimum standards through inspection and audits to one that incorporates accountability and excellence. To put it in ideological terms, quality assurance must emerge from a mind-set that is enabling and ameliorative, and not one that is castigatory and penal.

It is reasonable to begin the discussion on regulation and supervision of quality assurance with the International Network for Quality Assurance Agencies in Higher Education (INQAAHE), which is a worldwide association of over 200 agencies that are closely involved in the theory and practice of quality assurance in higher education. The association, referring to quality assurance, elaborates thusly,

> [Quality assurance] relate[s] to a programme, an institution or a whole education system. In each case, quality assurance consists of all attitudes, objects, actions, and procedures, which through their existence and use, combined with quality control activities, ensure that appropriate academic standards are being maintained and enhanced in and by each programme [sic]. Quality assurance extends to making the

process and standards known to the educational community and the
public at large (as cited in Stella, 2002, pp. 16–17).

In the Indian context, it would be fair to attribute the definition of
the concepts of quality and excellence in education to the National
Policy on Education (NPE) 1986. To its great credit, the Indian
higher education policy, especially following the period after NPE
(1986), has evolved a very intricate and thorough-going system of
"checks and balances" that oversees the functioning of one of the
largest higher education systems in the world. The UGC, positioned
at the very helm of affairs in this clustering, commands a great deal
of control. It is, in fact, bound by Section 12 of the UGC Act of 1956
to lay down the mechanism that regulates and coordinates the quality
control aspect of higher education in the country: "the determination
and maintenance of standards of teaching, examinations and research
in universities."

A cursory survey of the criteria and benchmarks reveals that in
the case of affiliating universities, the colleges are not really true
affiliates in the sense of being associates, rather they are subordinates.
The university prevails in all academic matters—grant of degrees,
examinations, curriculum, and so on. If this affiliating model has
proven counterproductive over time, it is because the number of
affiliating colleges has increased unanticipatedly. At the UGC end,
this translates into essentially two responsibilities pertaining to
quality assurance: formulating the eligibility criteria for institutions
and the suitability of existing institutions to receive monetary funding.
The observance of minimum standards is not limited to the Center.
The state governments have their own arrangement in place to ensure
compliance with the requirements. It is important to note that the
role of state governments is more about the fulfillment of obligations
than anything else. To bring this about, the state governments work-
up audits and inspections that monitor the activities of universities
and colleges. The effectiveness of this mechanism is of paramount
importance: after all the vast majority of higher education institutions
are of the state and not the central category. Further, the performance
of state universities and colleges has been an unrelenting challenge.
It has been demonstrated that of the whole gamut of institutions, the
ones in the state category fare the worst.

The UGC regulations frequently delve into the very nitty-gritty of operational details. This is especially true in the case of setting down minimum requirements; thus, the stipulations go into working hours, attendance, tutorials, and so on. In the context of the discussion, the instituting of the National Eligibility Test (NET) in 1989 and the establishment of the NAAC in 1994 count amongst UGC's landmark achievements. The UGC is also entrusted with the responsibility of taking on novel initiatives to enhance the overall quality of education.

It is relatable that the setting-up of inter-university centers and national facilities that specialize in defined areas is an encouraging enterprise. Some prominent initiatives include the setting up of Nuclear Science Centre, InterUniversity Centre for Astronomy and Astrophysics, Information and Library Network, Western Regional Instrumentation Centre, Crystal Growth Centre, and National Centre for Science Information. Along the same lines, UGC routinely launches schemes concerned with the enhancement of capacity-building in specified areas such as facilities, infrastructure, and so on. Similarly, UGC appoints working groups and projects for enrichment of existing institutions and organizations. Instances include Committee on New Models of University Management, the Committee on Accreditation and Assessment Council, and Action Plan cum Project Report for Setting up the Accreditation Agency.

As has been discussed previously, the growth of professional–vocational education in India has been nothing short of phenomenal. This stream is vastly different from general education on several counts. Bearing this in mind, the need for developing a separate regulatory framework is hardly stated. It is only fitting that professional–vocational institutions fall within the purview of a regulatory structure that is all their own. Whereas UGC is still responsible for coordination, determination, and maintenance of overall standards and disbursement of grants to select institutions, the statutory councils are entrusted with certification of institutions, authorization of professional licenses, and allocation of funds in some qualified instances.

An important discussion on the subject of quality and excellence is the one about private institutions. The concern is borne out of the simple fact that historically, education has been understood to be the nation-state's responsibility and this has been as true for India as it has been for other countries. In the Indian context, there are other forces at play that complicate the concern. The NPE of 1986 and Programme of Action of 1992 are counted as the foremost amongst these forces since the current policy orientation in higher education is guided by these rubrics. Further, UGC and AICTE wield enormous power to "coordinate and determine standards" in higher education. This power is customarily translated to imply methodization, as in forging homogeny and symmetry by drawing up a centralized scheme. In so doing, the notion of disparity is confounded with inconsistency. It follows, then, that it is the government's obligation to even out what is seen as inequity and imbalance. The regulatory plan that oversees higher education goes into the brass tacks of curriculum, examination, evaluation, teacher–student ration, and such. Add to this the cases that the regulators are sundry, the bureaucracy lumbering, and academia divorced from policymakers. It is no surprise then that this positioning renders policymakers distrustful of initiatives that are dynamic and self-motivated.

In the discussion on quality assurance, it is also important to be mindful of the consideration that in setting standards for the bare minimum, we do not lower the bar for higher education in general. Given the colossal unmet demand for quality higher education— in reality, higher education at all—and the astonishing diversity amongst both providers and recipients of higher education, it is important to ascertain that the higher education policy is one that upholds and honors this array of multiplicity. A country as blessedly disparate as India only stands to benefit from enhancing and utilizing opportunities for each one of the entities that makes the Indian higher education what Altbach calls "a giant monolith." The system indeed necessitates approaches that are diverse enough to target the large variety of demands and needs in the higher education demographic. Furthermore, the conventional publicly-funded system's failure to serve the cause of higher education optimally only bolsters the case for infusing innovative solutions that are really truly responsive to the needs of the populace. Interestingly, in contrast to the widely held reproach that academic rigor in private institutions is suspect, deemed universities—the vast majority of which are in the private sector—exhibit superior performance on that front.

Whilst the structure of checks and balances is rigorous enough, the concern about how effective it is in achieving the end goal of enhancing the overall quality of education persists. As noted earlier, the overburdening of the affiliating model, emergence of newer providers of higher education, and the altered context of internationalization have rendered the quality control aspect of higher education more ineffectual than before. The present higher education scenario is marked by an upsurge in information and knowledge. This casts a welcome quandary to educators: Whereas it is difficult to stay *au fait* with the ever growing expansion of specializations, interdisciplinary, and multidisciplinary streams, delivery modes, and so on, herein lie latent opportunities for all stakeholders.

If only one line of argument had to be identified in defense of greater autonomy to higher education institutions, it would have to be the monumental failure of the affiliating model. This has emerged out of findings of scores of working groups (Stella, 2002, pp. 52–62). More specifically speaking, it has been reinforced that institutions that have demonstrated continued excellence must be identified and granted autonomy. It would be fair to conjecture that the premise here is that these institutions have incorporated effective educational practices and that these can be trusted to deliver in the future as well. Such high-achieving institutions also serve as the seat of best practices for peers.

The NAAC: NAAC was established in 1994 as an autonomous body, under Section 12-CCC of the UGC Act 1956. Even though NAAC was founded through an UGC act, it functions with full autonomy vis-à-vis UGC. At the helm of affairs are the General Council and Executive Council. It is important to point out that these bodies are manned by eminent academics, educators, and educational leaders who are drawn from a very diverse pool of higher education institutions, UGC, MHRD, AIU, professional councils, and suchlike.

The primary goal of NAAC is to assess and accredit higher education institutions and their constituent units, such as centers, departments, and so on. The responsibility of assessment and accreditation is much more complex than it might seem at first. It includes several integral roles, such as the following:

1. Grade higher education institutions and their programs and courses
2. Enhance the overall quality of education in higher education institutions
3. Assist higher education institutions in realizing their mission and vision
4. Conduct periodic review of assessment and accreditation criteria
5. Strive towards achieving criteria that are objective and quantifiable
6. Promote and publicize criteria
7. Communicate assessment and accreditation results to higher education institutions
8. Help higher education institutions evolve their own modalities for self-evaluation
9. Initiate research studies in education administration and leadership.
10. Ascertain optimization of resources
11. Set up regional centers to facilitate NAAC's operations at all levels of the base of the pyramid

In the discussion on assessment, it is important to note that NAAC observes clearly outlined criteria in assessing the performance of higher education institutions: course and program design, pedagogical models, research, infrastructural support, student services, institutional planning and development, and innovation count amongst the most important indicators. The NAAC follows a three-step accreditation process. The first step is the Institutional Eligibility for Quality Assessment (IEQA) wherein the applicant institution identifies its eligibility for quality assessment. The second step relates to the preparation of a self-study report by the institution. This report is then submitted to NAAC for analysis. Last, a group of peer-reviewers assesses the institution for validation of the report; the findings of assessment accounts for the final grade award and accreditation by NAAC.

The AIU, although not being a regulatory agency per se, deserves note in the discussion on quality assurance. The AIU serves to improve the overall quality of higher education by functioning as a common platform on which higher education institutions collaborate and engage in the cross-exchange of ideas and information. The AIU is also a representative body: it speaks for and acts on behalf of its members. The membership includes traditional, open, professional, deemed-to-be universities, and "Institutes of National Importance." In addition, universities of neighboring countries are granted associate membership. The idea of bringing together higher education institutions on a common platform emerged from the deliberations of "Conference of the Vice Chancellors of Universities" in 1924. The InterUniversity Board (IUB) of India was subsequently formed in 1925 with the view of promoting camaraderie amongst institutions. The Board was ratified in 1967 as a Society under the "Societies Registration Act, 1860" and assumed its present name in 1973.

The inculcation of the element of internationalization into higher education has added a few uncharted concepts to the idea of quality assurance. The principal recommendation amongst these is the autonomous status of the accrediting body—the sense here is that these agencies should be free from political and bureaucratic influences. Also important are the instrumentation and methodology entailed in the evaluation of higher education institutions. It is of utmost importance that the assessment be based on criteria that are not random and arbitrary. In order to ensure that indicators and criteria are purposeful, it is imperative that peer review be at the heart of assessment. The concept of peer review is meaningful only if it is wide-ranging and steered by predetermined protocols. Finally, none of this would hold significance if the outcomes are not shared by all partakers; thus, communication of outcome must be transparent and unhampered.

As can be inferred from the discussion, the Indian higher education system has an expansive arrangement of checks and balances, which attempts to ensure that the participating institutions stand equal to the bare minimum that is expected of them. This configuration, as intricate as it is, tends to frequently cause situations where one regulatory-supervisory agency juts into another. There is room for improvement in coordination of collaborative activities of inspecting bodies such that higher education institutions are not overburdened with regulations and stipulations. Paradoxically, the large number of higher education institutions raises concerns about the quality control aspect of regulatory bodies—such as UGC, NAAC, and NIEPA—themselves. Looking farther ashore at international organizations and foreign counterparts might offer solutions.

Concluding Observations

The Indian higher education system makes an interesting study. The present is a rapidly maturing landscape, and one that is only remotely similar to what is was at the time of Independence—or even a few decades ago. The overall graph depicts progress across a number of dimensions; this upturn has occasioned on account of several factors, most of which are tied to the changes that the Indian economy has gone through and not so much to purposeful planning on the part of Indian Government.

As has been indicated earlier, of all the aspects of progress in higher education, three are easily identifiable as the most prominent—"massification," privatization, and internationalization. All of these trends are stepping stones to the democratization of higher education in the sense of making it available to a larger section of the populace as well as demographic groups that are putatively marginal or disadvantaged. It is also opportune that the higher education system is increasingly falling in step with global advances in pedagogy and education. Although late in the coming, Indian higher education can now be said to be awakened to the infinite possibilities that internation-alization brings along with it. Above all, policymakers have eventually upheld the inexorable correlation between higher education and skill formation from the standpoint of career-preparedness. It would not be fantastic to conjecture that the stage is all set for Indian higher education to scale unprecedented heights.

Notes

1. "For international comparability, GER has also been calculated taking 18–22 years population [sic] and it comes out to be 27.4 at All India Level" (AISHE, 2015, p. 3).
2. The Gross Enrolment Ratio in tertiary education is the total enrolment in tertiary education regardless of age, expressed as a percentage of the population in the five-year age group following on from the secondary school leaving age. Tertiary education is classified as International Standard Classification of Education (ISCED) levels 5 and 6. ISCED 5A programs generally equate to university undergraduate degrees, while ISCED 5B programs tend to be vocationally-oriented. ISCED 6 programs lead to the award of an advanced research qualification and are not based on course-work only.

References

Outlook Business. (2008, August 23). A for alumnus, b for business. *Outlook Business*, p. 91.

AISHE. (2015). *All India survey on higher education*. Retrieved from http://aishe.nic.in/aishe/reports (accessed on April 6, 2016).

Altbach, P., & Salmi, J. (2011). *The road to academic excellence: The making of world-class research universities*. Washington D.C.: World Bank.

Altbach, P. (2009). One-third of the globe: The future of higher education in China and India. *Prospects, 39*(1), 11–31.

Dahlman, C., & Utz, A. (2005). *India and the knowledge economy leveraging strengths and opportunities*. Retrieved January 13, 2012 from http://info.world bank.org/etools/docs/library/235713/India%20and%20the%20Knowledge %20Economy%20Leveraging%20Strength%20and%20Opportunities.pdf

EY-FICCI. (2009). *Making Indian higher education ready*. Retrieved January 17, 2012 from http://education.usibc.com/wp-content/uploads/2010/09/EY-FICCI-report09-Making-Indian-Higher-Education-Future-Ready.pdf

———. (2012). *Higher education in India: Twelfth Five Year Plan (2012–17) and beyond*. Kolkata, India: Ernst & Young Pvt. Ltd.

Gupta, D., & Gupta, N. (2012). Higher education in India: Structure, statistics and challenges. *Journal of Education and Practice, 5*(2), 15–20.

Business Standard. (2011, February 26). Making India a global education hub. Retrieved January 25, 2013 from http://www.business-standard.com/india/news/making-indiaglobal-education-hub/426592/

Ministry of Human Resource Development. (2014). *Educational statistics at a glance*. Retrieved from http://mhrd.gov.in/sites/upload_files/mhrd/files/statistics/EAG2014.pdf (accessed on April 6, 2016).

Mitra, A. (2015). Public spending in higher education in India a benefit incidence analysis. *Higher education for the Future, 2*(1), 71–91. doi: 10.1177/2347631114558191

Pathak, K., & Kanwar, D. (2012, December, 25). India is a world-class country without world-class universities: Philip G Altbach. *Business Standard*. Retrieved May 20, 2013 from http://smartinvestor.business-standard.com/market/story-149134-storydet-India_is_a_world_class_country_without_world_class_universities_Philip_G_Altbach.html

Salmi, J. (2009). *The challenge of establishing world-class universities*. Washington D.C.: The World Bank.

Sinha, K. (2015, September 15). In a first, two Indian institutes make it to world's top 200. *The Times of India*. Retrieved from http://timesofindia.indiatimes.com/home/education/news/In-a-first-two-Indian-institutes-make-it-to-worlds-top-200/articleshow/48964009.cms (accessed on April 6, 2016).

Stella, A. (2002). *External quality assurance in Indian higher education: Case study of national assessment and accreditation council*. International Institute for Educational Planning. Paris: IIEP Printshop.

The Indian Express. (2016, March 1). Union Budget 2016: Mixed reaction from education sector. *The Indian Express.* Retrieved from http://indianexpress.com/article/education/union-budget-2016-mixed-reaction-from-education-sector/ (accessed on April 6, 2016).

University Grants Commission. (2012). *Higher education in India at a glance.* New Delhi: UGC.

University Grants Commission. (n.d.). *List of autonomous colleges.* Retrieved from http://www.ugc.ac.in/oldpdf/colleges/autonomous_colleges-list.pdf (accessed on April 6, 2016).

World Bank. (n.d.a). *Expenditure on education as % of total government expenditure (%).* Retrieved from http://data.worldbank.org/indicator/SE.XPD.TOTL.GB.ZS (accessed on April 6, 2016).

World Bank. (n.d.b). *Government expenditure on education as % of GDP (%).* Retrieved from http://data.worldbank.org/indicator/SE.XPD.TOTL.GD.ZS (accessed on April 6, 2016).

World Bank. (n.d.c). *Gross enrolment ratio, tertiary, both sexes (%).* Retrieved from http://data.worldbank.org/indicator/SE.TER.ENRR (accessed on April 6, 2016).

2

Globalization and Internationalization

Theoretical Definition

The thematic concern of the book—internationalization of higher education—is embedded in the idea of globalization. Notably, globalization has been defined in countless respects, essentially because it has been studied by researchers from a large number of disciplines. Thus, the concept has been afforded just as many connotations and insinuations. It is important to point out that economists, in particular, have lessened the idea of globalization to integration of goods, resources, labor markets, and such.

At any rate, globalization refers to the coming together of people. It arises from the elemental human aspiration to unfold and reach out, which is at the nub of interactions between entities and groups. A continually occurring phenomenon, it is spurred on by advances in technology and communications. Knight and De Wit define globalization as follows: "The flow of technology, economy, knowledge, people, values . . . across borders. Globalization affects each country in a different way due to each nation's individual history, traditions, cultures, resources, and priorities" (1997, p. 6). Globalization is essentially a multifaceted phenomenon that results from technological advancements, which lead to reduction in the cost and obstacles to transportation and communication. This facilitates a more productive flow of goods, services, capital, knowledge, and human resource across borders, both political and physical. Altbach and Knight (2007) agree with this rendering:

> We define globalization as the economic, political, and societal forces pushing 21st century higher education toward greater international involvement. Global capital has, for the first time, heavily invested in knowledge industries worldwide, including higher education and advanced training. This investment reflects the emergence of the "knowledge society," the rise of the service sector, and the dependence of many societies on knowledge products and highly educated personnel for economic growth. (p. 290)

While technological advancement has always been the key stimulus driving globalization forward, two other developments are also remarkable in the discussion. The cessation of the communist *bloc* after the Second World War and the liberalization of a large number of economies across the globe in the 1990s also impelled globalization into the transformative force it is today. It need hardly be stated that globalization has proffered newer opportunities for all partakers. Not as obvious are the perils that come along with the promises: the increased interdependence amongst entities also increases their vulnerabilities. Be that as it may, globalization is an actuality that will continue to shape the future.

It is notable that globalization understates the notion of nation-states without invalidating it. Herein is introduced the concept of internationalization. The two are frequently misperceived to be substitutable: whereas internationalization arises out of globalization, it is not identical to it. Internationalization refers to an engagement of multinational, multicultural, and/or multilingual dimension into an entity or phenomenon. Altbach, Reisburg, and Rumbley (2009, pp. 23–24) mark the distinction succinctly:

> Globalization typically makes reference to "the broad economic, technological, and scientific trends that directly affect higher education and are largely inevitable in the contemporary world." Internationalization, on the other hand, has more to do with the "specific policies and programs undertaken by governments, academic systems and institutions, and even individual departments to deal with globalization" (Altbach, 2006, p. 123). A give and take between globalization and internationalization has been evident to many higher

education observers, but one of the key distinctions between the two concepts is the notion of control. Globalization and its effects are beyond the control of any one actor or set of actors. Internationalization, however, can be seen as a strategy for societies and institutions to respond to the many demands placed upon them by globalization, and as a way for higher education to prepare individuals for engagement in a globalized world. Indeed, internationalization has been conceived in many quarters as a necessary "process of integrating an international, intercultural, or global dimension in the purpose, functions, or delivery of postsecondary education." (Knight, 2003, p. 2)

Along the same lines, Van der Wende refers to internationalization as the "process of increasing cooperation between states or to activities across state borders" (cited in Powar, 2013). This description is important as it emphasizes the dissimilarity between globalization and internationalization based upon how each views the concept of nation-state. As stated earlier, globalization negates the significance of countries. On the other hand, internationalization upholds individualism of nation-states and other entities at a smaller level, such as institutions and organizations. Further, it espouses that cooperation and equity is possible amongst countries as they begin to interact more. It is important to point out that internationalization has the added underlay of considered and intentional prescriptive policies to that effect.

Internationalization in the Context of Higher Education

In the specific context of higher education, internationalization began to take on its conceptual silhouette in the early 1990s, and Knight and Altbach's formative work in the field accounts for much of the subject's substance. The literature on internationalization of higher education often goes into great detail about the concept and definition of internationalization. De Wit (2002) gives cogent reasons as to why such attention is useful:

It is not helpful for internationalization to become a catchall phrase for everything and anything international. A more focused definition is necessary if it is to be understood and treated with the importance that it deserves . . . . Internationalization needs to have parameters if it is to be assessed and to advance higher education. This is why a working definition in combination with a conceptual framework for internationalization of higher education is necessary. (p. 114)

In an oft-quoted definition of internationalization of higher education, Knight (1993, p. 21) states, "[I]nternationalisation is the process of integrating an international or intercultural dimension into the teaching, research, and service functions of an institution of higher learning." Knight's definition is arguably the most widely endorsed description of internationalization. Hans de Wit validated the definition on the grounds that Knight's approach was "process oriented . . . more global and neutral and . . . is a more bottom-up and instruction-oriented . . ." (cited in Knight, 1994). Altbach (2007) defines the concept as "specific policies and programs undertaken by governments, academic systems and institutions, and even individual departments." It is noteworthy that both researchers pivot the definition on infusion of an approach to reach out and interrelate with other nations. *Au contraire*, the proliferation of globalization is described as "tentacular spread" (Neave, 2001, cited in Powar, 2013). Thus, internationalization is not a goal unto itself, but means to an end; its value lies in enhancing pedagogy, research and innovation, and institutional engagement (Van der Wende, 1997, cited in Qiang, 2003).

The UNESCO's outline of internationalition of higher education bodies can be summed up as follows: "includes a broad range of elements such as curriculum, teaching, learning, research, institutional agree-ments, student/faculty mobility, and development cooperation" (IAU-AIU, n.d.a). Another apex advisory body, the International Association of Universities (IAU), defines "transnational education" as follows:

> all types of higher education study programs or sets of courses of study, or educational services (including those of distance education) in which learners are located in a country different from the one where the awarding institution is based. Such programs may belong to the education system of a State different from the State in which it operates, or may operate independently of any education system. (IAU-AIU, n.d.a)

Elements of Meaningful Internationalization

The notion of the extent of meaningful internationalization at the institutional level has been of concern to regulatory bodies for over a decade now. The AIU adopted a statement on internationalization in 2000, "It has often been taken for granted that universities are international . . . this impression only partially reflects the day to day reality of higher education institutions . . . and noting that internationalization of higher education is today more than ever a worthy goal" (IAU-AIU, n.d.a).

Internationalization of higher education has been categorized on the basis of its realm of activity into two classifications— "internationalization at home" and "internationalization abroad" (Knight, 2004).

> Internationalization at home typically consists of strategies and approaches designed to inject an international dimension into the home campus experience, for example, by including global and comparative perspectives in the curriculum or recruiting international students, scholars, and faculty and leveraging their presence on campus. Internationalization abroad, on the other hand, calls for an institution to project itself and its stakeholders out in the world. Key examples include sending students to study abroad, setting up a branch campus overseas, or engaging in an inter institutional partnership.

Middlehurst and Woodfield (2007) have observed that internationalization has impacted higher education primarily in two ways: first, it has made the higher education sector more competitive, and second, it has driven institutions to devise policy prescriptions at the organizational level. The former implies that higher education the world over is viewed as a global marketplace for international students, academics, and research funds. Thus, institutions and education providers do not interact with each other in a random fashion; rather, they engage in active competition. The latter impact refers to the increasing range and complexity of activities undertaken by higher education institutions. These strategies might be limited in their goal to increasing international student enrollment, or these might be more comprehensive and aim to transform the entire ethos of the organization so it is internationalized across manifold dimensions.

As stated earlier, internationalization has been defined using several approaches (Aigner et al., 1992; Arum & Van de Water, 1992; de Wit, 1995; Knight 1994, 1996, 1997, as cited in Qiang, 2003). Widely endorsed and cited is Knight's (1994) grouping of these approaches. In referring to "approach," the author refers to those techniques and methods that are construed to be the most effective means of attaining internationalization in an institution of higher education (see Table 2.1).

The author proposes a fourth approach, which is emerging to be increasingly more important in the present times—the "economics approach." This approach focusses wholly on the aspects that are related to the "economics" of internationalization, such as the

Table 2.1
Approaches to Internationalization of Higher Education

Approaches	Description
Process Approach	The process approach frames internationalization as a process which integrates an international dimension or perspective into the major functions of the institution. Terms such as infuse, integrate, permeate, and incorporate are used to characterize the process approach. A wide range of activities, policies, and procedures are part of this process.
Activity Approach	The activity approach describes internationalization in terms of categories or types of activities such as curriculum, scholar/students exchange, and technical cooperation.
Competency Approach	The competency approach looks at internationalization in terms of developing new skills, attitudes, knowledge in students, faculty, and staff. The focus is clearly on the human dimension not on academic activities or organizational issues.
Organizational Approach	The fourth approach focuses on developing an ethos or culture in the university or college that values and supports intercultural and international perspectives and initiatives. This last approach is closely linked with the process approach.

Source: Knight (1994, pp. 1–15).

following: first, the contribution that internationalization makes to regional economy and to the enhancement of country's "soft" power. The second aspect is about the contribution of internationalization to the enhancement of corporate competitiveness and comparative skill formation. The former example is discussed at length later in the section on "soft power" (as propounded by Harvard academic Professor Joseph Nye). The latter has been discussed, partially, by Brown (2001) and Brown, Green, and Lauder (2008) in their discussion on "high skills," and applied to the context of higher education by Yeravdekar and Tiwari (2014a).

The "economics-driven" approach has provided propulsive fuel to the internationalization of higher education all over the world. A key aspect of this is the contribution of internationalization to the enhancement of corporate competitiveness and comparative skill formation (Yeravdekar & Tiwari, 2014a). The rise of the knowledge economy and, with it, the need to train "knowledge-personnel" brings internationalization into the conversation.

Internationalization has redefined the dynamics within the graduate labor market. It has enlarged the sphere of higher education, intensifying the competition, and necessitating that, at national, multinational, and organizational levels, policy be devised to system-atize steps for the implementation of internationalization. At any rate, internationalization leads to the elaboration of an ethos that does away with randomness in the interactions between participants in the global higher education scene by ushering in "academic entrepre-neurialism" (Davies, 1992, cited in Knight, 1994), in other words, competition.

It also follows that a workforce that is to participate in the global employment market must be conversant with the requirements of the global work culture and work readiness skills. Brown (2001) and Brown, Green, and Lauder (2008), in their discussion on "high skills," posit that global economic competitiveness derives, in part, from the skill-base of the workforce.

Internationalization of higher education brings into the student portfolio many personal and professional properties that may be categorized as "global competencies"—cross-cultural competencies, interdisciplinary approach, "soft skills," and "high skills."

At the national level, internationalization of higher education is pursued as public policy prescriptions. In other words, the government issues mandates for institutions to encourage them to undertake internationalization and offers incentives to further reinforce the encouragement. At the institutional level, the diversification of modes of delivery and of providers of higher education, in response to the demand to broaden the bracket under which higher education cohorts are included, works to further drive internationalization.

The economics-driven approach well captures Teichler's (1999) prediction that internationalization, in the future, will have much greater a capacity to move from the "elitist" periphery to the "mass-based" center. It means that internationalization will transition to orient itself to the "substance of learning" (curricular and pedagogic aspects), away from the present orientation towards mobility.

Another important aspect of the "economics-driven" approach is that internationalization of higher education lends itself to the view that higher education is a tradable good, and it is not only an article of import and export but also one that can be evaluated on the basis of the extent to which it positively contributes to career prospects. Students who have the competitive edge of international education are better armed with the employability quotient. Apart from the above-mentioned reference to cross-cultural competencies, properties such as enhanced awareness of global business operations and better honed problem-solving and decision-making skills are also attributable to internationalization of higher education.

Perhaps the "economics-driven" benefit that gets the least credit is that students, faculty members, and institutions profit from the opportunities that come from building transnational knowledge and career networks across the globe:

> As important as they are, the benefits of international exposure in education and practical experience go beyond students. The higher education institutions also benefit from internationalization. It results in more revenue generation, cross-fertilization of academic and research intellectual knowledge, and stronger brand standing. The advantages to nation-states are manifold too. It strengthens politico-diplomatic ties between countries, fosters goodwill, and brings about familiarity and understanding of foreign people (Nye, 2005; Powar, 2012b).

The presence of foreign students also helps generate development of businesses and support services around higher education institutions to cater to this group (Whitaker, as cited in Yeravdekar and Tiwari, 2014a, p. 207).

The question also emerges as to what occasions and sustains internationalization. As with the multiplicity of definitions, the rationales to internationalization are many, coming from as many ideological models. As has been stated earlier, the "economic" model is the one most prominently elaborated on. It is argued that, higher education institutions, influenced by economic considerations, engage in competition, thereby spurring on internationalization of higher education. The understanding that internationalization of higher education adds competitive advantage drives institutions to incorporate the international element. This view perceives institutions to be partakers in the global marketplace of higher education as well as the multinational job market.

Teichler emphasizes the role of "entrepreneurialism," "marketization," and "competition" in the discussion on internationalization of higher education. Teichler has listed five areas of policies and activities with respect to internationalization:

(a) the knowledge dimension, particularly the border-crossing movement of knowledge; (b) the validation and recognition of teaching, learning, and research results; (c) issues of international homogeneity or the variety of structural elements of higher education; (d) the scope of actors' policies (e.g., national versus international policies of higher education); and (e) higher education steering as a whole (e.g., the role of national governments, national or international professional associations, international organizations, etc., as well as the modes of steering). (as cited by Altbach & Peterson, 2007, p. 112)

A more ideologically-driven liberal approach views internationalization of higher education as necessary in an interdependent world. As one might expect of the liberal democratic school of thought in social sciences, the world is a connected whole and the parts must cooperate if they are to grow. This perspective espouses internationalization of higher education on the grounds that it furthers mutual understanding and cooperation, which are important for building a responsible citizenry. Further, internationalization of higher education helps ingrain in citizens the sense of socio-political justice and responsibility. It would be fair to conclude that in reality all the rationales exert force to some extent, and that they are not mutually exclusive but work towards interplay.

What does internationalization entail? Put differently, how does one recognize it in an institution of higher education? Knight (1994) has identified several factors that are key ingredients in the internationalization process of a higher education institution. These are categorized separately into "academic activities and services," and "organizational factors." Knight (1994) also builds a charter of checkpoints to assess internationalization in higher education institutions around these elements.

1. *Academic activities and services*

   (i) Curricular innovations: This sub-category refers to the incorporation of disciplines and streams that have a distinct international and comparative dimension, such as area studies and international studies

   (ii) Exchange programs: emphasis on facilitating mobility of teaching and nonteaching staff in exchange programs

   (iii) Foreign language study

   (iv) International Development Initiatives: denotes opportunities to collaborate with peers in developing countries through development schemes

   (v) Inter-institutional collaborative schemes: dedicating set of services and resources for the purpose of building networks and channels of communication with higher education institutions in foreign countries and organizations associated with international higher education

   (vi) Research with international dimension: this refers to research with international/comparative focus, partnerships with international institutions and organizations, and dissemination of resulting knowledge through international networks and channels

   (vii) Area studies and theme centers: these centers are grouped either geographically or on the basis of cross-disciplinary concerns that have a distinct international focus

   (viii) Cross-cultural training: this training is primarily dispensed with the aim of increasing multi-cultural competencies

(ix) Institutional services and extra-curricular activities: this subcategory refers to services and activities that cater to international students or work to bring international and domestic students together

2. *Organizational factors*: commitment of senior management to internationalization, adequate funding, presence of an international office, policy statements, incorporation of internationalization as a criterion in hiring and reviewing faculty and nonfaculty members, inculcation of internationalization in communication and PR networks, and annual plan and budget

Indicative Information and Pointers in Internationalization

As internationalization has begun to feature extensively as a governmental and institutional policy item, a corresponding need to identify and consolidate the various points of reference has emerged, which become important as one ensures meaningful implementation of policies related to internationalization.

Performance indices, of which kind there are many, present a useful toolbox of resources for policymakers at the levels of the government and the institution as they plan strategies to implement internationalization. Literature review reveals that IAU–AIU (n.d.), Knight (2006), and Middlehurst and Woodfield (2007) have discussed the subject from many perspectives and offer several important pieces of advice and helpful hints. The benchmarking pointers discussed below cover the entire range of variables that can collectively or individually serve as markers of internationalization.

Internationalization As a Matter of Strategy

Internationalization features largely as an expressly stated mission in documents at institutional (higher education institutions), national (government policies), and international (international organizations such as UNESCO) level. "The 2006 International Association of Universities (IAU) survey (Knight, 2006a, p. 42) indicates that 73% of higher education institutions (HEIs) give internationalization a high priority, 23% a medium priority and only 2% a low priority" (Altbach & Peterson, 2007, p. 110). More recently, a similar survey titled "Internationalization of Higher Education—Growing expectations, fundamental values" was conducted by the IAU in 2014, in which analyses responses from 1,336 higher education institutions in 131 different countries were utilized. The findings present the largest and most geographically comprehensive collection of primary data on internationalization of higher education to date. Some of the important findings are reported as follows (IAU-AIU, n.d.b):

- Globally, higher education institutions are increasing their thrust on internationalization; however, the extent to which internationalization is incorporated in institutional policy varies considerably: "Over half of the respondents report that their institution has an internationalization policy/strategy, and 22% report that one is in preparation. Just over 15% indicate that internationalization forms part of the overall institutional strategy."
- Within institutions, areas that are accorded the highest priority are student mobility and international research collaboration.
- "Student knowledge of international issues is the most significant expected benefit of internationalization." This finding is consistent with the findings that came out of surveys in 2005 and 2009.
- Of the potential risks of internationalization, "international opportunities being available only to students with financial resources, was ranked by respondents as the most significant potential risk of internationalization for institutions while the most significant societal risk is noted as commodification/commercialization of education."
- The targeted region for drawing international students was the neighboring region. Europe is also a strong target.
- The biggest obstacle to advancing internationalization is lack of financial resources.

The Variables That Add Up to Internationalization of Higher Education

How does an organization ascertain if its efforts towards internationalization are worthwhile and fruitful or not? It emerges that a strategy guided by the fulfillment of quality-assurance goals is to be recommended. It is also brought to light that student experience counts as an important variable in the sum total of factors that make-up the rubric of institutional quality assurance management.

An important issue for regulatory and advisory bodies at international, national, and institutional levels has been to analyze the concept: what makes for meaningful internationalization of higher education bodies? A great deal of research studies have been undertaken in response to the concern. Since the year 2000, UNESCO has identified internationalization of higher education bodies as a priority area. Similarly, IAU issued the statement, "Sharing Quality Higher Education Across Borders: A Checklist for Good Practices," which was drafted by several authorities on transnational education. The statement includes the following principal goals for cross-border higher education (CBHE; IAU-AIU, n.d.b):

> to contribute to the broader economic, social and cultural well being of communities . . . strengthen developing countries' higher education capacity in order to promote global equity . . . instill in learners the critical thinking that underpins responsible citizenship at the local, national, and global levels . . . be accessible not only to students who can afford to pay but also to qualified students with financial need . . . meet the same high standards of academic and organizational quality no matter where it is delivered . . . be accountable to the public, students, and government . . . expand the opportunities for international mobility of faculty, researchers, and students . . . provide clear and full information to students and external stakeholders about the education they provide. (IAU-AIU, n.d.)

Quality Assurance and Student Satisfaction: The Heart of Institutional Performance Benchmarking

Quality-assurance-guided internationalization is important not only for regulatory bodies, but it is important as an element of internal benchmarking for institutions as well. International students are increasingly being offered more choices with respect to higher education institutions. It is not surprising then that international students are more selective and demanding. They have come to expect customized and consumer satisfaction-driven experience from higher education institutions in foreign countries. It is important to emphasize the "whole international student experience" factor since students now look ahead to more than academic enrichment; their expectation encompasses a much wider realm to include non-academic variables. Living and studying as an international student can be quite expensive and students can easily wind up incurring predictable and unpredictable expenses. The issue of acculturation and acclimating to foreign circumstances is just as big a challenge if not more. The higher education institutions cannot be called upon to take responsibility for the students' experiences outside the campus; however, the institutions are expected to take affirmative action to ensure that international students are reasonably aware of what they are up against as well as prepared to stand up to the challenges that they might face.

Middlehurst and Woodfield (2007) have outlined four essential composite elements that constitute the complete international student experience: educational, socio-cultural, administrative, and employment related.

Educational Elements: The educational element primarily includes the content of the study, including curriculum and other aspects of course or program, and its reputation for quality. The strategy about enhancing the international competitiveness of higher education institutions through the development of programs and curriculum that reinforce global dimension of the institution is an important one. Powar (2012b) in his discourse on ways to ensure relevance in internationalization, states his case for "academic restructuring." Along the same lines, Ching and Chin (2011) discuss the category "academic offerings and curriculum" as one of the key performance indicators of internationalization of higher education institutions. Thus, the stakeholders are responsible for staying attuned to the trends and competition in transnational education. This is a dynamic role and the institution should continually revise academic content such that it is responsive to the demands of the global job market and provide a competitive edge to students. Some pointers to achieve this are the specialization of programs, availability of foreign language programs, international internships and service opportunities, and ideas to incorporate practical training experience with businesses at home and abroad. The collaborations under the category widely known as "study abroad" refer to a higher education body's alliances with other international universities at home and abroad with the aim of promoting the exchange of ideas and mutually beneficial partnerships. Ching and Chin (2011) also mention "signing of student exchange agreements with partner universities abroad" among indicators of internationalization. This category includes initiatives such as promotion of element of overseas study into academic programs by assigning credit points to study abroad programs and "signing of a memorandum of understanding and/or agreements" with international universities at home and abroad.

The end goal of preparing graduates who are employable at home and abroad is crucial. In endorsing the significance of curriculum in attaining true internationalization, IAU discusses a checklist for cross-border higher education, which poses the question "do the institutions' cross-border programs encourage collaboration with the host country institutions and expand the opportunities for international mobility of faculty, researchers, and students?" (IAU-AIU, n.d.b). Other factors in this category include the quality of teaching, support from tutors and recognition of qualification for employment and further study, an international relevance of course and program content, opportunities for training in the medium of instruction, and so on.

Socio-cultural Elements: The socio-cultural experiences form a very crucial part of the international student experience. Broadly, these refer to the students' perceptions of the host country in terms of reception of international students, general hospitableness, and ease of living. There is much that higher education institutions can do to facilitate an easy transition to the foreign socio-cultural landscape. Some of the ways to bring this about are to embed a culture of international understanding and fraternity to ensure that domestic students are oriented to ethno-relative sensitivity and to improve support services and facilities that help international students improve their academic performance and adapt to the host country. Endorsing this view, Ching and Chin (2011) lists organizations and activities with "internationalized themes" as important factors to consider in an international university. Similarly, Powar (2012b) makes the case for promoting activities and services with the view of enhancing the students' socio-cultural experience.

Administrative Elements: The international students' perception of the administrative system is also an important component of their experience. The administrative aspect essentially refers to student and support services, especially the elements that serve international students, such as the scope and effectiveness of the international office. It has been widely observed that there is an increasing trend towards incorporation of nonacademic elements into the internationalization process of an institution—chiefly, as a way of differentiating the institution.

Amongst the subcategories of the administrative aspect, protocols related to immigration are noteworthy. Middlehurst (2001) and Powar (2012b, p. 255), advocating this stance, list customs and visa regulations as significant considerations in achieving internationalization of higher education institutions. Another important factor in this category is the incorporation of recommendations to human resource authorities to take concerted efforts to recruit academic and research staff with the advantage of international academic and professional experience. The institution must also undertake initiatives in staff development and training with the aim of encouraging multicultural awareness through travel and engagement with other institutions. The staff development and training ought to include opportunities to update IT and communication skills so as to keep up with the latest developments worldwide and stay conversant with modern technology and business culture. The role of world-class infrastructural support system in advancing internationalization has been addressed by several researchers.

As discussed earlier, the accessibility of information technology and the prevalence of a common medium of instruction and communication are the main catalysts of internationalization of higher education institutions. Powar (2012b, p. 251), underlining the significance of providing a support system around the medium of instruction, states, "It is necessary that . . . special English classes for international students are conducted for the first few months . . ." The author goes on to argue further that adequate English language training can potentially contribute to the student success and satisfaction. Similarly, foundation courses that are designed specifically for international students have the potential to assist international students tremendously as they transition to the Indian higher education system.

Employment Element: Last, international student experience also entails the extent to which international education serves to further career preparedness, employability, and future employment networks. With this in mind, higher education institutions are increasingly inclined to forge linkages between industry and academia. An instance of this element would be improving curricula such that the content provides students global career skills and competencies. The global milieu in which higher education bodies operate is constantly evolving and expanding. On the positive side, it means greater opportunities for higher education institutions. However, it also involves more competitiveness. In order to achieve more sustainable international partnerships, collaborative efforts by institutions have to step above and beyond the traditional focus on academics at the institutional level. A thrust toward building collaborative alliances at the corporate and communal level is necessary for improving international competitiveness. Work-study arrangements, such as internships that allow students to participate in the industry, are prominent ways to incorporate career skills into the academic component.

The Rationales for Practicing Internationalization

The drive to internationalize higher education is spawned by factors both external and internal. Among the institutional factors, increasing enrollment, "massification," and generation of greater revenues merit note. For these reasons and more, higher education institutions are beginning to consider internationalization as a multifarious phenomenon that hinges on the perception and satisfaction of students. To state the obvious, internationalization is now interwoven with student recruitment and retention. Related to this is the focus on nonacademic factors such as student support services.

The importance of identifying the rationale for practising internationalization of higher education is important at all levels: national, supranational, and institutional. The rationale lays down the motivation for internationalization. In other words, it answers the question "What are we trying to achieve by practicing internationalization?" It is an important question to be answered because internationalization does not come cheap. It requires a considerable investment of resources. In order to stay alert to the continued usefulness of such practices and processes, and to institutional accountability, it is only the purposeful to lay down, at the very outset, what the key motivations and objectives are and to spell out the guiding principles related to the workings and applications on the field. Knight states that "The importance of having clear, articulated rationales for internationalization cannot be overstated . . . Rationales dictate the kind of benefits or expected outcomes one would expect from internationalization efforts" (as cited in Powar, 2015, p. 6).

Several researchers have identified the chief rationales that motivate institutions, governments, and associations, such as the IAU, to undertake internationalization as an expressed mission.

Knight and De Wit have noted that, traditionally, "four types of rationales have been identified by scholars: academic, socio-cultural, political, and economic" (as cited in Powar, 2015, p. 6). As internationalization has evolved, it has been found that the above-mentioned four categories actually overlap in respect of their functions. Knight (2006) has stated that the rationales can only be properly grouped if they are first divided into two separate categories: national and institutional.

The four traditional rationales are as follows:

1. *Academic*: This category rationalizes internationalization on the grounds of the importance of "internationalizing" the academic component of higher education so that it is more relevant to the globalized milieu. The academic rationale concerns itself with the importance of increasing the knowledge base and competencies of individuals so that they can function optimally in the globalized world. The academic components such as curriculum, research, and teaching–learning processes are the focus.

2. *Socio-cultural*: This category emphasizes internationalization on the grounds of the significance of the social norms that reflect the changes which globalization has brought about. The social values of cosmopolitanism, global citizenship, multiculturalism, and world peace are considered to be the key forces that drive internationalization forward.

> Foreign students and scholars . . . are the "carriers" of knowledge across borders . . . They are the embodiment of cosmopolitan culture and they provide valuable expertise and a cross-cultural perspective. (Altbach, 1989, cited in Powar, 2015, p. 8)

3. *Political*: The political rationale speaks to the presence of "bloc" mentality in the post-World War II world. It emphasizes the importance of (political) indoctrination of future leaders through internationalization of higher education. Ever since the end of the Cold War between the US and the erstwhile USSR, the political rationale has shifted gears and made national interest its subject. In this discussion, internationalization of higher education is seen as "soft power," to be used as an instrument of exerting influence over other countries.

4. *Economic*: This line of argument is born out of the emerging reality of higher education being pursued as an article of cross-border trade. To state the obvious, internationalization is a means to add to the revenue stream of the institution. International students, who pay much more tuition fees than domestic students, are prized for that reason more than any other. The reduction of public expenditure on higher education across the world is, partly, responsible for the shift.

The more recent rationales, split across the two levels—national and institutional—are described as follows:

National-level rationales are, to put it broadly, the ones that justify internationalization on the grounds that it is a means to nation-building. The key thrust is that internationalization contributes to building the human resource base and fulfilling labor market requirements.

Institutional-level rationales are those that serve the specific interests of the institution. It includes factors such as brand-building, revenue-generation, and increasing the "catchment" area.

Powar (2015, pp. 11–12) cites Naidoo, who has outlined in his study, "trans-national higher education-related rationales: mutual understanding rationale" (increasing international cooperation and fraternity), "skill-migration rationale" (contributing to knowledge-economy and "brain-gain"), "revenue generation rationale," and "capacity-building rationale" (improving the skill base of the country). The typology of institutional rationales for internationalization is described in Table 2.2.

Table 2.2
Typology of Institutional Rationales for Internationalization

Rationales	Constituent Elements or Focus
Social and cultural	National cultural identity Intercultural understanding Citizenship development Social and community development
Political	Foreign policy National security Peace and mutual understanding National identity Regional identity
Economic	Economic growth and competitiveness Labor market Financial incentives Income generation
Academic	International dimension to research and teaching Extension of academic horizons Institution-building Profile and status Enhancement of quality and curriculum development International academic standards Research collaborations
Competitive	International branding and positioning Strategic alliances Knowledge production Knowledge transfer
Developmental	Student and staff development Institutional learning and exchange Capacity building Technical assistance

Source: Middlehurst and Woodfield (2007, p. 30).

Being that competition for international students is rising rapidly and that recruitment of these students is a significant institutional revenue model, higher education institutions are found to be concerned about improving the international student experience. Middlehurst and Woodfield (2007) note that a number of British universities view international students as "cash cows" since the tuition for this student group is significantly higher than domestic students. In an over-zealous attempt to increase recruitment, these institutions often "over promise and under deliver."

Possibly the authors are suggesting that to be fair to this student group, as well as bring about true internationalization, it falls to higher education institutions to identify what leads this student group to make informed choices and what constitutes student satisfaction with respect to internationalization. In order to contribute to internationalization, the institutions must monitor their performance and success in setting and meeting expectations. It is encouraging to note that several institutions that espouse internationalization of higher education as a matter of policy prescription have developed matrices to gauge international student experiences. Further, this research is being carried out both at the institutional—individually or in a benchmarking group—and sectorial levels. Instances of such audits and investigative studies include QAA, UKCOSA, and I-Graduate International Student Barometer in the UK. In common is the Education Services for Overseas Students (ESOS) Act in Australia, which is primarily a quality assurance regulatory body that oversees higher education institutions that recruit a significant number of international students. The ESOS Act is reputed to focus on upholding the welfare of international students as well as being an important service level agreement for international governments, students, and parents (Middlehurst & Woodfield, 2007).

Internationalization at Home

In its most frequent acceptation in research studies, policy-making, and institutional missions, the concept of internationalization of higher education refers to those processes and phenomena that are related to academic cross-border mobility, either outbound or inbound.

In the divergence from this reference, "internationalization at home" or "internationalization on campus" specifically denotes the aspects of higher education that can operate outside the realm of cross-border mobility. This orientation is exclusive of internationalization of such aspects as recruitment of international students, student exchange programs, and research projects that involve collaborations with universities in other countries. The literature on the subject does not address the question whether distance education or e-training and development count as internationalization at home or not.

Explaining the concept in a reductionist fashion, Wachter defines internationalization at home as "any internationally related activity with the exception of outbound student and staff mobility." He widens the definition by adding that "it has been avoided to freeze the concept into a simple rigid definition. One reason for this has been and still is that IaH should be the opposite of a concept cast in iron: It is meant to develop" (Wachter, 2000, cited in IAU-AIU, n.d.a).

Knight's (2008) definition is in line with the North American view, which uses "internationalization at home" inter-changeably with "internationalizing the campus":

> to give greater prominence to campus-based elements such as the inter-cultural and international dimension in the teaching learning process, research, extra-curricular activities, relationships with local cultural and ethnic community groups, as well as the integration of foreign students and scholars into campus life and activities.

According to Brewer (2004) and Mestenhauser (2003), the concept of internationalization at home was introduced by a European educationist, Bengt Nilsson, in 1999 and promoted by the European Association for International Education.

In the past, one of the key goals of the Erasmus program in Europe was to ensure that at least 10 percent European students are enrolled and studying at another European university. This goal turned out to be both unfeasible and faultily designed.

As the program was set up, it made student mobility the lone driver of international education. What it resulted in was neglect of other aspects.

[It] left institutions off the hook. Faculty did not need to change what they were doing, the curriculum did not need revision, nor did institutions need to commit resources to internationalization. Further, why were only 10% of the students to benefit? Were the remaining 90% not to be educated for citizenship in a Europe constantly facing new challenges? Were they not to gain the intercultural communication skills that would enable them to effectively interact with people from other countries? (Brewer, 2004, p. 2)

To be fair, it must be pointed out that complete dependence on student mobility was a factor of necessity, not design. In the past, resources were limited. To access information from other parts of the world, one had to travel. As opposed to the present times, the technology in communication was undeveloped and could not be relied on to establish dialogue or exchange information.

Perhaps a bigger reason was the climate of international politics at the time when study abroad was considered shorthand for student mobility, even internationalization. This is the era before globalization, when international education, as with international relations, was about specific interactions between nation-states with the attendant underlying vibe of "us" in relation to "them": the Cold War reference in student exchanges between erstwhile USSR and India comes to mind. In the United States, the most important guiding factor for investing in international education was to create "professional experts" in international relations, which could be consulted on matters related to foreign policy and other diplomatically oriented issues about other countries. It would seem that the higher education ecosystem has been unable to catch up with changes that have occurred in the politico-socio-economic realm.

Mestenhauser (2003, p. 3) notes that, according to official data, only nine percent of students receive any degree of international education. The author reports that, his personal estimation, based on the application of learning theories, is that an even smaller segment of the students in this nine percent group shows evidence of having the knowledge and skills that would qualify them as recipients of international education. He warns that the figures, appearing impressive, are exaggerated to paint a picture that is rosier than the reality:

> Researchers cite these figures to impress educators and policymakers in the hope that they will devote more resources and attention to this field. . . . These "case study" publications tout the so-called successful or promising practices on specific campuses. . . . While a very few are indeed outstanding, most lack any sophisticated treatment of what elements make a program successful and how this should be evaluated. (p. 3)

It would not be far-fetched to hold that the introduction and popularity of internationalization at home is due, in part, to the inability of study abroad programs, a mainstay of student mobility in Europe, to grow and adapt to the changing higher education landscape. Jenkins and Skelly pointed out that study abroad programs had failed to foster global citizenship. It was opined that these programs were overly commodified, as a result of which they were more about tourism than "immersion in the local culture" (Jenkins and Skelly, 2004, cited in Brewer, 2004, n.p.).

Why refer to internationalization at home in particular? Why not refer to just internationalization as it is generally understood to mean?

Internationalization of higher education, as it is generally known, is rather an elitist concept, which carries the risk of promoting inequitable selectiveness, thereby potentially running against the goal of "massification" of higher education. It may not be theoretically accurate, yet this is how it presents on the field, both at the levels of national policy-making as well as that of institutional strategies on internationalization.

The section on global rankings outlines the many ways in which global rankings, as an expression of internationalization, promote an elitist culture in the global higher education landscape. As it plays itself out, internationalization often passes for cross-border academic exchanges. This implies that internationalization is a capital-intensive proposition and only the countries and institutions that have selective access to massive funding are part of the center stage in global higher education. It also implies that only students who are intellectually the "cream of the crop" can reap the benefits of international education.

Thus, internationalization foregoes the proverbial "base of the pyramid," which, in a country such as India, would amount to the overwhelming majority of the higher education demographic. By the same token, internationalization reinforces the *dependencia* narrative of "center-periphery" in higher education, whereby a small coterie holds the center stage and the remainder of the participants is forever playing "catch-up."

It would be wise to consider further the possibility that internationalization can widen the present disparities in higher education systems at practically all levels. As an instance, it is frequently criticized that internationalization is concentrated in the Anglophone world; therefore, countries that do not follow the English language as the medium of instruction or the systems that do not follow the British or the American systems of higher education are out of the league.

Internationalization at home overcomes the limitations of this exclusivity. It is devised in the specific contexts of institutions and not so much that of policy-making at the national level or foreign institutions. Internationalization at home is more about the acquisition of international competencies that can be acquired in the absence of cross-border mobility on the campus, such as fostering cross-cultural proficiencies, introducing internationalization of curriculum, and modernizing pedagogic practices to bring them in step with global advances.

This is not to say that internationalization at home cannot coincide with thos forms of internationalization that involve cross-border mobility, but it is to say that it is possible to bring about the former without the latter.

As Knight's (2008) definition suggests, the pathway to internationalization at home is the campus, more specifically the classroom, which makes it possible for all institutions to take on internationalization and for all students within the institution to benefit from it. The most prominent ways to usher in internationalization at home are as follows:

1. Modernization of program and course structure to reflect international advances in curriculum development, pre-entry qualifications, assessment, and academic workload

2. Introduction of contemporary pedagogic practices in teaching–learning, instructional technology and library infrastructure
3. Addition of staff development and training programs to upgrade the teaching and nonteaching staff members' personal and professional skills and bring them up to step with global standards
4. Introduction of extra-curricular activities such as hosting international students' cultural festivals and providing student support services to this student group
5. Coordination with international organizations such as foreign embassies and participation in international conferences and conventions
6. Internationalization of the campus: undertake efforts to set up hostels for international students, introduce international cuisines, offer foreign language courses, and miscellaneous steps to modernize resources and facilities
7. Introduction of such student-support services as mentoring and counseling on living as an international student in India—the "buddy" service, wherein an Indian (domestic) student guides and counsels one (or more) international student serves as an example
8. Extension of scholarship to international students, especially those who are from developing countries

Internationalization at home is a useful approach to improve the mass of "learning outcomes" in a manner that makes them more inclusive of international innovations without having to make the students and other participants in the process travel abroad. It is a targeted methodology, which among other things, helps identify and instill those academic and career-preparedness skills that will allow students (and other participants) to succeed in further higher education and the global job market and create global competencies.

At the very top of the list of tools to foster internationalization at home is modernization of curriculum. Knight (1994) referred to curriculum as the backbone of internationalization at home. According to Leask (2009, p. 209), internationalization of the curriculum is about "incorporation of international, intercultural and global dimensions into the content of the curriculum as well as the learning outcomes, assessment tasks, teaching methods, and support services of a program of study" (cited in IAU-AIU, n.d.a).

Ensuring cross-border student mobility, it was assumed, facilitates sufficient exposure to global ethos and practices in higher education. The present-day higher education environment presents many characteristics that are unprecedented and pose an obstruction to this notion. The higher education demographic now includes a large segment of older students, who are also engaged in employment and, therefore, enrolled in programs that are not in the "fulltime" category. Higher education is also moving in the direction of "massification." It means that an increasing number of technical-professional programs and courses are being added to tertiary education; these typically cost less and last for a shorter duration. These circumstances make up a milieu in which global competencies must be delivered through the core learning processes and not as "add-ons" so that all students and institutions can benefit to some degree. Thus, curriculum, the core of teaching–learning processes, must be at the heart of internationalization at home.

Internationalization of curriculum must weave together relevant strains from other disciplines and other cultural contexts. The Indian curriculum has been criticized for being too centered on the Indian side of things and not including information and perspectives from other contexts.

The IAU (IAU–AIU, n.d.a) cites exemplary practices in the internationalization of curriculum at a few select universities—Oxford Brookes University, the University of Sheffield, and Glasgow Caledonian University. It also recognizes institutions that offer specific certificate programs as part of the initiative on internationalization at home: University of Hamburg, Queen's University, Salzburg College, University of Bremen, Grand Valley State University, International Center Clausthal, and University of Passau. These are useful "peer-study" models, and Indian educationists must analyze how well these can be applied to their own unique contexts.

A few strains run common through the resource kits that the above-mentioned institutions utilize: instilling global perspectives that relate to how the information in one's discipline is represented, widening one's frame of reference beyond the prevailing one, engaging in critical debate, and bringing in discussions on cross-cultural competencies, global citizenship, social justice, and sustainability.

Interestingly, the findings of a research study conducted by Soria and Troisi (2013) concluded that activities related to internationalization at home yielded greater perceived benefits than those that were related to student participation in study abroad programs. This large-scale study utilized a number of theories on intercultural development and examined the results of participation by undergraduate students in study abroad programs vis-à-vis outcomes of on-campus international activities in nine large public research universities in the United States. It could be concluded from the findings of the study that internationalization at home is a valuable tool to bridge the gap between on-campus and off-campus activities.

Mestenhauser (2003) brings a valuable aspect to the discussion by pointing out that there is room for improvement in identifying an important area for further research studies. The author notes that internationalization at home, as it is practiced, is poorly conceptualized. It lacks any appreciable application of learning theories. This is a field where the theoretical paradigm is neglected in the favor of an instrumentality-driven approach. Those who devise programs to promote internationalization at home are often not trained in learning theories, which emphasize the idea that all learning occurs in a relational context.

The disregard for learning theories comes with a price, not just in international education, but in education in all disciplines. All cognitive capabilities—critical thinking, relational reasoning, and the ability to contextualize concepts—function as tools with which to apply the intellect to disciplinary knowledge so that, with the assistance of learning, information is processed and stored as context-determined knowledge and, when there be a need, transformed to higher-order skills (such as problem solving), not merely continue as domain-specific knowledge.

The concept of internationalization at home or internationalization on campus must be brought to bear the ideal of *Vasudhaiva Kutumbakam*—the world is one family. In summary, internationalization "at home" or "on campus" means to bring in the international dimension to all aspects of education—academic, extra-curricular, cultural, diversity related, and, indeed, the organizational ethos. This must be seen as being antithetical to the elitist idea that internationalization is about organizing and facilitating investment-heavy movement of select students (or faculty members) across borders.

Internationalization of Higher Education: Changing Variables of Demand and Supply in a "Borderless" Development

Perhaps the most consistent enhancement in internationalization is with respect to increase in the incidence of pertinent activities and sophistication of strategies. It is remarkable that internationalization has been central to mission statements of the most institutions in the English speaking world. One might be hard pressed to find institutions that do not have international students on campus, collaborations with foreign institutions and organizations, exchange programs, and so on in Anglo-Saxon countries.

In their study of British universities, Middlehurst and Woodfield (2007) observe that, as welcome as the above-mentioned advancements are, these initiatives are often not coordinated within and without institutions. Communication and linkages between activities are not always fashioned well, resulting in suboptimal consistency and productivity. It is also noted that strategies related to internationalization are commonly not embedded into institutional planning and development. As activities related to internationalization expand in reach and investment, it becomes more important that institutions develop models to further internationalization by identifying effective, viable, and time bound policies (see Table 2.3). In an ideal

Table 2.3
Stages of Institutional International Strategy Development

Phase	Type	Description
Phase 1	International activity	Disparate and unconnected activities
Phase 2	International strategy	Co-ordination and beginning of alignment
Phase 3	Internationalization process	Effort to integrate, achieve leverage and added value

Source: Middlehurst and Woodfield (2007, p. 31).

expression, internationalization would be one of the core indicators of quality and excellence in an institution of higher learning and not merely a competitive differentiator in cross-border recruitment.

It is also observed that implementation of internationalization is a highly variable concept: it is understood to mean different things to different institutions. Stated differently, institutions approach it from a number of perspectives. To some, it is by way of self-improving goal; to others, it is a part of the ethos of the organization. Similarly, some institutions document their internationalization strategies in their vision or mission statements, whereas others create divisions and designatory roles to further internationalization.

The most prominent impact of internationalization of higher education pertains to the mode of international student recruitment. The increase in demand is accompanied with corresponding increase in diversity and competition.

The increase in multiplicity of types of providers and students engaged in international education is an important development in the internationalization of higher education. As can be seen from the following discussion, much of this generates from the competitive nature of the phenomenon of internationalization. Middlehurst and Woodfield (2007) hold that the drive to expand and diversify activities pertaining to internationalization is the result of some anxiety about "avoid[ing] an over-reliance on international student recruitment from a few source countries or related to particular kinds of provision" (p. 17). In an attempt to recruit students who might face restrictions related to factors such as mobility, finance, and so on, a number of institutions have come up with an ingenious provision, such as distance learning, international branch campuses, and likewise; Laureate Education is a ready example.

It is notable that international organizations related to higher education such as the Commonwealth of Learning (COL) and UNESCO have been expressly supportive of this "borderless" development. Often, these organizations view transnational education from the developmental perspective. It is maintained that distance education and the use of "open source" material, in particular, will help overcome the inequity in access to educational resources as well as in technology.

Another advantage of this "borderless" development is that international education is no longer merely overseas study experience; rather, it is that coupled with greater flexibility and diversity in delivery mode. At the end of providers, this has translated into greater opportunities. To begin with, the providers have a far larger base of prospective students to choose from. In addition, the student profile has diversified beyond recognition. Some decades ago, the reference to an international student would call to mind the image of a student from Europe or one of the Anglo-Saxon countries traveling to a university in the developing world to spend a whole year there. Of course, that has changed now.

There are noninstitutional factors that add to the prevalent competition including diplomatic relations amongst partaking countries, international trade relations, exchange rates, tuitions fees and other expenses, student perceptions of the host country, institution, and the contribution of education to employability, ease of immigration, and so on.

The global recruitment market of international students is an area of growing interest to the providers of higher education and other participants. The situation is doubtless one where institutions are driven to consider competitive differentiation with great importance. An important aspect of strategy building is with respect to salesmanship: an institution that hopes to eke out space in the global marketplace must be alert to competition from all quarters, watchful of emerging markets, and proactive about marketing its appeal to international students. Amongst some of the more popular approaches to improving marketing strategies are setting up international offices within the institution and overseas offices in key and emerging markets, commissioning market research, and strengthening the quality monitoring aspect of these initiatives. On the academic front, it has been demonstrated that bolstering international research collaboration (such as knowledge transfer partnerships and collaborative research projects) in addition to teaching–learning partnerships (such as student exchange and joint teaching programs) go a long way in consolidating an institution's prowess in recruiting international students (Wagner & Leydesdorff, 2005, cited in Middlehurst & Woodfield, 2007). Some prominent examples include European Research Area, Worldwide Universities Network (WUN) and the League of European Research Universities (LERU).

Obstacles to Meaningful Internationalization of Higher Education: Multiple Concerns Related to Quality Assurance

In time, the expansion of transnational education has revealed roadblocks to the movement of higher education across borders. Middlehurst (2001) has identified seven obstacles to the effective internationalization of universities: national legislation in the larger context and in relation to higher education, regulation policies with respect to qualification, customs regulations, immigration, telecommunication laws, intellectual property legal policies, and bureaucracy (cited in Whitaker, 2004, p. 9).

In addition to the above, it has been reiterated that research on internationalization is woefully limited and this presents a serious challenge in forward movement. One of the main obstacles to comparative analysis and benchmarking of data on transnational education is the problem that there is not ample quantifiable data on the subject that can be used for the purpose of locating points of reference. Adam (2002) shares his frustration in conducting research on internationalization of universities: "virtually no country maintains statistical data on it and few educational experts had considered the phenomenon in any detail" (cited in Whitaker, 2004, p. 9). In the discussion on challenges in benchmarking, a persistent barrier is the lack of regulation at national or international level. For instance, accreditation system is, more often, than not, a decision-making process at the institutional level, and there are few policies at the national or multilateral level to abide by. Adam (2001) regrets that "currently many of the organizations that offer codes of practice to guide in the administration of transnational education provide only voluntary guidelines" (as cited in Whitaker, 2004, p. 9). Altbach and Knight (2007, p. 300) share a similar sentiment:

Many countries—lacking capacity or political will—do not have the regulatory systems to register or evaluate out-of-country providers. Regulatory frameworks for quality assurance or accreditation, even when they exist, usually do not apply to providers outside the national education system. This loophole permits bona fide and rogue foreign providers to avoid compliance with national regulations in many countries and makes monitoring their activities difficult . . .

The issue of quality assurance in international education is another roadblock in standardization of transnational education. Altbach and Knight's (2007, p. 139) writing captures the challenge lucidly.

[I]t will be of strategic and substantive importance to recognize the roles and responsibilities of all the players involved in accreditation and quality assurance. These include individual institutions/providers; national quality assurance systems; non-governmental and independent accreditation bodies; professional bodies; and regional/international organizations—all of whom contribute to ensuring the quality of cross-border education. Much is at risk if rogue providers or fraudulent qualifications become closely linked to cross-border education.

Evidently, cross-border universities proliferate across several levels, resulting in confusion with respect to the terms of accountability. Adams (2001) states that "the responsibility for quality assurance of transnational education is seen to be shared between the national authorities of the importing country, the receiving institution, the authorities of the exporting country, national quality assurance agencies, and a new supranational authority" (as cited in Whitaker, 2004).

References

Altbach P., & Peterson. (2007). *Higher education in the new century.* Rotterdam, Netherlands: Sense Publishers.

Altbach, P. (2006). Tiny at the top. *The Wilson Quarterly, 30*(4), 49–51.

Altbach, P. (2007). *Tradition and transition: The international imperative in higher education.* Rotterdam, Netherlands: Sense Publishers

Altbach, P., & Knight, J. (2007). The internationalization of higher education: Motivations and realities. *Journal of Studies in International Education, 11* (3–4), 290–305, doi: 10.1177/1028315307303542

Altbach, P., Reisberg, L., & Rumbley, L. (2009). *Trends in global higher education: Tracking an academic revolution.* Paris: UNESCO.

Brewer, E. (2004). *From student mobility to internationalization at home.* Conference on New Directions in International Education: Building Context, Connections and Knowledge. Beloit, WI: Beloit College.

Brown, P. (2001). *High skills: Globalization, competitiveness, and skill formation.* Oxford: Oxford University Press.

Brown, P., Green, A., & Lauder, H. (2008). *High skills: Globalisation, competitiveness and comparative skill formation.* Oxford: Oxford University Press.

Ching, G. S., & Chin J. M. C. (2011). *Managing higher education institution internationalization: Contemporary efforts of a university in Taiwan.* Retrieved from http://www.consortiacademia.org/index.php/ijrsm/article/view/9, 2011 (accessed on April 6, 2016).

De Wit, H. (2002). *Internationalisation of higher education in the United States of America and Europe: A historical, comparative, and conceptual analysis.* Westport, CT: Greenwood Press.

IAU-AIU. (n.d.a). *Internationalization.* Retrieved from http://archive.www.iau-aiu.net/internationalization/i_definitions.html (accessed April 6, 2016).

IAU-AIU. (n.d.b). *AIU global surveys.* Retrieved from http://www.iau-aiu.net/content/iau-global-surveys

Knight, J. (1993). *Internationalization: management issues and strategies.* International education, Ottawa, Canada: CBIE.

———. (1994). Internationalization: Elements and checkpoints. Canadian Bureau for International Education, Ottawa, Canada: CBIE.

———. (2003). Updated internationalization definition. *International Higher Education, 33*(), 2–3.

———. (2004). Internationalization remodeled: Definition, approaches, and rationales. *Journal of Studies in International Education, 8* (1), 5–31. doi: 10.1177/1028315303260832

———. (2006). Quality assurance and cross-border education: Complexities and challenges. In N. Furushiro (Ed.), *Developing evaluation criteria to assess the internationalization of universities.* Japan, Osaka: Osaka University.

———. (2007a). *Implications of crossborder education and GATS for the knowledge enterprise.* Commissioned Research Paper for UNESCO Forum on Higher Education, Research and Knowledge. Paris: UNESCO.

———. (2007b). Cross-border tertiary education: An introduction. In *Cross-border Tertiary Education: A way Towards Capacity Development.* Paris: OECD, World Bank and NUFFIC.

———. (2007c). Cross-border higher education: Issues and implications for quality assurance and accreditation. *Higher Education in the World 2007: Accreditation for Quality Assurance: What is at Stake?* Barcelona, Spain: Global University Network for Innovation.

————. (2008). *Higher education in turmoil: The changing world of internationalization*. Rotterdam, Netherlands: Sense Publishers.

Knight, J., & Altbach, P. (2007). The internationalization of higher education: Motivations and realities. *Journal for Studies in International Education, 11*(3–4), 290–305. Retrieved from http://dx.doi.org/10.1177/102831530730 3542

Knight, J., & De Wit, H. (Eds). (1997). *Internationalization of higher education in Asia Pacific countries*. Amsterdam: European Association for International Education.

Mestenhauser, J. A. (2003). Building bridges. *International Educator, 12*(3), 6–11.

Middlehurst R. (2001). University challenges: Borderless higher education, today and tomorrow. *Minerva, 39*(1), 3–26.

Middlehurst, R., & Woodfield, S. (2007). International activity or international strategy? Insights from an institutional pilot study in the UK. *Tertiary Education and Management, 13*(3), 263–279.

Nilsson, B. (1999, spring). Internationalisation at home—Theory and praxis. *EAIE Forum, 12*.

Nye, J. (2005). *Soft power: The means to success in world politics*. New York: Public Affairs.

Powar, K. B. (2012a). *Indian higher education revisited*. NOIDA, India: Vikas Publishing.

————. (2012b). *Expanding domains in Indian higher education*. New Delhi, India: Association of Indian Universities Publications.

————. (2013). *Understanding internationalization of higher education*. Pune: DY Patil.

————. (2015). *Changing landscape of international higher education: An Indian perspective*. Pune: DY Patil.

Qiang, Z. (2003). Internationalization of higher education: Towards a conceptual framework. *Policy Futures in Education, 1*(2), 248–270.

Soria, K. M., & Troisi, J. (2013). Internationalization at home alternatives to study abroad: Implications for students' development of global, international, and intercultural competencies. *Journal of Studies in International Education*. doi: 10.1177/1028315313496572

Teichler, U. (1999). Research on the relationships between higher education and the world of work: Past achievements, problems and new challenges. *Higher Education, 38*(2), 169–190.

Whitaker, A. M. (2004). *The Internationalization of higher education: A US perspective*. Retrieved January 17, 2013 from http://scholar.lib.vt.edu/theses/available/etd-06202004-192329/unrestricted/WhitakerMP.pdf

Yeravdekar, V. R., & Tiwari, G. (2014a). Internationalization of higher education and its impact on enhancing corporate competitiveness and comparative skill formation. *Procedia—Journal of Social and Behavioral Sciences, 157*, 203–209. http://dx.doi.org/10.1016/j.sbspro.2014.11.023

3

Cross-Border Higher Education: A Constantly Evolving International Student Market

Introduction

Higher education is an article of global trade. It crosses physical and political borders as easily as do capital, goods, and services. It is also as susceptible to market forces as other tradable commodities. Powar (2012b) states that cross-border higher education is "institutionalization of the provision of higher education across national boundaries." Transnational higher education, borderless higher education, and offshore higher education refer to the blurring of external boundaries; however, the broad consensus is that cross-border higher education is an umbrella term that encompasses other designations.

The idea of cross-border higher education commonly calls to mind the image of a student traveling to another country for degree or diploma in higher education. Although this movement is quite correctly an expression of cross-border education, it is not the only such. The idea of what constitutes international student is affixed to the broad concept of cross-border higher education, which refers to the mobility of one or more elements of higher education, including students, faculty, academic programs, and institutions across borders.

Cross-Border Higher Education:
Elements of Mobility

1. *International student mobility* is regarded as the most important aspect of internationalization of higher education, and not just because of its easy visibility. The UNESCO Institute of Statistics (UIS) defines international students as "students who have crossed a national border to study, or are enrolled in a distance learning program abroad. These students are not residents or citizens of the country where they study. Internationally mobile students are a subgroup of "foreign students," a category that includes those who have permanent residency in the host country" (UNESCO, n.d.).

2. *Program mobility* is the second most common form of cross-border education (subsequent to student mobility), and is a more recent occurrence.

> It [program mobility] involves cross-border distance education, including e-learning, generally supplemented by face-to-face teaching in local partner institutions, but mainly takes the form of traditional face-to-face teaching offered via a partner institution abroad. The relationships between foreign and local institutions are regulated under a variety of arrangements, from development assistance to for-profit arrangements. (OECD, 2004, p. 3)

Knight (2007b, pp. 134–46) elaborates on the numerous methods of cross-border mobility of programs: franchising, twinning, double/joint degrees, validation, distance/virtual, and various articulation models.

a. *Franchising* is an arrangement wherein a provider in country x authorizes provider in country y to deliver its program or course in country y. The degree or the diploma is granted by the provider in country x, and the regulatory compliance is carried out with respect to the framework of country y.

b. *Twinning* is an arrangement is the same as franchising, except that the two providers develop an articulation system whereby students can take course credits in either or both of the two countries. Semester-exchange programs may fall under this category.

c. *Double or joint degree* is an arrangement where two or more countries participate to offer a program for which students receive credits or joint award from the collaborating partners. In a departure from the above two, operational arrangements and regulations are customized for each collaborative initiative and for each of the country in which the program is offered.

d. *Articulation* is an arrangement wherein, as in double or joint degree, the providers can be many and they can be spread across many countries. The idea here is to allow "students to gain credit for courses and programs offered by all of the collaborating providers. This allows students to gain credit for work done with a provider other than the provider awarding the qualification" (p. 137). Validation arrangements between providers in many countries allow provider y in receiving country to award the qualification of provider x in source country (p. 138).

e. *Virtual/distance mode*, as the name suggests, is an arrangement whereby courses or programs are delivered online, by correspondence, or other such "off campus" arrangements.

Amongst the "for-profit" arrangements in cross-border mobility of programs, the popular modes of operation include franchises and twinning programs. A franchise is generally a provider of higher education in the host country that is accredited or endorsed by an institution in the home country to offer whole or part of a program. Under a twinning program, students are enrolled with a provider outside their countries and follow the curriculum of the foreign provider. Further, the program is completed in institutions "at home" and abroad. Thus, twinning programs involve both student and program mobility.

3. *Institution mobility* is the most recent of the three forms of cross-border higher education. Knight (2007b, p. 138) terms this form of cross-border higher education "provider mobility" because she makes a distinction between institutions and companies:

> Cross-border mobility of providers can be described as the physical or virtual movement of an education provider (institution, organisation, company) across a national border to establish a presence so as to offer education/training programmes and/or services to students and other clients. The difference between programme and provider mobility is one of scope and scale in terms of programmes/services offered and the local presence (and investment) by the foreign provider. A distinguishing feature between programme and provider mobility is that with provider mobility the learner is not necessarily located in a different country from the awarding institution, which is usually the case in programme mobility.

Most commonly, it refers to the setting up of international branch campus in the host country by an institution in home country. Less commonly, it may refer to the setting up of an institution from the ground up, and this new institution might or not be affiliated or endorsed by the "home institution" abroad. There are also instances in which an institution is "taken over" by the "home institution."

Knight (2005, p. 20, cited in Knight, 2007b, p. 138) identifies the following classifications:

1. By a branch campus, we understand an arrangement whereby the provider in country x offers programs and courses in a satellite campus in country y; the degree is awarded by the provider in country x.

2. "Independent institutions" refer to an arrangement wherein a provider in country x sets up an independent institution in country y. In this case, the provider in country y is self-determining and awards its own degrees.

3. Acquisition/merger, as the name suggests, refers to a case where provider in country x buys all of, or part of, an institution in country y.

4. In the case of study center/teaching site, a provider in country x sets up study centers or teaching sites in country y to assist students in country y who are enrolled with the provider. The study center/teaching site could be independent or part of another institution.

5. Affiliations/networks are arrangements whereby providers of many kinds engage in "innovative" partnerships to offer programs and courses in home or the host country.

A large number of operations serve as prominent examples: The University of Phoenix (owned and operated by the Apollo Group Company), the Netherlands Business School, and Laureate Education (Knight, 2007b, p. 135). As seems likely, institutional mobility does not afford to the international student the same breadth of international education. On the upside, it entails fewer risks from the business standpoint.

An important development in the proliferation of cross-border mobility of providers or institutions is that several Asian countries, which were long-time "sending countries," have begun providing cross-border higher education through institutional mobility. Some familiar examples are Manipal Academy of Higher Education, Aptech, and NIIT in India; Raffles LaSalle, Informatics, and Hartford in Singapore; SEG and Stamford College in Malaysia. Knight (2007b, pp. 135–45) notes that the cross-border activities of the UK, Australia, and New Zealand are concentrated in the Asia-Pacific region (see Table 3.1). The primary reason for this is that the Asian countries have a substantial and growing demand for tertiary level education that the countries, by them, cannot meet. The author states that several studies project that Asia will be the center stage of activities in cross-border higher education. In particular, Malaysia, Singapore, China, Thailand, India, and Vietnam, in no definite order, have been the most popular destination countries in the last decade or so. On the flip side, these countries have figured out the workings of cross-border higher education enough that they can venture to turn it on its head. "As of June 2003, Hong Kong had 858 degree level programmes from 11 different countries operating in [the] SAR [South Asian Region] and Singapore had 522 degree level programmes from 12 foreign countries" (Observatory on Borderless Higher Education, 2002–05, cited in Knight, 2007b, p. 135).

Evolution of Cross-Border Higher Education

The oldest mode of cross-border higher education, international student mobility, can be traced to the imperial policy of encouraging select students from the colonized country to seek higher education in the country that wielded colonial power with the aim of conditioning these students so that they would serve the interests of the imperial power. The British practice of encouraging Indian students to seek higher education in Britain comes to mind.

The next era can be said to have emerged after the Second World War when the newly independent (formerly colonized) countries undertook developmental activities that necessitated skills and specialized training. Given that almost all developing countries were lacking well-functioning higher education systems, the governments in these economies encouraged students to seek higher education in

Table 3.1
Comparative Data on Programs Offered Across Borders

	United Kingdom	Australia		New Zealand
Year data collected	2002/03	2003	1999/2000	2001
Percent of HEIs delivering cross-border program	88% of universities			47% of all (38) public HEIs (88% of universities)
Number of Students in cross-border program	101,645 students	97,751 students	34,905	2200 students (increase from 380 in 1997)
Number of cross-border program		1569 program		63 program (increase from 6 in 1997)
Primary locations	Hong Kong	China, Hong Kong, Singapore and Malaysia represent 70% of cross-border delivery	Hong Kong, Malaysia and Singapore	Malaysia 23% China 9% Australia 9% Hong Kong 6% Singapore 6%
Level of degrees	Undergrad 56% Graduate 44%			Sub-degree 34% Undergrad 39% Postgrad 27%
Primary disciplines	Business 44% Joint Degrees 21% Law 13% IT 8.5%	Business Administration Economics		Business/Commerce 15% Special Medicine 15% Computer science 14% Management 13%
Spread of activity among HEIs	10 institutions account for 8% of cross-border enrolments	3 institutions account for 55% of all cross-border program delivery		
Mode of delivery				42% through campus based teaching 32% through distance only 26% used combination
Source of data	HESA 2002/03 London External 2002/03 – As reported by OBHE July 2004	AVCC Offshore Program of Australian Universities 2003	DEST Overseas student statistics 2000	Ministry of Education 2002

Source: Knight (2007c, p. 136).

the developed countries. It is relatable that the popular subject areas were reflective of the employment opportunities in the emerging areas of developing economies: engineering was the most popular subject in the postcolonial era, followed by business management and computer science (Varghese, 2008). Ever since then, the volume of students crossing borders has been on the ascent. According to UIS (2006), student mobility across borders has been rising continuously. It has increased by nine times between 1963 and 2006 (cited in Varghese, 2008). According to Project Atlas, IIE, the number of international students in 2014 stood at 4.5 million.

It would be fair to trace the origins of cross-border higher education—insofar as it is a result of globalization—to the decade of the 1990s, or perhaps even a little earlier. The 1980s saw the initiation of issuing of policy statements with respect to international education: International Committee for the Study of Educational Exchange (ICSEE), National Association for Foreign Study Affairs (NAFSA), United Kingdom Council for Overseas Student Affairs (UKCOSA), the Australian Vice Chancellor's Committee (AVCC), and Australian Committee for Directors and Principals in Advanced Education (ACDPAE; Snehi, 2012, p. 5). Varghese (2008, pp. 10–11) points out that it would be erroneous to neglect factors other than globalization: reduced public subsidies and state regulation in higher education, increased participation of market forces and private partakers in higher education, dissolution of communism in Eastern Europe, and advances in technology and communication. It was during this time that institutions began to enlist internationalization as part of their "cost recovery" plan (p. 10). This marks an important transference in institutional policy with respect to international students. Being that this student group typically pays more than domestic students, international students were commonly homed in on. Universities, at least the notable ones, came to acquire a dual aspect—an active pursuance of internationalization while continuing to be national in ownership and management.

Although border-crossing in higher education had existed earlier, the scale of participation of international providers and students hereafter was so large as to mark a defining moment. The end goal of higher education was a product for the global market. Thus, the key academic elements, including curriculum and pedagogy had to be put in order so that they prepared a candidate who was ready to become a successful member of the workforce in the global labor market. The prospective student, who placed a premium on the internationalization in academic institutions on account of the increased possibility of higher returns, was willing to invest more money on his education. In consequence, both the providers and patrons of higher education were inclined to making higher investments in education.

Yeravdekar (2012) has identified *four levels that denote distinctive patterns in the evolution of cross-border higher education*. The *first* level is categorized on the basis of student mobility. The author has demonstrated that this is the earliest form of cross-border higher education, and occurs on account of a number of factors: the strength of higher education institutions in the home country might not be sufficient to accommodate the growing population of students; the quality of institutions might be suspect; the students might be guided by their aspirations to add foreign experience to their portfolio and the prospect of enhanced employment. The *second* level is grouped on the basis of program mobility. The most common manifestations of this phenomenon are twining programs, semester abroad program, joint research program, and summer schools. It is notable that instances wherein faculty members of a university move to a foreign university to conduct academic programs leading to the award of diplomas and certificates by the parent university are also examples of program mobility. The *third* level is characterized by the incidence of branch campuses. This is an instance wherein a university operates its branch campus in another country. *Finally*, the inception of education hubs marks the onset of the fourth level.

Varghese (2008) outlines two distinct modes of cross-border higher education: "international/transnational providers and students seeking cross-border education."

Garrett and Verbik (2003) propose that in the first case—cross-border education through transnational providers—the reference is to the delivery mechanism wherein both program and instruction are made available from one country or more to another country or several other countries without the need for students to physically move away from their home country (cited in Varghese, 2008). Typically,

South-East Asian countries enjoy prominence in this spectrum. Hong Kong, Malaysia, and Singapore are notable instances of countries that have concentrated presence of transnational providers offering courses in domestic markets. The other mode of cross-border higher education—students seeking cross-border education—refers to the scenario where students physically move from their home country to the host country in pursuit of higher education; the traditional overseas study program is a case in point. Among the countries that demonstrate considerable evidence of outflow of students for this mode of cross-border higher education are China, India, and Korea. A directly correlated causal relationship in this regard is the one between internationalization of higher education and labor market. Varghese (2008) hypothesizes that increase in demand for skilled and specialized labor results in a corresponding increase in the premium placed on foreign degree. Consequently, the foreign education beneficiary expects additional compensation for his/her foreign education as it is construed to offer a competitive edge over those that are not armed with it.

The international student market, which is marked by declining public input and increasing private participation, is massive and competition-ridden. It draws millions of students and accounts for billions of dollars. As stated earlier, according to Project Atlas, IIE, the number of international students in 2014 stood at 4.5 million. It is projected that cross-border higher education is likely to grow rapidly. Bohm, Davies, and Meares (2002) have estimated that the demand for cross-border higher education is likely to increase to 7.2 million by 2025 (cited in Varghese, 2008, p. 11). Historically, the two most important factors that impacted cross-border higher education were colonial legacy and political patronage. This has changed and given way to "market principles" in the present times. The profit motive is not surprising given that international students are often charged more for tuition and the living expenses they incur; the "Open Doors 2010" report records that international students in US spent to the tune of $20 billion while they were present there.

Varghese (2008) further outlines the following primary factors that impact students' decision-making in their selection of higher education institution:

1. *Finance*: international students evidently consider lower tuition and cost of living a huge advantage. A case in point is the recent trend of Indian students' preference for Australia as a host country.

2. *Political inclination of the state*: political leanings have traditionally gone a long way in influencing the basis for prioritizing nations in their capacity as host countries for cross-border higher education. By way of illustration, socialist inclination contributed enormously to the wave of cross-border higher education exchanges between India and Soviet Union during the Cold War and post-Cold War era.

3. *Medium of instruction and lingua franca*: a cursory examination of interregional flow clearly indicates that proficiency in the medium of instruction in the universities in host country plays a decisive role in determining the students' preference. It would not be a stretch to connect the Indian students' tendency to opt for English speaking countries to the English language.

4. *Perceived academic superiority*: the students' perception of the quality of higher education institutions contributes enormously to decision making. For instance, Bangladeshi and Nepali students demonstrate a clear preference for India in pursuit of higher education.

5. *Attainment of culture and language*: acquisition of culture and linguistic competency are key factors that contribute to gaining "experience in working in a multicultural context."

6. *Employment opportunities*: cross-border higher education instruments, such as study abroad programs, are popular not just because they enhance academic credentials but also for the opportunities they proffer in terms of building networks for career. A case in point is the large number of Indian student who go to US for higher education in techno-engineering fields like IT, find job opportunities and settle there.

7. *High economic growth in the home country*: economic growth translates into better affordability of foreign education among students. The increasing number of Indian cross-border higher education students following the trade liberalization of the 1990s illustrates the argument.

8. *Ease of immigration formalities*: The sharp decline in the number of students moving to the US for higher studies after 9/11 can be attributed, at least in part, to increase in visa restrictions.

Perils of Cross-border Higher Education

Cross-border higher education is not without its tribulations. It comes with the high likelihood of wearing down national autonomy in higher education. It is probable that in some countries, especially those that are developing, the national agenda on higher education addresses concerns that are specific to the country and might even run contrary to the international standard in curriculum or other such academic elements. To let global market forces play at liberty might well result in nonfulfilment of national interests in higher education.

Cross-border higher education also runs the risk of leading to brain-drain—the incidence of which is worryingly high in some countries. Students from developing countries such as India and China often do not return to their home countries upon completion of higher education in host institutions in developed countries.

Another way in which cross-border higher education can be perilous is with respect to the difference in quality and mission between "mother institution" and its branch campuses and other operations. It is commonly observed that the "mother institution" in a developed country upholds higher vision and standards than its branch campus in a developing country. This difference can well mislead the student who expects comparable measure of merit in orientation and operation. What is much worse than this disparity is that cross-border education is fraught with deceitful practices. There are many untrustworthy providers of cross-border education who take cover in the confusion that arises from the absence of a well-formulated regulatory framework to direct cross-border higher education.

Cross-border Higher Education: A Profitable Proposition

Cross-border movement of higher education is a matter of much significance to all participants in higher education, and this importance is likely to not only continue but reify in the years to come. At the heart of this is the indisputable fact that cross-border higher education brings voluminous revenues to governments and institutions. In the face of reducing public investments in higher education and increasing competition for students, the revenues from cross-border higher education are going to become more coveted in the future. Powar (2015) notes that it was the advent of "Thatcherism" in the UK in the 1980s that marked the beginning of differential tuition fee structure for students on the basis of whether they were "domestic" or "international." Since that time, tuition fee for international students has come to be seen as an important avenue for revenue generation. The government's policy in this respect in the UK, Australia, and the US has been discussed earlier. However, it must be pointed out that not all countries identify with this line of thinking. Many European countries provide higher education free of cost, whereas many other charge the same fees for both domestic and international students.

Powar (2015) notes that of the top eight "hosting" countries, five (the US, the UK, Australia, Canada, and New Zealand) collect and make available financial data related to cross-border higher education. The other three (Germany, France, and Japan) do not share the information related to finances that are involved in cross-border higher education, and it is estimated that their financial gains are nowhere nearly as high as those of the five that do share data. Bashir (2005, cited in Powar, 2015, p. 50) noted that, in 2005, the five above-mentioned countries "exported education" to the tune of US$28 billion. The US accounted for US$14.1 billion. Vargheses (2010, cited in Powar, 2015, p. 50) reported that this figure for the US jumped to US$17.8 billion in the 2009. One must bear in mind that it is not just the tuition fees that contributes to the economy, but also living expenses.

According to Project Atlas, IIE, in the year 2010–11, the annual revenue generated in the following five countries through international students is as follows: US (20 billion US dollars), Ireland (900 million Euros), Australia (18.5 billion Australian dollars), and Canada (5.5 billion Canadian dollars; Powar, 2015, p. 51).

In the case of India, the figures vary considerably, indicating that there is no one particular agency in charge of collecting and analyzing these numbers. Perhaps, these are merely estimates. Khare (2011, cited in Powar 2015) reported that, in the year 2010, the outbound international students from India spent five to six billion US dollars on tuition and other expenses. Ghosh (2012, cited in Powar 2015) estimates this figure to be 13 million US dollars. (Interestingly, the former figure was reported by a Government of India official and the latter by an FICCI official.) In 2014, it is estimated that 220,000 Indian students were registered in an institution abroad. Given that the estimated annual expenditure for each student is 30,000 US dollars, it emerges that these students spent 7 billion US dollars (Powar, 2015, p. 51).

Similar figures for inbound international students in India can only be rough estimates and it is questionable whether guesswork, which is not based on a large scale survey, would yield reliable numbers. Powar (2015, p. 52) cautiously estimates that inbound international students spend a mere 150 million US dollars in India. This figure is as low as it is because of many reasons. First, the number of international students is not high (25,000). Second, the majority of students come from neighboring countries in Asia and Africa, which are typically developing countries and record low to medium per capita income figures. There is a widely held impression that these students subsist on a peppercorn of a budget. Powar (2015) cites Choudaha (2011) and Khare (2011), both of whom recommend that enhancement of capacity-building is the way to go in higher education if the country is to realistically hope to meet the demands of domestic and international higher education cohorts. Capacity building in higher education will also go a long way in generating revenue for institutions and for ancillary businesses that are organized around students. In the context of internationalization, collaborative partnerships with foreign governments must be the first "line of attack" for overcoming the inertia that has beset the system for so long. The UK–India Education Research Initiative (UKIERI) and the Indo-US 21st Century Knowledge Initiative (formerly known as the Obama–Singh Knowledge Initiative) are welcome steps and one hopes to see more of these in the years to come.

The Rising Concerns About Accreditation and Quality Assurance in Cross-border Higher Education, with Special Reference to India

Much of the concern about the lack of regulatory framework and confidence in cross-border higher education comes from an insufficient availability of underpinning data. This, for its part, is a result of the newness of the more recent forms of cross-border higher education, such as institutional provider and program mobility. It would seem that the more recent the form of cross-border higher education, the more likely it is to be beset with questionable legitimacy, more accurately, perceived questionable legitimacy.

This is definitely true of provider-institution mobility. Between the traditional and the "new or alternative providers," the latter is more frequently called into question in respect of its trustworthiness. Although issues related to accreditation, recognition, and quality assurance benchmarking in higher education are knotty enough at the national level, the same concerns assume complexity of a much larger scale at the transnational level. Yet, to be completely fair to those on whom a doubtful eye is cast, one must acknowledge that all of us engaged in cross-border higher education are on a learning curve. Several forms of the phenomenon, such as international branch campus, twinning, articulation, and study center are not well-precedented—they have not been around long enough for the gaps and cracks within to break the surface. It is hoped that cross-border higher education will mature to see to the many calls for approbation that it evokes at the present time.

As things stand at the moment, the most crucial question related to the legitimacy of the partaking institution is whether it is accredited by an above-board body or not. In respect of this, the typical traditional higher education institution is, by and large, not suspect. In more cases than not, the institution is endorsed by a national regulatory body. The apprehension is with respect to "rogue providers" such as "accreditation mills" and "degree mills" (Garrett, 2005, cited in Knight, 2007b, p. 137): These could be "publicly traded companies such as Apollo (USA), Aptech (India) and Informatics (Singapore), corporate universities such as those run by Motorola and Toyota . . ."

(Knight, 2007b, p. 137). Another distinguishing feature of the latter class of providers is that, unlike the former, the institution does not undertake "research and other scholarly activities" (Knight, 2007b, p. 137). The case that institution-provider mobility involves give-and-take between two or more bodies across borders is at the root of why perceived legitimacy of the participating bodies is held in skepticism, especially the nontraditional kind.

In particular, a common area to look into is whether the delivering foreign provider is within the purview of the regulatory system of the receiving country. If that is not the case, then many red flags are raised: is the institution being monitored by the regulatory framework of the receiving country? Is the institution complying with the accreditation and quality assurance benchmarks of the receiving country? Although most countries that engage in cross-border higher education have a serviceable system in place to monitor domestic providers, many have none or unsatisfactory guidelines to "map the terrain" in respect of foreign providers that operate in the country, in which case, the foreign provider is free to operate at liberty. As a result, it is not just that higher education is compromised, but also that general confidence in cross-border higher education is left eroded.

A common interpretation of regulations that report on foreign providers is one of the impositions of state-induced restriction to free trade. The ideological grounds for defining higher education as a freely tradable commodity have been presented as a case for border crossing in higher education. This is a vast departure from classifying higher education as an instrument of public good. Possibly the most important implication is that the metaphorical "invisible hand of the market" comes to assume a place of permissibility, and even predominance.

There are two important points in this regard: first, General Agreement on Trade in Services (GATS) and other trade agreements do not lay down rules for quality assurance and accreditation. Second, there is limited awareness about regional UNESCO conventions that do cover quality assurance and accreditation in cross-border higher education.

Regional UNESCO conventions on the recognition of qualifications were established more than 25 years ago and have been ratified by over 100 member states in Africa, Asia and the Pacific, the Arab States, Europe and Latin America. They are uniquely legally binding instruments that deal with cross-border mutual recognition of qualifications. There is a limited general awareness of these instruments except for in the case of the European regional convention, which was jointly updated in 1997 by UNESCO and the European Council at the Lisbon Convention. In 2001, the same two organizations established a Code of Good Practice for Transnational Education that is now a recognized part of the Lisbon Convention. At the present time, there is discussion on how these UNESCO conventions could be used as instruments to complement trade agreements and assure students, employers and the public that there are systems in place to recognize academic and professional qualifications. Given the growth in academic mobility, the increased mobility of the labour force and the fact that the GATS is encouraging greater professional mobility, there is a clear and urgent need for national education policy-makers to address the issue of recognizing qualifications (Knight, 2007b, p. 140).

Similar to UNESCO conventions are national, regional, and international codes of conduct, which are not binding but serve as guidelines to achieve "best practices." Some examples are Quality Assurance Code of Practice: Collaborative Provisions—UK Quality Assurance; Code of Ethical Practice in the Offshore Provision of Education and the Educational Services by Australian Higher Education Institutions—Australian Vice-Chancellors Committee; Principles of Good Practice for the Educational Program for Non-US Nationals; Code of Good Practice in the Provision of Transnational Education—UNESCO/CEPES and the European Council; and Code of Practice for Overseas Education Institutions Operating in Mauritius (Knight, 2007b, p. 141).

It would seem that cross-border higher education is far from having achieved what Altbach, Reisberg, and Rumbley (2009, pp. 50–65) term "convergence," not to put too fine a point on it. Nonetheless, there is a growing bid to harmonize national regulatory frameworks by which we understand a supranational attempt to bring the participating systems in agreement with each other. Higher education systems are finding themselves increasingly strained to hold in balance the necessary equilibrium between international codes of conduct on the one hand, and national self-determination and domestic goals on the other.

The road to methodizing quality assurance benchmarking and achieving quality in cross-border higher education is even more "long and winding" than working out accreditation and other regulatory matters. First, the notion of quality in higher education is both conjectural and adaptive (as in responsive to other changes, such as trends in graduate labor market). Therefore, quality in higher education is not a rigid, unchanging concept. For instance, work-preparedness training and research output, which were peripheral concerns earlier, have moved inwards to gain center stage in higher education institutions of high standing. This ambiguity does not, however, get in the way of perceived significance of quality assurance. Nor do protests that standardization of quality assurance impedes "institutional autonomy, national culture, and the importance of relevance to local contexts further complicate the discussion" (OECD, 2004; ENQA, 2007; cited in Altbach, Reisberg, & Rumbley, 2009, pp. 50–65). If anything, benchmarking measures, such as institution of "key performance indicators," figure more in the conversation than ever before.

Another identifiable emerging strain in quality assurance is the emphasis on "learning outcomes," by which we mean the attainment of academic objectives by students that were outlined by the institution of higher learning. A ready example would be the growing popularity of "student satisfaction and engagement surveys." This trend is demonstrated by the OECD's introduction of "The Assessment of Higher Education Learning Outcomes" (AHELO) project, which was launched in 2006 to put in place a design to evaluate teaching–learning capacity. The project focuses on the following key aspects:

- *Physical and organizational characteristics*: observable characteristics such as enrolment figures or the ratio of male to female students
- *Education-related behaviors and practices*: student–faculty interaction, academic challenge, emphasis on applied work, and so on
- *Psychosocial and cultural attributes*: career expectations of students, parental support, social expectations of higher education institutions, and so on

- *Behavioral and attitudinal outcomes*: students' persistence and completion of degrees, continuation into graduate programs or success in finding a job, student satisfaction, improved student self-confidence, and self-reported learning gains claimed by students or their instructors (OECD, n.d., cited in Altbach, Reisberg, & Rumbley, 2009, p. 59)

In the context of globalization, it could be said that quality assurance in cross-border higher education, as with higher education itself, is an evolving process—a "work in progress," if you will, rather than a preset charter of checklists. Quality in higher education was defined at the 1998 UNESCO world conference as follows:

> Quality in higher education is a multidimensional concept, which should embrace all its functions, and activities: [sic] teaching and academic programmes, research and scholarship, staffing, students, buildings, facilities, equipments, services to the community, and academic environment. (van Ginkel and Rodrigues Dias 2007, p. 39, cited in Altbach, Reisberg, & Rumbley, 2009, p. 53)

Almost a decade thereafter, UNESCO-CEPES definition spoke to the increasing complexity of the higher education landscape.

> Quality in higher education is a multi-dimensional, multi-level, and dynamic concept that relates to the contextual settings of an educational model, to the institutional mission and objectives, as well as to the specific standards within a given system, institution, programme, or discipline (Vlasceanu, et al., 2007, cited in Altbach, Reisberg, & Rumbley, 2009, p. 53).

The chief drivers of this evolution are increase in the diversity and international orientation of providers and program. Maassen (1987) and Neave (1994) point out that a universal shift has occurred in the realm from "ex ante" regulation (establishing standards and limitations beforehand) to "ex post" evaluation (measuring and evaluating performance after the fact; Maassen, 1987) with ex post-evaluation usually being conducted and coordinated by new parastatal agencies" (cited in Altbach, Reisberg, & Rumbley, 2009, p. 52).

Thus, quality assurance plays out quite differently now than it did in the past. There is a trend of adding in self-evaluation (by means of benchmarking against institutional vision and mission statements, for instance) and evaluation against peer-performance (a representative example is to have oneself participate in international academic rankings). This shift relieves an institution of its susceptibility to fall into complacence when it is called upon by parastatal regulatory body, such as UGC or NAAC in India, to make a passing grade, not to say, show evidence of the bare minimum. More to the point, the newer is a more distanced approach to quality attainment—one that is not overly self-referenced and one that serves to prod the institution towards exceptionalism. To sum up, attaining quality is an ongoing process that concerns itself with enhancement across many parameters. Coming from this perspective, the regulatory body must examine institutions with an eye to improving the score on quality that the institutions achieve. The regulatory body must also go further to help the institution build up the organizational apparatus that undergirds the fluid process of ensuring that the institution does not lose ground.

Cross-border higher education necessitates that some shared reference points be determined to get to a working level of equivalence and achieve effective transferability of credits and such. An interesting aspect of the need to achieve cross-cultural understanding in higher education pertains to building a common vocabulary and having higher education institutions from across countries commit to it as signatories. It has been widely suggested that an internationally accepted vocabulary is crucial to capturing important definitions and explanations, such as determination of a postsecondary student's qualifying ability to undertake higher education in a foreign country.

Adelman (2009) and Crozier, et al. (2006) have pointed out the importance of fair and accurate recognition of a student's educational qualifications (cited in Altbach, Reisberg, & Rumbley, 2009, p. 55), which was driven home in the "Lisbon Recognition Convention" in 1997 (UNESCO, 2004, cited in Altbach, Reisberg, & Rumbley, 2009, p. 56). The "Bologna Process" merits note in the discussion. It refers to a set of agreements that aims to bring comparability in the standards and quality of higher education systems in Europe.

The Bologna process was named after the Bologna Declaration signed in 1999 by ministers in charge of higher education from 29 European countries. At present, the Bologna Process brings together 47 countries. The key objective of the Bologna Process is to create a European Higher Education Area (EHEA), with the broader goal of facilitating international mobility of students. Another important landmark is the launch of UNESCO's "Portal of Higher Education Institutions" to provide information that will help stakeholders weed out unauthentic documents and providers from those that are not.

Many other agencies and agreements that may be lesser known but still relevant are the INQAAHE, the European Association for Quality Assurance in Higher Education (ENQA) in 2000, the European Quality Assurance Register (EQAR), the Asia-Pacific Quality Network (APQN) in 2003, the Iberoamerican Network for Quality Assessment and Assurance in Higher Education (RIACES) in 2004, the European Quality Improvement System (EQUIS), Global Initiative for Quality Assurance Capacity (GIQAC), and the Arab Network for Quality Assurance in Higher Education was established (ANQAHE; Altbach, Reisberg, & Rumbley, 2009).

Powar (2015) notes that, in 2005, UNESCO and OECD jointly issued "guidelines for quality provisions in CBHE" (p. 43). These recommendations touch upon the following key issues:

1. *Guidelines for governments*: fair and transparent system of registration for CBHE providers; capacity for quality assurance and accreditation; availability of information; and membership of multilateral associations and partnerships with other governments
2. *Guidelines for institutions/providers*: quality of programs is consistent across borders; competence in faculty members; internal quality management system; respect for the practices of the "host country;" and transparency in providing information on the financial status of programs
3. *Guidelines for student bodies*: active involvement and increase in awareness
4. *Guidelines for quality assurance and accreditation bodies*: ensuring inclusion of all modes within CBHE; establishment and consolidation of networks; collaborative links between participating countries; reciprocal arrangements for recognition and partnerships;

composition of review panels, benchmarking and assessment procedures; and formulation of codes of conduct

5. *Guidelines of academic recognition bodies*: inclusion of all modes in the quality assurance and accreditation arrangements within CBHE; strengthening of networks, availability of information in a transparent manner; reciprocity and partnerships between participating entities; formulate peer review panels and assessment bodies; and develop guidelines for benchmarking

6. *Guidelines for professional bodies*: platforms for exchange of information; cooperation with other accreditation and quality assurance bodies; and professional recognition of qualifications in the labor market

In the discussion on the subject of quality assurance in cross-border higher education in India, it is important to focus on international collaborative degree programs, such as, double/dual, joint, and consecutive degree programs. As of now, joint degree programs are not in operation in India, but dual or double degree programs are widely followed by Indian higher education institutions. Although there are no official records that reflect the prevalence of these initiatives in numbers, there is the impressionistic knowledge that these initiatives are widely undertaken and eagerly sought by Indian students. The popularity of these collaborative initiatives is echoed in other countries as well. As the interest in these programs increases, so too does the concern that establishing their validity is a complicated affair, caught up in many regulatory bindings, spread across two or more higher education systems. Although many educationalists promote these programs as an organic outcrop of program mobility, others eye them as problematic new-fangled models that harbor room for duplicity and deception. An array of factors is at play in the dynamics: diversity of programs and providers, ambiguity in arriving at what count for legitimate mechanisms for controlling entry qualifications, academic workload, quality assurance, and evaluation. It would seem as if the terminology itself is ambiguous: "double, multiple, trinational, joint, integrated, collaborative, international, consecutive, concurrent, co-tutelle, overlapping, conjoint, parallel, simultaneous, and common degrees" (Knight, 2011, p. 299) are some of the popular names that refer to international collaborative programs.

These programs have been defined previously, but it would be helpful to recapitulate in this discussion. Upon completion of a joint degree program, the international student is awarded one qualification by the collaborating institutions. A student generally completes this program in the same time that he would have completed a conventional program. The student does not necessarily cross-border, as either other components, such as teaching staff, instructional, and delivery facilities are moved across the physical or virtual scope of the program.

A double (or dual) degree and its cousin, multiple degree programs, are different from joint degree programs.

> "A double degree program awards two individual qualifications at equivalent levels upon completion of the collaborative program requirements established by the two partner institutions." A multiple degree program is essentially the same as a double degree program, except for the number of qualifications offered: "A multiple degree program awards three or more individual qualifications at equivalent levels upon completion of the collaborative program requirements established by the three or more partner institutions." . . . The duration of a double or multiple degree program can be extended beyond the length of a single degree program in order to meet the requirements of all partners participating in the collaborative program. (Knight, 2011, p. 301)

It is easy to see why dual degree programs are popular in India and in general. The acquisition of two degrees from two institutions, each of which is located in a different country, has proven attractive to the international student. There are many advantages: first, a degree that combines international and domestic aspects of the discipline clearly widens the student's professional repertoire. Second, many students are convinced that the curriculum of these programs is more extensive. Third, some students see such degrees as "two pops for the price of one."

International collaborative degree programs, such as dual degree programs, have been one of the mainstays of internationalization in India. Contrary to the branch campus education hub set-up, collaborative programs are a stable continuing way of bringing in internationalization. "In India, for example, 631 foreign institutions were operating in 2010, of which 440 did so from their home campuses, 186 had twinning or some other arrangements with local institutions . . ." (Lawton & Katsomitros, 2012). Although there are no official records to rely on, there is the impressionistic knowledge that private institutions lead ahead of public institutions on this score. Symbiosis international University, Birla Institute of Technology, Shiv Nadar University, Manipal University, SRM University, and OP Jindal University, all of which are private institutions, boast a prospering record of twinning programs, dual degree programs, and study abroad programs.

In the case of these collaborative degree programs, it is assumed that each one of the collaborating institutions is recognized by the respective domestic accrediting body. Therefore, the degree awarded by each of the collaborating institutions is recognized in the respective country. Although the legitimacy-related and administrative aspects of the awarded degree are in the clear, other areas are not necessarily so. The setting down of requirements related to curriculum and workload is not an easy task. It is often the case that curriculum and workload are duplicated and, in other instances, the academic integrity of the program is in jeopardy. The key challenges are of technical and procedural natures: dealing with two or more academic calendars, credit systems, tuition fee structures, pedagogic practices, and assessment requirements.

It would appear that both joint and dual degree programs take place largely at the masters level as programs at that level are the shortest and the most flexible, making international collaboration easy to bring to completion. It is also observed that the vast majority of joint and double degree programs take place in business administration, management, and engineering disciplines. This is easy to make sense of; students in these streams are the most internationally mobile anyway. Often, the international mobility component is introduced into the program by the means of international internship or other work-study mode.

Consecutive degree programs are beginning to emerge on the cross-border higher education map. They remain the least popular and bogged down by considerations of the authentic worth of the awarded degrees.

> A consecutive degree program awards two different qualifications at consecutive levels upon completion of the collaborative program requirements established by the partner institutions. . . . [the degree is] awarded when program requirements for each degree, as stipulated by the awarding institutions, are completed. For the international consecutive degree program, the two awarding institutions are located in different countries. In this case, it is usual for a student to be mobile and complete the course work and research requirements for the first degree in one country and the requirements for the second degree in the partner institution located in another country. The duration of the program is usually longer than a single program, but shorter than if the two degrees are taken separately. (Knight, 2011, pp. 301–02)

An important aspect of collaborative programs is that they work to reflect the (supposedly high) quality of partnering institutions. This is especially true when the partnering institutions are of unequal stature, and the lesser "rides on the coat's tails" of the greater. Many such undertakings are forged between institutions from developing and developed countries, in which case, the institution from the developing country utilizes the collaboration for "brand-building" purposes.

It is the lure of the degree with the foreign association that so draws the student that often times he does not care to look into the credentials that come with it. Far too frequently, the student, as well as the employer who is reviewing the student's academic portfolio, focuses on the reputation of the partnering institutions and not on the academic content of the program. Knight (2011) suggests three frameworks in which to situate completion requirements: "the number of completed courses/credits . . . student workload . . . required outcomes/competencies." This line of reasoning would lead us to believe that double and multiple degrees, if they are built around specified essential courses and result in predetermined learning outcomes and competencies, can be easily judged as academically rigorous and valid or not. The knotty part is about identifying what adds up as legitimate coursework, not the completion requirements as such.

In light of the several considerations playing at supranational, national, and institutional levels, it falls to the regulatory bodies in India to work in partnership with institutions to come up with a rubric to iron out the issues of authenticity and reliability in collaborative programs.

Branch Campuses in India: A Jagged Path

International branch campuses or offshore campuses are one of the most recent modes of cross-border higher education. Typically, in this arrangement, a higher education institution from a developed country sets up an offshore campus in a developing country. The thrust of branch campuses are diploma/certificates, undergraduate and postgraduate courses in professional programs. Research and other scholarly activities are, characteristically, not an area of focus.

Lawton and Katsomitros (2012) define an international branch as follows:

> [A] higher education institute that is located in another country from an institution which either originated it or operates it, with some physical presence in the host country, and which awards at least one degree in the host country that is accredited in the country of the originating institution. (cited in Powar, 2015, p. 135)

This definition, in addition to referring to the original definition of branch campus (an offshore physical presence of an institution, operated by the "mother" institution or by a joint venture with a local partner, and one that offers, at least, one degree program by the "mother" institution), widens the concept of branch campuses to include the institutions that award degrees accredited in the home country and institutions that conduct articulation programs (degree programs in which only a part of the program is carried out at the branch campus). It is important to note that the following are not included in branch campuses: study abroad programs, programs conducted by consortium of universities, foreign institutions that are located in the host country and given degree-awarding powers, non-degree granting operations, and research centers of foreign universities that are established in collaboration with host countries.

UGC (2010, cited in Powar 2015) defines an off-shore campus thusly, ". . . an approved [by the Central Government] centre of the institution . . . beyond its campus and outside India." Previously, UGC (2008) had defined an overseas campus as: [A] campus of the university established by it outside the country, operated and maintained by it as its constituent unit, having the university's complement of facilities, faculty, and staff. (cited in Powar, 2015, p. 136)

In 2011, there were 209 international branch campuses and, at least, 37 were in the process of being planned (Lawton & Katsomitros, 2013, cited in Powar, 2015, p. 128). The number of branch campuses has risen sharply since 1996: 15 branch campuses in 2000, 24 in 2002, 82 in 2006, 162 in 2009, and 200 in 2011. OBHE expects the number to increase to 250 by 2015 and 280 by 2020 (Lawton et al., 2013, cited in Powar, 2015, p. 138). It is interesting to note that branch campuses represent a radically progressive trend in internationalization—only 50 percent of the movement has been North to South, the rest has been South to South or North to North. What is even more encouraging to Indian educationists is that the South to South movement is primarily Indian "home" institutions setting up branch campuses in Gulf and other countries in the South. Remarkably, there have even been a few instances of South to North movement.

The most popular region for setting up branch campuses is the Middle East. This is so for obvious reasons: abundance of financial resources, readily available infrastructural support, positive interest in institutions in developed countries, and a missing "home" tradition of excellence in higher education. Lawton et al. (2013, cited in Powar, 2013, p. 138) note that, in the last few years, South-East Asia and East Asia have replaced the Middle East.

Thus, sustainability is clearly a challenging issue. The reasons for this are interrelated: truly competent faculty members are often unwilling to move to the "host" institution, the locally hired faculty members fall short of internationally competitive standards, and enrolment volume is insufficient to work as a long-term revenue generation avenue.

Indeed, insufficient funding is a major reason for the failure of branch campuses, as is the cynical eye with which branch campuses are seen by educationists. Branch campuses are a very costly affair. Home institutions are often guarded about pumping investment in the host country, without there being certainty about long-term viability.

Verbik and Merkely (2006, cited in Powar 2015) have outlined three major approaches to funding: first, home institution funding the project in its entirety; second, funding from external sources; third, support by way of facilities provided by the local government or private company as an incentive for setting up branch campuses.

Lane and Kinser (2013, cited in Powar 2015) have identified five ownership-funding models for branch campuses, derived from their survey of 50 branch campuses:

Model one: Entirely owned by the home campus
Model two: Owned by host government or its agency
Model three: Owned by a private partner (investment firm or property developer)
Model four: Rented from a private partner
Model five: Owned by an academic institution

Research studies have been few; therefore, confirmed information on the subject is missing. Moreover, branch campuses have a history of failures and shut downs—more have closed shop than continued. Powar (2015) notes that, in the last few years, as many as 18 international branch campuses have closed operations, of these 11 were US-based institutions. Further, the contribution of branch campuses to overall internalization has not been consequential. Choudaha (2014) points out that of 600,000 students involved in transnational education in the UK in 2012–13, only three percent were enrolled in branch campuses (cited in Powar, 2015, p. 128).

We conclude that, for an operation to qualify as an international branch campus, it does not necessarily have to be plentiful in terms of academic offerings or physical infrastructure. It could be a very small operation but as long as it satisfies the conditions of some physical presence and a minimum of one degree program, it passes as an international branch campus. It is frequently seen that branch campuses offer professional education more than general variety, with management education being the winner. Powar (2015, p. 137) notes that the executive MBA degree is a staple at international branch campuses.

Branch campuses have been mentioned in the literature on internationalization, but they have not been objects of detailed study. The OBHE has been at the forefront of whatever little statistical data is available on branch campuses. Becker (2009) points out that international branch campuses offer various advantages to home and host countries.

Advantages to home countries are as follows:

1. Generation of revenues through tuition fees
2. International brand standing
3. International experience to "home" faculty members
4. Opportunity to develop new and varied curriculum and other teaching–learning practices
5. Cross-cultural knowledge and experiences

The advantages to the host country are as follows:

1. Development of local capacities and infrastructure
2. Prevent loss of outflow of foreign exchange and brain drain
3. Income generation for local businesses that are organized around higher education institutions
4. Widening of intellectual horizons

The students benefit from branch campuses too. They have the opportunity to secure foreign degrees without leaving the country. As a result of this, they not only enjoy greater convenience, but also save on tuition and living expenses.

Indian Branch Campuses

In the Indian context, branch campuses have worked only one way—India as the "home" country, that is to say, Indian institutions, the overwhelming majority of which are privately managed, have succeeded in opening their branch campuses in other countries. "India leads overseas higher education provision from non-Western countries, with at least 17 campuses abroad, 10 of them in the United Arab Emirates, 4 in Mauritius and others in Malaysia, Singapore, and countries in the West" (Sharma, 2012). This number marked an increase from 12 in 2009 and 16 in 2010 (Pawar, 2010, cited in Powar, 2015, p. 141). In a research study of Indian branch campuses in popular source countries, OBHE (2006) noted that the vast majority of these were private institutions (cited in Agarwal, n.d.a). In the majority of cases, the Indian private institution was invited by the "host" country to set up a branch campus, in a gesture of confidence in the "home" institution's capability (Sharma, 2012). An example of a successful Indian branch campus abroad is the presence of Manipal Global in Dubai's International Academic City in Dubai. Many Indian institutions that decide to open branch campuses abroad do so because they find the potential for long-term growth in India to be stunted. The regulatory structure that governs internationalization is rigid and punitive. The institutions that are eager to grow with respect to internationalization find that there are far too many hoops in India to jump to keep them encouraged. These institutions are privately managed, and held in high regard by students and institutions in "host" countries; therefore, the decision to move the operations abroad is an easy one. Quite commonly, the Indian branch campuses are extensively patronized by the students who are Indian by descent, such as members of the Indian Diaspora, or students who are nonresident Indians, such as members of the Indian expatriate community. In these cases, the students are familiar with the brand identity of the "home" institution and are keen to associate themselves with an Indian institution. It is no wonder that the popular destinations for Indian branch campuses are often countries that record a strong presence of people of Indian origin, for instance, countries in the Gulf region, the Caribbean, Mauritius, Fiji, Nepal, and South-East Asia.

As it has been discussed earlier, the future of branch campuses is uncertain, going by the number of downright closures and partial failures. Indian branch campuses have not done as badly as many of the branch campuses of developed countries in the Middle East, but several have fared poorly or shut down. The highest number recorded for Indian branch campuses, which is 17, was for the year

2011. Although it is certain that the total number of campuses has come down, there is conflicting data on the exact figure of campuses that are actively in operation: OBHE puts the number at 10, Powar (2015) at 14 (pp. 142–43).

Of the 14 campuses that are in operation, based on Powar (2015), two were set up in 1994 and the rest between 2000 and 2010. The programs run from diploma/certificate and bachelors to masters; the study did not list any doctoral programs. These disciplines clearly belonged to the category of "professional" education, and business administration management education was the most popular choice. Host countries included Nepal, Malaysia, UAE, Oman, and Mauritius. The home institution included Manipal College of Medical Sciences, BITS, Symbiosis International University, Mahatma Gandhi University, S. P. Jain Institute for Management and Research, JSS Education Foundation, Institute for Management Technology, Welingkar Institute of Management Development and Research, Madurai Kamraj University, and D. Y. Patil Medical College.

Conversely, the picture of "host" branch campuses in India is as discouraging as it is complex. A large number of "home" foreign institutions are "straining at the leash" to set up branch campuses in India, driven by the long-term goal of finding a place for themselves in a regional education hub in the country. The MHRD was wise in drawing on caution in its decision to allow admittance of foreign providers. However, as things turned out, in place of well-considered judgment, the Indian Government made use of procrastination— the Foreign Education Providers Bill being the case in point. In the face of acute policy paralysis, the message that went out to foreign providers was that the question of entry of foreign providers is in an indeterminate state, not that the government is sufficiently invested in the matter. In a representative example, the Canadian York University, which was all set to open a branch campus of Schulich School of Business in Hyderabad, had to shelve the project, faced with "prolonged delay of the proposed legislation" (ICEF Monitor, 2013).

What is the path ahead with respect to the setting up of branch campuses and education hubs in India?

In light of the above-mentioned several reasons, it would seem that the setting up of branch campuses in India is an issue ridden with many challenges. Education hubs, along the lines that one sees in the Gulf region or in South-East Asia, might not be the most feasible possibility in the near future. To begin with, legal bureaucratic challenges pose considerable obstructions and added to this are the manifold problems related to quality assurance.

Powar (2015, p. 159) points out that, in the late 1990s, the Indian Government did debate the idea of setting up free education zones within free economic zones. The two major factors that caused this plan to be abandoned were that large tracts of land around the fringes of metropolitan cities had to be acquired and that massive investments had to be planned before the project could even be envisaged. Similarly, in 2011, the Planning Commission toyed with the idea of creating education hubs on fallow lands around four or five locations. It was thought that some large public sector enterprises could be brought in by applying the concept of Corporate Social Responsibility (CSR). Again, the familiar roadblocks of massive capital investments in infrastructure arose. It was forecasted that a gestation period of two or three decades would likely be required before profits could be reaped. This time, too, the scheme was abandoned.

In consideration of the fact that the Indian Government has taken the initiative of debating the feasibility of education hubs and deserted the plans before taking any steps towards execution, it seems as though the country is not ready. The wide array of developmental challenges that the country is ridden with do not presage a promising outcome. As things stand, it is improbable that resources can be sufficiently mobilized for the purpose of setting up education hubs by nudging the politico-bureaucratic-legal framework of the higher education system out of its well-worn position of *statis*.

The failure of education hubs in the Gulf region must be borne in mind as a sobering forewarning. Many education hubs, although supported by astronomical investments and incentives such as tax-breaks and institutional autonomy, fell flat because there was no homegrown culture of academic excellence. The transplantation of foreign talent, no matter how plentiful, cannot sustain hubs in the long-term by itself.

Perhaps, it would be the more plausible thing to do to groom cities that show potential for advancement into centers of excellence in international education. This concept is inspired by the idea that regional growth in higher education must be osmotic and self-generative, evolving in its own time and through its own natural course. Although favorable public policy and effective executive structure are necessary, an educational ecosystem that is not prepped and primed from the grounds up will not be able to sustain a breakthrough of the nature of hubs. Cities that are the bastions of international education, such as Pune, have evolved over many decades, some might say a hundred years or more, and have been nourished by a culture that is not only conducive to higher education institutions, industry, and research and development but also hospitable to international students. Pune, which is hailed as the capital of international education in India, does, indeed, offer a working model for the Indian Government. Patil (2014) notes that in the year 2014, the population of international students in Pune stood at 10,166. This figure includes the figure released by AIU—7290—which reflects the official enrollment in higher education institution at the graduate and postgraduate levels (cited in Powar, 2015, p. 161). Universities, colleges, and other higher education institutions, which are many in number and cover practically all streams and levels, have a long-standing culture of excellence. There are also many research centers and laboratories that frequently work collaboratively with higher education institutions. The large network of multinational companies and enterprises add to the cosmopolitan culture of the city and offer career opportunities to graduates.

Education Hubs: New Pathways in Institutional Mobility

International branch campuses and education hubs are considered to be the most novel manifestations of international education. These are shining examples of the dynamism and innovativeness that are salient characteristics of internationalization of higher education in the present times.

The precipitous expansion of branch campuses and hubs in the Gulf region and South-East Asia is remarkable. The reverberations from the growth, such as it is, have sparked interest in other parts of the world—a self-referential introspection about how well this model could be transplanted in one's own higher education system.

In India, as in many other countries, there have been policy discussions about the system's readiness to receive branch campuses and hubs. India's enthusiasm is easy to understand. The country shares much with both the regions—the "geographic proximity, similarities in socio-politico-economic landscape and shared colonial past" (Yeravdekar & Tiwari, 2014, p. 165). The concern about the Indian system's suitability to host branch campuses and hubs in a sustaining manner is a reasonable one, as is the one about quality assurance management. The limited success and the unexpected roadblocks that campuses and hubs in the above-mentioned regions have encountered cast further uncertainties.

Theoretical Definition and Background

Unparalleled expansion in cross-border higher education in respect of volume of participants (both students and providers), modes of program delivery, variety of collaborations, and a general move towards "supra-territoriality" (Scholte, 2007, cited in CII-AIU, 2014, p. 63) have set the stage for the entry of hubs.

It must be pointed out that the ushering in of education hubs has been hurried and rather unforeknown. Perhaps, the need for providers to find unchartered territories in the face of unrelenting competition in the international education market is the main reason.

According to Knight (2011), education hubs are the newest era in cross-border higher education. Education hubs are regional nodes that are characterized by a clustering of higher education institutions and ancillary industries and businesses. Knight (2011, p. 225) defines the concept thusly: "an education hub is a concerted and planned effort by a country (or zone, city) to build a critical mass of education/ knowledge actors and strengthen its efforts to exert more influence in the new marketplace of education."

[W]hile countries' rationales for taking on education hubs might vary greatly, there are two constants: the enterprise of education hubs is typically taken up when a "relatively small" country makes a policy decision to switch from an economy based on manufacturing and natural resources to a "knowledge economy." (Knight, 2011, cited in Yeravdekar & Tiwari, 2014, p. 167)

Lane and Kinser (2011b), who have researched branch campuses and education hubs extensively, share Knight's viewpoint.

An educational hub is a designated region intended to attract foreign investment, retain local students, build a regional reputation by providing access to high-quality education and training for both international and domestic students, and create a knowledge-based economy. An education hub can include different combinations of domestic/international institutions, branch campuses, and foreign partnerships within the designated region. To date, the term appears to be primarily a rhetorical tool used to attract attention and drive the development of governmental policy (p. 82, cited in Yeravdekar & Tiwari, 2014, p. 167).

One can see how international branch campuses are related to hubs. The term "international branch campus" refers to the *physical* presence of the mother or home institution in the host country (in order to mark it out from other modes of cross-border higher education). Wilkins (2010) elaborates, "the term 'international branch campus' implies a brick and mortar approach, whereby an institution has a physical presence in a foreign country. Students receive their education in premises owned or leased by the foreign institution, solely or jointly with a local partner . . ." (p. 390, cited in Yeravdekar & Tiwari, 2014, p. 167). Thus, hubs house branch campuses along with supporting infrastructure and services.

The foundation stone of hubs was laid in India when the country made proclamations to liberalize higher education. "The advent of globalization in the early 1990s, and the signing of the General Agreement on Trade in Services (GATS) in 1995 provided, at least theoretically, a pathway for the entry of both foreign providers and foreign investment, into India" (Powar, 2012b, p. 237).

In contrast to the platitudes about recasting India as knowledge economy and embracing internationalization, the public policy has been unclear and prohibitive to foreign providers: "Verbik and Jokivirta (2005), in their six fold classification of regulatory models, place India in their fourth category—'moving from liberal to more restrictive' regime" (Altbach, 2012, p. 238).

The Indian Government's stance on education hubs has fairly consistently been tied to the goal of positioning India as a center of knowledge and innovation. Yeravdekar and Tiwari (2014) chronicle important discussions on public policy on hubs:

> The Federation of Indian Chamber of Commerce and Industry (FICCI) Higher Education Summit 2012 (was sponsored by the FICCI, the Ministry of Human Resource Development, and the Planning Commission); and the Planning Commission (in its Eleventh Five Year Plan, 2007–12) pronounced goals to attract foreign talent in higher education through public-private partnership. It was in the last context that the goal of setting up of fourteen "innovation universities aiming at world class standards" as "Global Centers of Innovation" in "identified cities" was stated. (p. 169)

These centers were to embody the Indian government's vision of education hubs where an interdisciplinary approach to higher education, global advances in research and innovation, and entrepreneurship were to be showcased to the world (Kasturi, 2008).

> [I]t is proposed to establish 14 new CU [central universities] aiming at world class standards. These universities . . . serve as benchmarks of excellence for other universities and colleges . . . The proposed 14 World Class Universities (WCU) need to be carefully planned to have various schools including medical and engineering. Their establishment should be implemented in a creative mode, by setting up an autonomous project team comprising eminent people for each of the proposed WCU, who would design and implement the project creatively. The location decision should balance the desire for achieving a greater geographical spread and the potential synergies arising from colocation with the existing reputed institutions and laboratories . . . so as to enable India to become the global knowledge hub and set benchmark for Central and other universities. (Government of India, n.d.)

The Planning Commission, in an attempt to build a model of a global education hub, came up with the plan for "Mohali Knowledge City":

> It is planned to build a knowledge city in Mohali, Punjab with a vision to promote innovation and startup [sic] companies. The cluster

includes, on a single campus, the Indian Institute of Science Education and Research (IISER), National Agri-food Biotechnology Institute, Nanotechnology Institute . . . a Technology Park for start-ups, and a host of other shared facilities. Governance, as a cluster is so designed as to allow dynamic contact and collaboration within the cluster and with all existing local institutes and enterprises. (Government of India, n.d.)

The Planning Commission's notion of education hubs could be described as "acropolis hub," which is one of the categories based on Lane and Kinser's (2011b) taxonomy: "[acropolis hub is] where there is a purposeful decision that institutions are to be located in very close proximity to each other, thus creating a focused site for the hub" (p. 84). The other category is "archipelago hub," which refers to hubs in a developing country where the institutions are not clustered but placed in a diffused manner.

It is notable that the Indian Government's plans related to education hubs are in contrast with those of the countries in the Gulf region and South Eastern Asia. In India, the attempts at setting up of hubs involve a regional cluster, not the entire country (as it is in the cases of Singapore and Malaysia). In the Gulf region and in South-Eastern Asia, a salient feature of the government's policy on hubs is the presence of a national plan (and investment) to enable the country to project it to the world as an education hub. It is this feature that distinguishes initiatives in these two regions from those in larger countries such as China, India, or the United States, where specific geographic areas are being promoted as hubs, not the country as a whole (Knight & Morshidi, 2011, p. 594).

Altbach and Jayaram (2008) and Altbach (2012) point out that the Indian higher education system is marked by a significant lack of homogeneity in regional terms. The clusters that house institutions of some international standing are contingent on infra-structural resources, along with corporate and industrial networks in research and innovation. Yeravdekar and Tiwari (2014) note that three metropolitan regions in India show potential to develop as global education hubs: Pune, Bangalore, and Hyderabad. Although upcoming regions are being promoted as hubs (for instance, Lavasa, in Maharashtra, and the "Rajiv Gandhi Education City" in Sonipat,

Haryana), but given the lack of supporting infrastructure, the sustainability is doubtful.

The notion of clustering higher education institutions and ancillary businesses carries all the advantage of "cluster regions" (Whitaker, 2004) because these agglomerations have self-generative properties resulting from the mutually interdependent relationship of the participating entities. The Planning Commission echoed this line of thinking in developing hubs in India:

> Building cluster in strategic location enables innovation. Characteristically, in a cluster, research, technology management, investment and business skills, technology incubators and parks for startups are colocated, functionally linked, based on a common vision. The vision of such a cluster is to create necessary synergies and sharing of resources, ideas, and facilities. (Government of India, n.d.)

The guiding goal is to come up with a regional hub that brings together higher education institutions, the IT industry, and other ancillary businesses. The MHRD's expression "hub and spokes model," models the notion that what the system needs the most is an encouragement to adopt entrepreneurship, which, along with publicly-funded infrastructural support, would result in a chain reaction of excellence in higher education. This argument agrees with the government's favorable stance on Public Private Partnerships (PPP).

It would be helpful to note that, in the recent years, the governments of Andhra Pradesh and Kerala have undertaken many initiatives to launch education hubs in their respective states. The author, a member of consultative committees related to these projects in both states, has highlighted the need to heed the following important considerations in developing international hubs (academic cities, higher education zones, and so on):

1. There is a need to create a government-managed entity that would look into the management of education city, including management of infrastructure and efforts toward sustainable success.
2. It important to ensure that the above-mentioned entity be economically feasible (in the sense of generating self-sufficiency). A reliable way to ensure this is to make available common infrastructure.

This will likely help in two ways: first, it will allow for the government entity to have recurring income; second, it will allow educational institutions to focus on academics and not be bogged down by upkeep of infrastructure and so on.

3. The construction and facility management must be of high-quality so that it meets international standards.

4. The quality of partnering institutions must be good because this is the key determinant of success.

5. The participants must attempt to infuse the ethos of "multiversity."

6. The policymakers must set up a relatively independent and non-partisan body to manage quality assurance concerns related to administration. A model to study in this regard would be the Government of Dubai's Knowledge and Human Development Authority.

7. It is important to emphasize the "international" nature of hubs in branding—all the way from nomenclature to other aspects of promotions.

8. It is important to attract ancillary industries and small businesses around hubs. It is just as important to offer incentives to R&D centers to operate in and around the hubs and partner with institutions in areas of common research interests. The guiding goal must be to set up a "research community." For this purpose, collaborative research program and activities must be conducted in partnership with Government-aided research institutions such as Department of Science and Technology (DST), Council of Scientific and Industrial Research (CSIR), ICAR, Department of Biotechnology (DBT), and Department of Information Technology (DIT).

9. The importance of interdisciplinary approach to curriculum design and teaching–learning must be emphasized.

10. The hubs must bring private participants in higher education into the heart of the initiative. The PPP model, discussed elsewhere, must be considered for its advantages over a model that is either public or private singularly.

This will allow the hubs to benefit from private funds, thereby easing the state's burden. The educational model will likely be more responsive to global advances, given that private institutions in India have demonstrated a track record of staying in step with global pedagogic practices.

The inclusion of private participants will also instill the entrepreneurial spirit in the higher education ecosystem, a result of which would be that graduates will likely be better ready to thrive in the global job marketplace as professionals as well as entrepreneurs, who create employment and innovation.

Private interests can be expected to place a stronger emphasis on technological skills and professional–vocational training. Private institutions in the country offer more innovative technological resources and facilities; it is likely that their inclusion will enhance this aspect in hubs.

Finally, transitioning from a centralized governance system to one that enjoys more diverse autonomic governance will go a long way in ensuring the success of hubs.

Several recommendations emerging out of working groups have stated that education hubs will not only help strengthen internationalization but also improve the overall quality of education. Institutional collaborations such as those seen in hubs can potentially imbue a "culture of excellence," especially in respect of research, which is India's paramount failing. This has the benefit of cultivating the capacity for international competitiveness from the grounds up through international collaborations, as opposed to "importing" foreign excellence. An indigenously-cultured ecosystem of meritocracy in higher education has more long-lasting value than a few "imported" goods and services from institutions abroad.

It is important to ask introspective questions that look into how well the Indian institutions are equipped to collaborate with foreign institutions, considering that curriculum, teaching–learning, caliber of professoriate, and infrastructure are far from being to the standards of trans-Atlantic universities. The limited success of branch campuses in the Gulf region and South Eastern Asia is partially explained by the consideration that the higher education systems in the host countries were not primed and prepped to receive and replicate the trans-Atlantic model of higher education, which accords importance to institutional autonomy, research, and the competence of professoriate:

> Wilkins (2002) builds on Sutton and Tse's (1997) argument which cautions against overlooking the differences in pedagogic methods

between home and host institutions. Wilkins illustrates his case by pointing out the dismal failure of student success and retention at Dubai Polytechnic on account of the students' unfamiliarity with the more progressive teaching-learning methods of the British home institution (cited in Wilkins, 2010, p. 395).

Along the same lines, Knight is skeptical about the less than realistic goals of Educity in Iskandar, Malaysia, on account of cross-cultural dissimilarities: "the challenges of recruiting the right mix of foreign universities, researchers, and R&D companies to work in a cross-cultural and disciplinary environment should not be underestimated" (Knight, 2011, p. 228; Yeravdekar & Tiwari, 2014, p. 177).

Several researchers have alerted Indian policymakers to the motives and long-term goals of foreign providers who are interested in partnering with Indian institutions:

> [T]hese schools will offer the programmes in India that they feel will attract students and may well have little commitment to either a long-term presence in India or to maintaining good quality . . . with very few exceptions, foreign providers are not interested in investing in high-cost academic infrastructures such as science laboratories and re-search facilities. They wish to minimise the investment and maximise the profit, like any corporation. (Altbach, 2012, p. 242)

The question about elitism is an important one too. Will a system ridden with inequality in access to higher education be served well by branch campuses and hubs? Collaborations with foreign providers, across all modes of cross-border higher education, are characteristically costly and oriented to the trans-Atlantic model. It is likely that international branch campuses and hub will worsen the prevalent mindset, which values "brand stature" and elitism in a higher education system more than service to nation-building and developmental goals. The concern about ill-advised emulation of the Western ethos of higher education, a vestige of the colonial heritage, merits note too. Education hubs have a propensity to create a set of circumstances where a limited number of providers monopolize the competition—this certainly does not presage welcome outcome in the Indian context.

India faces cutthroat competition from its neighbors to the South East, especially from Malaysia and Singapore. These governments, for their part, are eyeing the Indian market for enrolment and for partnerships.

> [O]ne of the target objects is the prospective Indian student looking for the international education experience: "The plan is to gain greater access to the regional education market especially from the three Asian population giants, India, China, and Indonesia" (Knight, 2011). Yahya (2008) argues that Singapore . . . through education hubs will need to join hands with India. He . . . contend[s] that the mere presence of Indian students will raise benchmark for higher education institutions in Singapore. (Yeravdekar & Tiwari, 2014, p. 188)

There are many challenges related to regulations, which result from the case that numerous governments and institutions participate in education hubs. Each of these participants has their own motives and stakes, and frequently there comes a situation where regulatory structure gives way—at the "crossroads of policy arenas" (Lane & Kinser, 2011b).

Operational and academic issues that harbor room for duplicity and confusion are countless: rules and regulations related to qualifying criteria, assessments, academic coursework, matching of credits and credit equivalencies, and student visa protocols. The fact that branch campuses and hubs are relatively newer phenomena explains the lack of inter-institutional and supranational networks to devise regulatory structures. Developing countries, such as India, must be further cautioned against the possibility of losing academic autonomy and institutional self-governance as they partner with foreign providers.

References

Agarwal, P. (n.d.a). International India a turning point in educational exchange with the US. Retrieved from http://www.usief.org.in/USIHEC/Chapter%204/Internationalization%20of%20Indian%20Higher%20Education.pdf (accessed on January 13, 2013).

Agarwal, P. (n.d.b). Privatization and internationalization of higher education in the countries of South Asia: An empirical analysis. New Delhi, India: Indian Council for Research on International Economic Relations (ICRIER).

Altbach, P., & Jayaram, N. (2008, October 23). Towards creation of world class universities. *The Hindu*. Retrieved from http://www.hindu.com/2008/10/23/ stories/2008102355501000.htm

Altbach, P. (2012). *A half-century of Indian higher education: Essays by Philip G Altbach*. New Delhi: Sage Publications.

Altbach, P., Reisberg, L., & Rumbley, L. (2009). *Trends in global higher education: Tracking an academic revolution*. Paris: UNESCO

CII-AIU. (2014). *Trends in Internationalization of Higher Education in India*. Retrieved from http://www.cii.in/PublicationDetail.aspx?enc=j+Bre1cn EnR7Sgogrka6KohkwpLy3x9ujfczyTnGBH8Pk1aE4ly77FRtKBZo0 YzFiVaGJLen1cG0O7iLKWe0szJJQOYv17/2Ud9piEIB1wUYJCzxAaL 6W6HZ0zrocFkdwNvqqO5gbqDAYy8PbqfcNF4MgwGKS4CIAGsf4 gwYhRVEQZuVQeUSm/p9oCvxp9Ll (accessed on April 6, 2016).

Government of India. (n.d.). *Eleventh five year plan*. Retrieved from http:// planningcommission.nic.in/plans/planrel/fiveyr/11th/11_v2/11th_vol2.pdf (accessed on April 6, 2016).

ICEF Monitor. (2013). International branch campuses: this is the year to hit "pause" before "go". Retrieved from http://monitor.icef.com/2013/01/ international-branch-campuses-this-is-the-year-to-hit- pause-before-go/ (accessed on April 6, 2016).

Kasturi, C. S. (2008, December 22). 'World-class' pursuit without a plan— Ministry asked to refer to other institutions for new law's framework. *The Telegraph*. Retrieved March 01, 2013, from http://www.telegraphindia. com/1081222/jsp/nation/story_10285611.jsp

Knight, J. & Morshidi, S. (2011). The complexities and challenges of regional education hubs: focus on Malaysia. *Higher Education, 62*(5), 593–606.

Knight, J. (2007a). *Implications of Crossborder Education and GATS for the Knowledge Enterprise*. Commissioned Research Paper for UNESCO Forum on Higher Education, Research and Knowledge. Paris: UNESCO.

———. (2007b). Cross-border tertiary ducation: An introduction. In *Cross-border tertiary education: A way towards capacity development*. Paris: OECD, World Bank and NUFFIC.

———. (2007c). Cross-border higher education: issues and implications for quality assurance and accreditation. In *Higher Education in the World* (p. 136). Retrieved June 5, 2016, from https://upcommons.upc.edu/revistes/ bitstream/2099/8109/1/knight.pdf

———. (2011). Education hubs: A fad, a brand, an innovation? *Journal of Studies in International Education, 15*(3), 221–40.

Lane, J. & Kinser, K. (2011a). Multinational colleges and universities: Leading, governing, and managing international branch campuses: *New directions for higher education, 2011*(155), 1–4.

Lane, J., & Kinser, K. (2011b). The cross-border education policy context: Educational hubs, trade liberalization, and national sovereignty. *New Directions for Higher Education*. doi: 10.1002/he.446.

Lawton, W., & Katsomitros, A. (2012). *International branch campuses expanding, geopolitical landscape changing*. Retrieved from http://www. universityworldnews.com/article.php?story=20120118205237531 (accessed on April 6, 2016).

OECD. (2004). *Building capacity through cross border tertiary education*. Retrieved from www.oecd.org/education/skills-beyond-school/33784331. pdf (accessed on April 6, 2016).

Powar, K. B. (2012a). *Indian higher education revisited*. NOIDA, India: Vikas Publishing.

———. (2012b). *Expanding domains in Indian higher education*. New Delhi, India: Association of Indian Universities Publications.

———. (2015). *Changing landscape of international higher education: An Indian perspective*. Pune: DY Patil.

Sharma, Y. (2012). Indian university expands overseas branch campuses. *University World News*. Retrieved from http://www.universityworldnews. com/article.php?story=2012031600441660 (accessed on April 6, 2016).

Snehi, N. (2012). *Student mobility at tertiary level in India status, prospects and challenges*. Delhi: NUEPA.

UNESCO. (n.d.). *Global flow*. Retrieved from http://www.uis.unesco.org/ Education/Pages/international-student-flow-viz.aspx (accessed on April 6, 2016).

Varghese, N. V. (2008). *Globalization of higher education and cross-border student mobility*. Paris, France: International Institute for Educational Planning (UNESCO) Printshop.

Yeravdekar, V. R. (2012). *Internationalization of higher education in India*. Unpublished doctoral dissertation, Symbiosis International University, Pune, India.

Yeravdekar, V. R., & Tiwari, G. (2014). Internationalization of higher education in India: How primed is the country to take on education hubs? *Procedia–Journal of Social and Behavioral Sciences, 157,* 165–182. doi:10.1016/j. sbspro.2014.11.036.

4

Regulations and Reforms to Promote Internationalization

The state is responsible for the achievement of planned growth in higher education. National objectives, which are set out periodically, guide enabling actions to promote higher education for the purpose of public welfare. Although the Indian Government has undertaken many initiatives to enhance the provisions related to internationalization of the Indian higher education system, the impact at the level of institutions has not been as impressive as one might have hoped for. It is to be pointed out that many Indian institutions have been slow to respond to the recent wave of internationalization. Several recent research studies and Government of India reports (National Institute of Educational Planning and Administration, 2004; Powar, 2015) have suggested legislative action to effect revisions in the UGC Act so as to facilitate the admittance and management of foreign providers in India.

Constitutional provisions entrust the Central Government to regulate the higher education system in the country. Some of the constitutional provisions have significance for the operation of foreign universities in India, even if not expressly. There is an urgent need for revision of regulatory provisions to facilitate the dynamics of the present day globalized higher education landscape.

Some working groups have been instituted now and again, and recommendations have been issued. The counsels that have come out of these committees are highly rhetorical and declamatory in nature, without the pairing of concrete mandates that could be translated into action or cause to enforce accountability. Alternatively, it is possible that these committees had, to begin with, no power to bring forth schemes that could be materialized. Although public knowledge and information on follow-up action is not available, it is likely that no significant reformative action resulted from the workings of these committees.

The vast majority of reformative proposals are initiated through the Government of India agencies mentioned subsequently.

Association of Indian Universities (AIU): The AIU, which is a 95-year-old organization entrusted with the responsibility of coordinating the activities of Indian higher education institutions, began collecting and disseminating data on international students in 1990. Since then, it comes out with information and recommendation on international students every now and then. The AIU has organized two roundtables on internationalization of higher education—the first in Mysore in 2001 and the second in Amritsar in 2002. Both the working groups came out with documents to report their findings and recommendation, which are respectively called Mysore Statement and Amritsar Statement. These documents were forwarded to government agencies and institutions for the purpose of implementation. In a nutshell, their recommendations included the following policy areas: directives to Government of India agencies to undertake urgent steps to finalize policy decisions on promotion of Indian higher education abroad, mandates to institutions to take up concrete steps to improve infrastructural and academic component such that the institutions are conducive to internationalization, and recommendations regarding promoting study abroad programs.

The University Grants Commission (UGC) and the All India Council for Technical Education (AICTE): The UGC undertook the first initiative on internationalization in 1996 by organizing a study group, which recommended some new modalities to provide educational opportunities to foreign students and to generate resources. It was in 2003 that the Commission identified for the first time internationalization as a thrust area by launching Promotion of Indian Higher Education Abroad (PIHEAD) as a coordinated national initiative (UGC, n.d., cited in Powar, 2015, p. 199). The Standing Committee of PIHEAD prepared a report detailing the vision, strategy, and operative plan of PIHEAD. In 2009, an expert committee appointed by UGC prepared an Action Plan on Internationalization of Indian Higher Education (UGC, 2009, cited in Powar, 2015, p. 199).

The UGC exercises its responsibility with respect to foreign education providers through UGC (Promotion and Maintenance of Standards of Academic Collaboration between Indian and Foreign Educational Institutions) Regulations, 2012. These regulations apply to all "foreign educational institutions" that operate in India through collaborations with Indian institutions, except those that are "technical institutions."

The AICTE was constituted in 1945 as an advisory agency in matters related to technical education. For quite some time, it had no statutory powers but still contributed to the growth of technical education in the country. During the 1980s, when there was a tremendous expansion of technical education—some of it without adequate regulatory supervision and planning—concerns were expressed by working groups to rectify the lack of coordination and management. The National Policy on Education of 1986 mentioned the need to make AICTE a statutory body. The AICTE became a statutory body through the Act of Parliament 52 in 1987.

The AICTE, for its part, oversees the regulations that apply to collaborative partnerships between foreign providers and Indian institutions "in the field of technical education, research and training."

The AICTE and UGC have set down some broad guidelines to regulate collaborations and initiatives with foreign education providers—these are posted on the respective websites, and some pertinent provisions are noted below:

Recognition of Qualifications and Statement of Equivalence

The issues of recognition of qualifications and statement of equivalence are important for the following reasons:

1. *Registration*: For the purpose of registration, many factors are considered, such as the eligibility criteria, course syllabus, academic work load, duration of program or course, assessment, and

recognition of qualifications. The AIU is responsible for ascertaining the validity of the above-mentioned factors.

2. *Employment with the Indian Government*: The Central or State Governments validate the "equivalence" of foreign degree in India for the purpose of making a decision on the academic and professional merit of persons seeking employment with the Indian Government.

3. *Higher Education*: The Indian institution, in conjunction with the AIU, settles the issue of equivalence. As stated earlier, regulations are insufficient, as a result of which standardization often gets compromised.

It is counseled that equivalence be made more adaptable and accommodating. In place of out-and-out accepting or rejecting a foreign degree as equivalent of an Indian degree, the system must move towards figuring out how a foreign degree might be brought up to par with an Indian degree. One must bear in mind that internationalization is a dynamic phenomenon, and it does not help to maintain a rigid stance in judging the relative value of academic standards. As an instance, a way of giving due credit to a foreign degree that is assumed to be substandard is to suggest supplemental academic courses, instead of flat out rejecting it as equivalent of an Indian degree.

The Association of Indian Universities follows certain guidelines for evaluating the equivalence of foreign degrees to Indian ones— the guidelines make an assumption about collaboration between foreign and Indian providers (as opposed to the foreign provider operating independently). Some guidelines to manage international collaborations are as follows:

1. The Indian institution must have sufficient infrastructural resources, and this must be ascertained by a Review Committee appointed by the AIU.

2. The academic programs in question must receive equal measure of contribution from the Indian and foreign institutions.

3. The foreign institution must certify that the awarded degree or diploma (awarded to Indian students) is equivalent to the corresponding degree or diploma awarded by the "mother" or "home" university.

The AICTE issued regulations for admittance and management of foreign institutions (those that offered technical–professional programs in India) in 2003.

According to Powar (2004), the objectives of the above-mentioned regulations are as follows:

1. Facilitate collaboration and partnerships between Indian and foreign institutions in technical areas
2. Systematize the operation of foreign institutions already operating in India
3. Safeguard the interest of the Indian student community
4. Enforce accountability on the part of the foreign providers
5. Prevent the entry of non-accredited institutions
6. Safeguard the nation's interests

The documents mention the following regulations related to registration of foreign providers:

1. The foreign provider must obtain "No Objection Certificate" from the respective Embassy or High Commission in India.
2. The foreign provider must submit a detailed "Project Report" to AICTE for evaluation.
3. The foreign provider must establish operation on its own or in collaboration with an Indian institution.
4. The foreign provider must be accredited in the home country.
5. The foreign provider must certify that the awarded degree or diploma will be recognised in the home country.
6. The partnering Indian institution must be an Indian university or an affiliated institution, preferably accredited by the National Board of Accreditation of AICTE.
7. The nomenclature of the degree offered in India has to be the same as that which exists in the parent (home) country.
8. It is the responsibility of the foreign provider to ensure that infrastructural resources are provided.
9. The AICTE will determine the tuition fees and limit on intake of students.
10. There are other minor clauses that describe "overall control of operations by AICTE" and assurance of protection of Indian students (cited in National Institute of Educational Planning and Administration, 2004, p. 23).

It emerges that the regulations set forth by the AIU and the AICTE are neither precise nor detailed. For provisions to be sufficiently helpful, they must offer separate stipulations for each of the circumstance of collaboration—joint or dual degree programs, articulation, franchise arrangement, branch campuses, and so on. It is recommended that, in addition to the above-mentioned provisions, there be in place amendment of the UGC Act to accommodate the present reality of foreign providers wishing to operate in India.

The Complexities of "Academic Entrepreneurism" and the Need for a Balancing Act

Altbach (2008) notes that India is quite possibly "the world's largest single market for foreign universities." The author cautions Indian policymakers to exercise deliberateness in allowing foreign education providers to step in on the Indian grounds. The crux of the author's argument is that a number of foreign bodies see internationalization of higher education as academic entrepreneurialism. In other words, higher education is just another tradable commodity, which is imported and exported across borders according to the dictates of the market.

The pivotal concern in the discussion is about the extent to which higher education, especially, as it presents itself in response to globalization, be allowed to work as a function of the demand and supply principle. The idea of a market molding the form that international higher education takes runs in contradiction to the idea of higher education as *public good*—the notion that higher education is responsible for shaping citizenry by fostering rhetorical thinking. A number of considerations are embedded within this line of thinking: is it a good idea to allow high-demand streams and disciplines to flourish at the cost of those that are low-demand? What if doctoral and other research-oriented programs are not amongst the high-demand programs? If that is the case, which is a very high-probability scenario, then research will likely be neglected even more. Will international collaborations result in reinforcing elitism in higher education? Will there be stipulations for institutions to make available subsidies, scholarships, and other incentives for meritorious students and for those who are underprivileged? What if national interests in higher education are vitiated?

An important apprehension relates to the case that there are newer kinds of global higher education providers and consumers joining in the mainstream ever so often: the for-profit companies, testing companies, and governments and parastatal agencies in countries such as Australia and the UK. This increase in the kind of entities that hold stake in global higher education poses challenge for those who have an investment in being informed of the credibility of providers and the reliability of operations. Guided by the business imperative of minimum investment and maximum returns, the providers, with very few exceptions, steer clear of research programs, which, typically, require huge investments to be set up.

Altbach (2008) states that the governments of many countries, such as the UK and Australia, are driven by an express national policy to earn profits from higher education exports. In this, they are backed by intermediary bodies, such as the British Council, which operate across borders to further the objectives of their respective governments. The US differs from the UK and Australia in that the American institutions' interest in exporting higher education to India and other countries is not guided by a national agenda. More to the point, there is no national agenda, as higher education goals vary across states. But, this must not obviate caution on part of the Indian government. If anything, the likely problems are even many more. Those American institutions that are the most invested in exporting higher education are the "low-end" private ones.

> The two largest players [in US] are Laureate Education Inc. and the Apollo Group (owners of the University of Phoenix and other institutions). Laureate's strategy is either to purchase existing universities outside the United States (they own 29 universities and postsecondary institutions on three continents) or to establish new schools. Laureate started a university in Andhra Pradesh, a state friendly to foreign providers, but pulled out when the regulatory environment seemed too complex. (Altbach, 2008)

The challenge in respect of regulatory deficits in the management of cross-border higher education India is no different from what is quite likely the scenario in other countries. As has been noted earlier, a big part of the problem is the recentness of cross-border higher education. As the Ministry of Human Resource Development works to set down regulations, it is to be hoped that the directives will be enabling and not punitive.

Proposal for Consortium for International Education (CIE)

The UGC proposed the setting up of the CIE, which was to function in collaboration with the AIU. The project never could take off, but was implemented on a very small scale by establishing an International Education Cell (IEC) within the AIU's Student Information Services Division. The CIE was to originally serve the following purposes (Powar, 2002, pp. 190–91):

- Identify select universities and institutions of higher learning in respect of their standard, infrastructural facilities, and performance, with the view of preparing a directory of centers of excellence (for international education) where international students can be admitted, and to update the directory from year to year
- Project Indian universities/institutions in other countries and function on their behalf
- Function as a clearing house for information on courses offered, availability of seats, the fees charged, the financial assistance available, and possibility of on-campus and off-campus housing accommodation for individuals and families
- Publish and distribute guides and handbooks for the promotion of international education programs in the country
- Coordinate education and training of international students of the universities/institutions of higher learning in the country
- Network, liaise, collaborate and interact with relevant institutions, individuals, and other agencies, within and outside the country, with the view to facilitating the promotion of international education cooperation programs

- Provide help to Indian universities/institutions of higher learning in obtaining approvals of the various ministries of the Government of India in respect of international education cooperation programs
- Promote, coordinate, and monitor—jointly with the Indian universities/institutions—the international students' affairs
- To represent Indian universities/institutions at international fairs on higher education and to organize similar fairs in India
- Undertake, with the help of individuals and universities, ethnographic studies on international students with a view of understanding more about the experiences of individuals, and also to make informed generalizations about specific nationality groups
- Develop norms and guidelines for ensuring quality in international education
- Do all other things which are incidental or, as the Consortium thinks, conducive to the attainment of the main objects of any of them

The Mysore Statement

The Association of Indian Universities organized a roundtable titled "Internationalization of Indian Higher Education," at the University of Mysore, Mysore, in 2001. Many educationists and policymakers participated in the discussions. The participants were broken down into three separate working groups to deliberate on administrative and academic restructuring with the view to bring in internationalization into the higher education system. At the end of plenary meetings, a number of resolutions were adopted under the title of "Mysore Statement."

The Amritsar Statement

The Association of Indian Universities organized a roundtable discussion on "Internationalization of Higher Education" at the Guru Nanak Dev University, Amritsar, in 2002. It was attended by representatives of the higher education systems of the US, Australia, Germany, France, and India. This conference was possibly a follow-up to the Mysore Statement of 2001. The resolutions that emerged from the conference came to be known as the Amritsar Statement.

The Ministry of Human Resource Development

In 2002, the Ministry constituted a Committee for the Promotion of Indian Education Abroad (COPIE) with the objective of formulating a policy framework for undertaking educational ventures abroad. The Committee could not make much progress.

The Prime Minister's Office in 2008 circulated a document titled "Welfare of Foreign Students," which recommended procedures for institutions and organizations that are involved with the internationalization. It also detailed recommendations for other Indian ministries, embassies, consulates, and high commissions abroad to take steps to promote Indian higher education abroad and ease the many processes that international students have to undertake to begin and complete their education in India.

The CNR Rao Committee

In January 2005, the MHRD set up a working group, headed by CNR Rao, which was entrusted with the responsibility of advising the Indian Government on the entry of foreign universities into India (David, Sanyal, & Wildemeersch, 2006, p. 8). Some of the major recommendations made by the committee are as follows:

1. Foreign institutions that intend to operate in India must secure approval of the Indian Government.
2. Foreign institutions must be given only a limited period within which they can operate in India. The institution's performance in this period will determine whether it be allowed to operate in the long term or not.
3. The recommendations are to apply to all modes of operation and delivery: branch campuses, franchises, and study centers.
4. In order to ensure that only trustworthy and well-meaning participants are allowed to operate in India, it is suggested that binding conditions, such as placing of security deposits by the foreign institution, be put in place.

Foreign Education Providers Bill

In order to facilitate and regulate the admittance of foreign education institutions into India, the Indian Government introduced in the Parliament, in 2007, the "Foreign Educational Institutions (Regulation of Entry and Operations, Maintenance of Quality and Prevention of Commercialization) Bill 2007." The stated intent was to ensure that only institutions of considerable quality and reputation be allowed admittance into the system, and to winnow out fly-by-night operators and other substandard providers. After "hanging" in the Parliament for three years, the Bill was withdrawn and a revised bill along the same lines was introduced. The revised bill was titled "Foreign Educational Institutions (Regulations of Entry and Operations) Bill 2010."

The Foreign Educational Institutions (Regulation of Entry and Operations) Bill, 2010, was introduced in the Lok Sabha on May 3, 2010. The Bill could not muster sufficient support and was withdrawn in 2014. At present, the bill is considered "lapsed" (not passed by the Indian Parliament due to lack of consensus).

The Bill sought to regulate the entry and operation of foreign educational institutions that seek to impart higher education. Some key features of the Bill are as follows:

1. Every foreign education institution intending to operate in India has to be notified as a foreign educational provider by the UGC on behalf of the Central Government. The application has to be endorsed by the High Commission of the foreign country in India.
2. Foreign education providers have to maintain a fund of a minimum of 500 million rupees. Further, up to 75 percent of income generated from the fund must be utilized for developing the institution in India and remaining amount is to be put back in the fund.
3. The Central Government may waive the regulatory conditions for any institution; the only exceptions are the penalty provisions and the ban on revenue repatriation, both of which cannot be waived.
4. A "foreign educational institution" is defined as any institution established outside India that has been offering higher education for a minimum of 20 years and proposes to offer programs that will be taught through classroom teaching methods. (It excludes

distance education offered independently or through collaboration, partnership or twinning arrangement.) The Bill also lays down separate guidelines for foreign institutions that offer certificate programs.

5. The Central Government, based on the recommendation of UGC, is authorized to withdraw recognition of a foreign educational provider if the latter fails to fulfill any regulatory conditions.

6. The programs that are offered by the foreign providers have to conform to the regulatory guidelines laid down by the relevant body—UGC, AICTE, or other councils—with respect to curriculum, teaching–learning methods and suchlike.

7. Every foreign provider that plans to operate in India must publish a prospectus two months before the admissions open to students. The prospectus must include the amount of fees, amount of fees that is refundable, approved number of seats, conditions of eligibility, and details of the appointed teaching faculty.

In the wake of the failure of the Foreign Education Providers Bill, the MHRD worked on a proposal to permit foreign universities to operate in India, open their campuses, and issue their own degrees under UGC and in line with the Companies Act. The proposal mainly lists rules on "the Establishment and Operation of Campuses of Foreign Education Institutions." The proposal was accepted by the Department of Industrial Policy and Promotion (DIPP) and the Department of Economic Affairs (DEA) under the Company Act.

The announcement, an executive order, does not need parliamentary approval and is essentially seen as a way to bypass legislative impasse.

The main difference between the executive order and the lapsed bill is that the former allows the issue of degrees by a foreign institution and the latter—had it become an act—would have allowed the award of the degree by an Indian institution.

Under the executive order, only those foreign institutions will be allowed to set up branch campuses that are registered as "not for profit" entities, have been in existence for at least 20 years, and are registered by an accrediting agency of the home country or by an international system of accreditation. The order also mandates that the institution, in order to be eligible, must feature in the list of top

400 institutions in, at least, one of three global rankings: the Times Higher Education (THES), Quacquarelli Symonds (QS), or the Shanghai Jiao Tong University Academic Ranking of World Universities. The institution must also offer programs that are of a quality comparable to the programs offered by the home institutions.

In another noteworthy move, the Government of India submitted a paper to the International Education Summit, which was held at Washington D.C. in 2012 (Powar, 2015, p. 201). The paper was intended to convey to the higher education authorities and institutions the Indian Government's keen interest and enthusiasm in promoting Indian higher education abroad and in collaborating with American higher education bodies. The paper covered the following items: research, teacher mobility, joint degrees, program collaboration, articulation arrangement, and twinning arrangements. Further, it admitted the part about the Indian Government's failings with respect to regulating the entry of foreign education providers. It also emphasized the Government's inclination in favor of program mobility rather than institutional mobility, as well as, facilitation of mobility through credit transfer and quality assurance mechanisms and mutual recognition of academic awards.

The AIU come out, in 1999, with the "Guidelines for Grant of equivalence to Degrees Awarded in India by Foreign Providers." These guidelines apply to those foreign providers that have partnered with an Indian institution. The following conditions were outlined for the grant of equivalence to degrees of foreign institutions operating in collaboration with accredited Indian institutions:

1. The Indian institution has adequate infrastructure and facilities, as validated by the report of a Review Committee of the AIU.
2. The program be implemented jointly by the foreign university and an Indian university, or an academic institution affiliated to an Indian university, with both contributing to the academic program in approximately equal measure.
3. The foreign university gives an undertaking that the degree/diploma awarded to the student in India would be considered as equivalent to the corresponding degree/diploma awarded by the university at home, and that it would be recognized in that country as being equivalent to the corresponding degree/diploma of the awarding university (Powar, 2015, pp. 201–202).

The AICTE issued in 2005 the "AICTE Regulations for Entry and Operations of Foreign Universities in India imparting Technical Education, 2005." These regulations are applicable to foreign universities intending to both enter into collaborative arrangement with Indian academic institutions and to establish their own campus. The regulations require foreign institutions seeking to operate in India—directly or through collaborative arrangements with an Indian institution—to fulfil the following objectives: become accredited in its home country; apply for permission, along with a no objection certificate issued by the concerned high commission or embassy in India; offer an understanding that the degree/diploma would be recognized in the home country; find partnership with an Indian university or an affiliated institution, preferably accredited by the NBA of AICTE; and offer assurance that the nomenclature of the degree offered in India is the same as that which exists in the "mother" country. In addition to this, there are other clauses that provide the AICTE with the authority to control operations (Powar, 2015, p. 202).

The UGC, by passing the regulations "Promotion and Maintenance of Standards of Academic Collaborations between Indian and Foreign Educational Institutions" in 2012, lay down three important conditions:

1. Only the most highly-regarded and accredited foreign education institutions be allowed to enter into partnerships with institutions in India.
2. The Indian institutions that enter into partnerships with foreign educational institutions must be those that are accredited with a grade not less than "B" and have an experience of not less than five years in offering educational programs at the level of degree or postgraduate diploma. Those institutions that are maintained by the central government, state governments, and union territories are exempt from these conditions.
3. Any foreign or Indian educational institution that already has a collaborative arrangement must comply with the regulations within a period of six months of the regulations coming into force.

It is lamentable that follow-up on these initiatives has been thoroughly dissatisfactory. Powar (2015, pp. 203–04) notes a number of lapses in this regard. The AIU continues to issue status reports on the inflow of international students into India, but, since 2008–09, it has stopped furnishing these reports to the IIE, as a result of which this information is not disseminated widely and does not find place in international databases, directories, and other publications. This is all the more regrettable in light of the fact that, more recently, UGC and MHRD, through the program "All India Survey of Higher Education," have also been collecting and analyzing data on international students.

Further, there has been no follow-up on the report of the Standing Committee of PIHEAD (UGC 2004, cited in Powar 2015) or on the Action Plan on Internationalization of Indian Higher Education (UGC 2009, cited in Powar 2015). The activities of PIHEAD are not only limited, but also intermittent. Most of its work is limited to coordinating the activities of Indian universities, with the aim of representing them in education trade fairs abroad.

The AICTE regulation of 2005, which requires foreign institutions operating in the country to register with AICTE, has been pretty much ignored by the handful of foreign education providers that are operational in the country.

The UGC regulations of 2012 have met a similar fate. A large number of partnerships between Indian and foreign institutions do no pass as entirely legitimate when judged on the basis of eligibility norms that are laid down by the regulations. The Indian Government has neither identified those institutions that are in breach of the regulations nor has it devised a plan to deal with those that are in violation of the compact.

Finally, the withdrawal of the Foreign Educational Institutions (Regulation of Entry and Operations) Bill, (2010), indicates that the Indian Government is not in the favor of allowing foreign providers to set up branch campuses in India.

Choudaha (2010) has identified three sets of universities that might be interested in moving to India (cited in Powar, 2012, pp. 204–05):

1. Prestige-enhancing universities (top research universities): the key goal is the enhancement of brand stature and not revenue generation.
2. Prestige-seeking universities (next-tier research universities): the key goal is building brand stature through internationalization and revenue generation is a secondary goal.

3.   Revenue-maximizing universities: the key goal is revenue generation because these universities do not have the funds to set up branch campuses. The main modes are twinning (articulation) arrangements and franchising.

Although the Government bodies claim to extend admittance to only the above-mentioned first two categories, in reality, it is the last category that is the most interested in partnering with Indian universities. The targeted Indian universities are either tier one universities, such as IITs and IIMs, or research-intensive institutions, such as Jawaharlal Nehru University, which are known for research productivity in specific areas. Private universities that have been awarded grade "A" by NAAC are also targeted because they offer the combination of opportunities for profitability along with academic rigor.

Powar and Bhalla (2001), Powar and Bhalla (2006), and Rahaman et al. (2012) point out the increase in the number of providers that have entered the Indian higher education system to partner with institutions: from 144 in 2001 to 438 in 2006, followed by 651 in 2010. It is certain that the number at present is higher than the last recorded figure. The majority of these partnerships are franchise operations or articulation arrangements. It seems that these providers have entered the Indian system by doing what McBurnie and Ziguras (2011) call "slipping between the regulatory cracks," which means that they have not been scrupulous about following the conditions that have been laid down by the home and the host governments. They have, instead, exploited the loopholes in the system or found a way to dodge the regulatory system in India or the system in the other participating countries (cited in Powar, 2015, pp. 198–206).

The MHRD has entrusted the AIU with the responsibility and task of holding consultation with the various stakeholders of internationalization of higher education as part of the initiative to formulate the New Education Policy. It is commendable that the present government accords importance to internationalization and has plans to include it in the forthcoming New Education Policy.

The New Education Policy

The New Education Policy marks a welcome development in the goal of internationalization of higher education. An initiative of the MHRD, the project is being extensively discussed at several levels within many Government of India agencies and other organizations. It seems likely that the outcomes will be more along the lines of review and recommendation than those that have some authority to assert corrective enforcement.

As mentioned previously, many committees and symposia have been instituted by the Central Government, but they have yielded results that are advisory at the best—their presence would not have affected the processes at the institutional level all that much. In light of the long-continuing scarcity of working groups on internationalization and an even more sparse practice of the counsel that comes of such groups, one is inclined to be hopeful that the new initiative will prove salutary.

In the specific context of internationalization, the discussions on the New Education Policy raise a few important themes. A guiding idea is that education must be seen as "public good." Further, the discussions underscore the importance of ensuring that national autonomy continue unthreatened as foreign providers operate in the country, and that these providers comply with the guidelines set forth by UGC and AICTE. The discussions have led to the conclusion that commercialization of higher education is not advisable.

The key rationales for internationalization are as follows: first, the presence of international students brings diversity; and, second, the lack of international students contributes to India's non-presence in the global rankings landscape. It was pointed out that the number of "foreign students" in India is only around 28,000, and no Indian institution is close to the "15 percent ceiling" (of "foreign students"), which is recommended by the regulatory authorities. From the preliminary report on the discussions, it would appear to the policy-makers that the presence of international students is the most important aspect of the internationalization. The following points were covered as part of the consultative discussions:

(i)   Indian institutions must improve their branding efforts in order to bring in international students. Dissemination of information (related to curriculum, medium of instruction, research etc.) amongst prospective international students is an important step.

(ii) Strengthening and modernization of infrastructure goes a long way in attracting and retaining international students.

(iii) Matters related to visa, registration and extension at Foreign Registration Office (FRO), and "tax regime" must be made more user friendly.

(iv) Curricula and goals related to learning outcomes must be enhanced such that they have greater international appeal.

(v)   Indian institutions must target "fast-growing" economies in the SAARC region (South Asian Association for Regional Cooperation), Central Asia, and Africa as catchment area.

(vi) Many international students come to India because of the appeal of the Indian culture. Therefore, curriculum must be revised such that it better caters to this supportive factor.

(vii) Centers of excellence must be developed in high-performing institutions to attract international students and faculty members.

(viii) More funds must be allocated to institutions as incentive to attract international talent.

(ix) Many international students find it difficult to cope with the level of rigor that Indian curriculum sometimes requires. Foundation and English language courses can resolve this challenge and improve student success.

(x)   Formalities and protocols related to the entry of international faculty members and researchers must be made more conducive. Similarly, the processes related to organization of international conferences must be made more lenient and streamlined.

The key rationales for internationalization are as follows:

1. Presence of international students
2. The consultations also raised the point that policy-level interventions are necessary to facilitate "mutual degree recognition." A suggestion was made to the effect that a viable approach in this regard would be one where the accreditation of joint or dual degrees in Indian institutions is recognized. This would benefit students at both the sides

3. The discussions included suggestion that a gradual transition from "years-based" to "credit-based" system would be helpful. It was also suggested that the range and norm of "credit-based" system must be specified in order to bring more uniformity
4. Internationalization must be encouraged as a two-way process, where both international and Indian institutions cross-borders and engage in exchange of information and skills
5. Many Indian institutions are not oriented to the global higher education landscape. A policy intervention must be made for encouraging institutions to consider being part of the competition for global rankings
6. Exchange programs and research collaborations must be led by faculty members, not the participating institution

The initial discussions on the New Education Policy bring internationalization into the heart of the discussions on the higher education system. The above-mentioned points are incisive and comprehensive. It bodes well for the Policy that the finer points related to implementation have not been left to chance.

Private Institutions and the "Obstructionist" Regulatory Structure

Private universities in India are called "self-financed" universities and "deemed-to-be-universities." These are governed by section 3 of the UGC Act, and, in states, these universities are established through the Private University Act. The "self-financed" in the taxonomy is accurate because they do not receive any funding from the Government. Mostly, they rely on tuition fees to fund their operations.

The growth of private institutions has been phenomenal in the last few decades. This is to be explained by the fact of their having responded successfully to the demands of those in the higher education cohorts. These institutions have contributed significantly to the enhancement of the employability aspect, thereby increasing their appeal amongst a broader base. Indeed, much of the recent successes of private universities are to be attributed to the case that their offerings include a much larger share of career-oriented programs, such as engineering, management, and architecture. On the other hand, public universities have traditionally focused on "general education" programs in science, humanities, and social sciences, and it continues to be that way. Although public universities are bringing in professional programs, it is not enough to meet the needs of the higher education demographic. Failure to respond to the emerging demands that come with "massification" is perhaps the biggest reason why private universities have found space to step in and carve out a substantial share of the total enrollment for them.

It is relatable that the progression of private institutions has occurred on account of very pressing demands in the higher education demographic, not public policy thrust on private institutions. That private institutions have been able to accomplish this all on their own is quite remarkable.

> The last decade has witnessed phenomenal growth of the private sector: In the year 2002, India had nearly 4,400 professional colleges of which about 3,150—upwards of 70 percent—were in the private sector (Powar & Bhalla, 2005, cited in Powar, 2012). This growth has continued unabated: In the year 2012, the total number of diploma granting institutions stood at 12,748, of which 9,541 were in the private sector. More importantly, the private sector has recorded growth at the broadest level: in the year 2012, as many as 64% of higher education institutions were in the private sector. This growth was reflected in other parameters as well—59% of student enrolment in higher education was in the private sector. (Yeravdekar & Tiwari, 2014, p. 331)

In light of this, it seems unfair that the Indian Government has laid down more elaborate regulatory structure for private institutions, whereas public universities, which are supported by public funding, are allowed to function with much simpler regulatory mechanisms.

As with private institutions the rest of the world over, private institutions in India have gained enormously from "massification" in striding forward. Massification refers to a giant shift within the higher education system wherein the system moves from serving elites to serving the masses. This landmark moment, which could refer to a decade or more, marks a transformation not only in enrollment, but also in the extent and nature of demand for higher education.

The government's failure to address the demands of the teeming millions has occurred at many levels. First, public expenditure in higher education has not kept pace with the requirements. Not only that, there is not much surplus capital to be invested back into the higher education sector. Second, public institutions have failed to consolidate knowledge and innovation within the higher education system. Private institutions, on the other hand, have demonstrated dynamism, successfully capturing niche and emerging markets. Third, private institutions have shown superior management of the quality assurance aspects. They have generally performed well in NAAC assessments, featured high on the list of rankings of academic institutions, generated positive reputation amongst students, media, and the wider higher education circle, and succeeded in enhancing the employability of their graduates.

> Of the top ten US universities in the QS World University Rankings® 2013–14, all are private institutions. In India, deemed universities, the vast majority of which are in the private sector, received higher grades by NAAC than did their public universities (Powar, 2012). (Yeravdekar & Tiwari, 2014, p. 332)

Fourth, internationalization, which represents a new frontier in higher education, has been espoused by private institutions more prominently. All the modes of cross-border higher education, from student mobility to program mobility, have found more expression in private institutions. The case of Indian branch campuses in Asian countries, especially in South Asia and the Gulf region, is quite remarkable. Almost all these branch campuses are privately owned and managed (OBHE, 2006, cited in Agarwal, n.d.a).

The Indian Government's regulatory structure is not well suited to help private participants thrive. Overly burdened with centralized bureaucratic and political regulations, private institutions are reduced to functioning suboptimally.

> The federal structure of the system, especially in the wake of the Forty-second Amendment to the Constitution" (1976) renders the system susceptible to political vagaries, even mishandling. The UGC regulations, often punitive in nature, work to clamp down on private institutions' autonomy and self-determination . . . The Ministry of Human Resource Development's approach to higher education policy is largely governed by a rubric that derives from NPE (1986)

and PoA (1992) . . . None of these reforms would be possible until the policy makers decide to remodel a rulebook that was drafted over twenty-five years ago (in fact, the original version of NPE was drafted in 1968). (Yeravdekar & Tiwari, 2014, p. 332)

The reports and the recommendations that are elaborated by the Indian Government typically have strong "social-democratic rein-forcement" (Yeravdekar & Tiwari, 2014, p. 332). These recommenda-tions fail to take into account the changes that are necessitated by the forces of globalization. Thus, the system is not primed and prepared to embrace the more progressive innovations in pedagogy, curriculum, and research and development that bring higher education to serve knowledge economy.

The UGC and AICTE are armed with the authority to lay down stringent measures to ensure supervision of the system:

[The UGC and the AICTE have the power to] "coordinate and determine standards" in higher education. This power is customarily translated to imply methodization, as in forging homogeny and symmetry by drawing up a centralized schema. Thus, the government assumes a paternalistic and directorial stance, leading to the locus classicus "over-regulation and under-governance." The "over regulation" is, in point of fact, fault-ridden at many levels: the enacted edicts are drafted with the intent to schematize not just the bigger pieces of the puzzle, but the "nuts and bolts" as well. (Yeravdekar & Tiwari, 2014, p. 332)

As a result of this, the regulations go into the nitty-gritties: coursework, assessments, curriculum plans and such. In addition, the offices that regulate are many and spread across many levels; the bureaucracy is a "lumbering behemoth"; and educationists are not invited to work complementarily with the policymakers. The end result is that the policies lead to a scenario that perpetuates *statis* and one that frankly clamps down dynamism, motivation, and initiative.

How Dynamism in the Private Sector Propels Internationalization

Private institutions, the world over, are considered to have heralded internationalization of higher education. The emergence of private institutions has not merely coincided with but is correlated to globalization. The breaking down of physical and political boundaries, combined with decentralization of governance and businesses, has been a powerful impetus for privatization of higher education. The vast majority of private institutions entered higher education in response to a pressing need for new participants in the field, a need following on from the failure of public institutions to meet the requirements of the higher education cohorts. A representative example of this would be the Indian system, where state universities were (and still are) trudging along as they bear circumstances of deprivations in funding and having to manage more affiliated colleges than can come close to doing.

The very case that private institutions have made a space for themselves by filling in serious gaps in a rigid, unyielding system, offers evidence of their dynamism and resourcefulness. Private institutions have embraced many progressive properties in higher education far better than their public institutions: internationalization, career competencies, interdisciplinary approach, and extracurricular skills, particularly those that are defined as "high skills."

Indeed, these institutions have infused fresh energy and vitality into the system, opening the system to authentic competition, meaningful public accountability, and newer benchmarks in quality assurance management.

Private institutions, by and large, do not benefit substantially from public funding; typically, they subsist on tuitions and other self-generated sources. In India, the stance of the government is positively "obstructionist" and punitive, as has been discussed previously; therefore, the private institutions' forward movement is commendable.

Tierney (2012, cited in CII-AIU) has listed three factors that account for the private institutions' lead in internationalization of higher education: first, the inclusion of newer entities (in terms of demographic profiles and education requirements) in the student population; second, private institutions' superior incorporation of technological advancements; third, expansion of tertiary education and the public institutions' inability to be fully responsive to this transformation. The end result of these three occurrences is that public institutions have not developed the capacity to meet the growing demands of the higher education cohorts, have not been able to carve out new markets for them, and have not been able to add to their revenue stream (CII-AIU, 2014).

It is difficult to miss how well these occurrences find match in the Indian higher education system. In India, private institutions have led the way in internationalization, but this phenomenon is nested within a broader trend—the powerful sway of private participants in the higher education system The EY-FICCI (2014) present some figures to demonstrate the strength of private participants in the last two decades.

> private institutions account for 64 percent of the total number of higher education institutions in the country, and 59 percent of the total enrolment. Even more remarkable is the rate of annual growth: "state private universities have witnessed an annual growth of 33.8 percent since 1995 . . ." (EY-FICCI, 2012, p. 14)

Private institutions in India have succeeded in promoting internationalization across all the modes—in partnering with foreign universities, in hosting international students, and in expansion of the "home" (Indian) institution abroad.

> The Anglophone world has displayed keen interest in partnering with Indian institutions (Mishra, 2012). Altbach (2008) notes that India is quite possibly "the world's largest single market for foreign universities" (n.p.). The vast majority of these foreign institutions eye private institutions in India that specialize in management and other professional streams and disciplines (Altbach, 1999) . . . The more recent expression of internationalization in India's neighbourhood, for instance, in South East Asia and the Gulf region, has been in the form of privately owned and managed international branch campuses (Agarwal, n.d.a; Knight, 2011; Wilkins, 2010) . . . In a research study of Indian branch campuses in popular source countries, the Observatory on Borderless Higher Education (OBHE; 2006) noted that the vast majority of these were private institutions (cited in Agarwal, n.d.a). In the majority of cases, the Indian private institution was invited by the "host" country to set up branch campus, in a gesture of confidence in the "home" institution's capability. (Sharma, 2012, as cited in CII-AIU, 2014, p. 60)

Sharma (2012, cited in CII-AIU, 2014) notes that, most of the time, the private institutions, in deciding to open branch campuses abroad, are motivated to do so on account of their frustration with the regulatory structure in India and a sense of hopelessness that things will ever improve enough to allow for potential for long-term growth in India. Frequently, these institutions, successfully drawing in students and building brand stature in India and abroad, are too discouraged by the perennial challenges in the system and conclude that to limit to India is to "have their wings clipped." Thus, the decision to expand abroad is guided by operational challenges, among other things.

International Branch Campuses (2013) cites that the Canadian York University, which was all set to open a branch campus of Schulich School of Business in Hyderabad, had to shelve the project, faced with "prolonged delay of the proposed legislation" (cited in CII-AIU, 2014, p. 60). The Indian regulatory system, which has been criticized for its inability to make decisive choices and move policies and projects forward, signals the message that advances in higher education are not a matter of priority.

Whereas the private institutions' contribution to inbound student mobility is well-documented, the same for program mobility is not so. Dual degree programs, twinning programs, and study abroad programs, which have demonstrated success in popularity and effectiveness, are carried out almost predominantly by private institutions. But, the regulatory system poses roadblocks to a successful outcome of institutional mobility. The UGC stipulations that oversee collaborations with foreign partnering institutions are "insufficiently detailed" in laying down the processes and criteria used to draw up collaborations. The scouting of opportunities and finalizing of partnerships call for the ironing out of many variables at the end of all partners.

> . . . diversity of programs and providers, ambiguity in arriving at what count for legitimate mechanisms for controlling entry qualifications, academic workload, quality assurance, and evaluation . . . The UGC regulations, which are titled "Promotion and Maintenance of Standards of Academic Collaboration between Indian and Foreign Educational Institutions Regulations, 2012," for instance, go into "procedure for approval" [of memorandum of understanding (MoU)] and the "consequences of violation" [of regulations], but not delve into the academic content of collaborative partnerships, such as, twinning programs: Thus, questions such as what constitutes academic coursework, evaluation of credits, assessment criteria, and so on are left unattended. (CII-AIU, 2014, p. 61)

The success of private institutions in the realm of internationalization is to be explained by their utilization of progressive means to devise solutions to chronic and widely-prevalent challenges. Anecdotal experience shows that relative freedom in self-governance assists these institutions in gaining adaptive skills in their operations. Motivated to thrive in the face of competition, private institutions go the distance and bring home the benefits that accrue from global advances in infrastructure, pedagogy, instructional technology, work–study opportunities, and career competencies. The end result is that students graduate with the personal and professional capabilities that help them succeed as contributors to knowledge generation and dissemination, as members of the global workforce, and as global citizens.

The question about the positioning of private institutions vis-à-vis public ones is not one of India's alone; it is being raised all over the world. Massification, receding public contribution to higher education, and increasing competition—all outcrops of globalization—have created a "quasi-market situation within and between the public and private sectors" (Slaughter & Leslie, 1997; Teixeira, Dill, Jongbloed, & Amaral, 2004, cited in Altbach & Peterson, 2007, p. 79).

The dichotomous nature of ownership of higher education institutions across private and public lines marks a watershed moment. It denotes many transformations: a breaking down of boundaries between public and private ownership in the management of higher education, the moving of private institutions inwards to the center, increasing interconnectedness between knowledge and career networks across the globe, and so on. The Indian public policies on higher education, posing an obstruction to growth and out-of-true with the changing realities, are due a revisit. It is now for Indian policymakers to integrate the transformative shifts in paradigm into public policies that regulate governance and funding.

Thus, the coming together of public and private ownerships in higher education across the world and the broader trends of decentralization, liberalization, and homogenization could be placed within the larger paradigm of globalization as an all-in phenomenon, which is described by Scholte (2007) as "a reverberation of the larger dilution of boundaries that split nation states as entities engaged in struggle for power. In place of a state-centric world, globalization brings forward the notion of 'supra-territoriality'" (cited in CII-AIU, p. 63).

In Scholte's (2007) lexicon, the world is becoming a sum of territories, and moving away from the center-periphery mode of functioning. The variables in the equation of higher education, as in other realms, are increasing in number and across spheres of relevance. It could be extrapolated that government-managed institutions, by virtue of being defined as such, are incongruent with the notion of "supra-territoriality" and, therefore, due a reevaluation.

Opportunities for Foreign Education Providers in India

If higher education systems in the Anglophone world have turned to India to look for pastures a new, it is with a good reason. India has undergone expansion in higher education that is out of the ordinary in both absolutistic and relative terms.

> The Indian education space is by far the largest capitalized space in India with Government spend of USD 30 bn and private spend of USD 50 bn . . . In terms of number of collaborations forged by Foreign Universities with Indian Educational Institutions, in 2011 alone, a total of 161 collaborations were reported . . . While Foreign Direct Investment (FDI) in the Regulated segment ["regulated segment" refers to "formal" higher education segment] is not feasible as of now due to restrictions imposed on the form of legal entity to be set up (viz. trust/ society/ section 25 company), FDI in the Un-Regulated segment ["un-regulated" segment refers to "un-formal" or "semi-formal" higher education segment] is seeing a considerable inflow: it was USD 492 mn during the period April 2000 to January 2012. (PwC, n.d., p. 4)

This growth is more of an osmotic response to developments in the higher education milieu in India and abroad and less of an outcome of policy planning at the governmental level in India. That said, the Indian Government has exhibited an inclination to liberalization of the higher education system and favorable reception of foreign education providers in the country. The factors that drive foreign education providers to scout opportunities in India are no different from those that further internationalization of higher education.

- Unmet demand for higher education (especially in the nontraditional modes of delivery and in streams that are skill-oriented and service-industry focused)
- Greater participation of private education providers
- Increased inflow of Foreign Direct Investment (FDI) in the higher education sector
- Better awareness of and connectivity with untapped markets
- Introduction of bills that are indicative of Indian Government's revived interest in partnering with foreign providers, such as Foreign Educational Institutions (Regulation of Entry and Operations) Bill, 2010, and Educational Tribunals Bill, 2010
- Increased pressure in the Anglophone world to look for unexploited markets
- Stimulus amongst higher education systems in the developed world to bring higher education closer to international students rather than draw international students to home campuses

The regulatory framework that governs entry and operation of foreign education providers is not remarkably different from the organizational structure that oversees the Indian higher education system (see Figure 4.1).

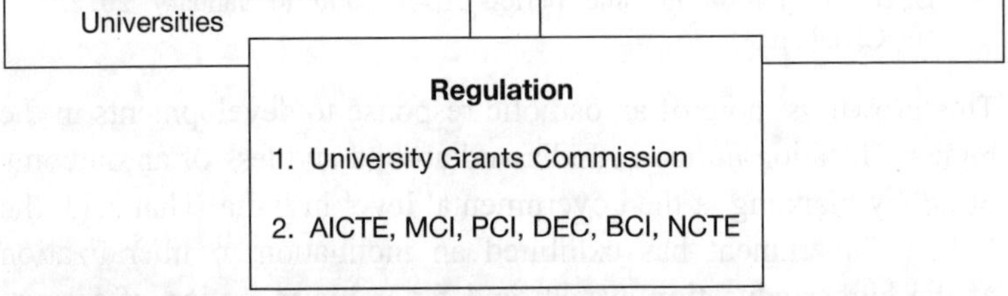

Policy-Making

1. Ministry of Human Resource Development (Higher Education Department)

2. Association of Indian Universities

Accreditation

1. National Board of Accreditation

2. National Assessment and Accreditation Council

Regulation

1. University Grants Commission

2. AICTE, MCI, PCI, DEC, BCI, NCTE

Figure 4.1 From Regulatory Framework Within Which Foreign Education Providers Operate

Source: PwC (n.d.).

The GATS and Internationalization
of Higher Education

The General Agreement on Trade in Services (GATS), which came into force in 1995, is a World Trade Organization (WTO) treaty that laid down the legalities of multilateral trade agreements in trade in services. The overarching rationale is to liberalize international trade in services by eliminating those barriers to trade that are perceived to be excessive or impeding. The GATS is the first ever treaty to regulate multilateral trade in services, and its significance derives from its association with WTO. The WTO agreements that constitute GATS are ratified by the majority of the world's trading nations. Therefore, the agreements are legally enforceable and all of the signatories are bound to the set of contracts.

The GATS is composed of many segments: general guidelines, inventories of countries' specific engagements as to the interaction between domestic sector and foreign providers, and qualifying conditions and restrictive clauses. The treaty outlines four "modes of supply" by which one understands the ways in which trading in services comes about—these are as follows:

Cross-border supply: This is defined as the provision of services where the services cross the territorial boundaries of one member state to that of another without necessitating movement of the consumer across physical boundaries. In the context of cross-border higher education, this mainly refers to distance education mode of delivery by means such as online programs and courses.

This mode is directly correlated to technological advancements in the instructional technology. The most common trend in the movement is from developed to developing countries. The developed countries clearly enjoy an advantage here, given their upper hand in education technology. Developing countries are catching on, but typically the movement is within developing countries and not from developing to developed countries. India has undergone a significant growth in this sphere in the last decade—an illustrative example is the wide range of programs and courses that the IGNOU offers to students in neighboring countries and Africa. The expansion of this mode in India is likely on a steep ascent. Since the overwhelming majority of distance education presupposes Internet usage, trends in Internet access and subscription make for an important investigation. In India, Internet access is an area of phenomenal growth.

> India has bypassed Japan to become the world's third largest Internet user after China and the United States, and its users are significantly younger than those of other emerging economies . . . The Telecom Regulatory Authority of India (TRAI) pegged the number of Internet subscribers in India at 164.81 million as of March 31, 2013. (*The Hindu*, 2013)

The next big leap in this mode is MOOCs, and it has been suggested that MOOCs will go a long way in addressing the issue of access to higher education in developing countries such as India.

Consumption abroad: This is defined as the provision of a service in the territory of one member country to consumers of another member country while involving the movement of the consumer to the country of the supplier. In the context of cross-border higher education, this mode would translate into the traditional mode of delivery—the physical movement of students from "home" to the "host" country. It is needless to state that this is, by far, the most prominent and voluminous mode of delivery of cross-border higher education. The operational complexities of this mode are to be found mainly in student visa formalities, recognition of awarded degree, and qualifying postsecondary education. In this mode, the upper hand belongs to developed countries as they benefit from the financial gains that come from the inflow of international students and from defining the operational guidelines for incoming students. The skewed presentation of this mode in India—low inbound and high outbound student mobility—has been discussed earlier. The spillover result of this imbalance is the oft-cited issue of "brain drain."

Commercial presence: This is defined as the supply of a service by the supplier of one member country in the territory of another member country by establishing "commercial presence," which implies setting up of branch offices, franchises, and subsidiaries. In the context of cross-border higher education, the illustrative examples that readily come to mind are education consulting offices, branch campuses, twinning, franchising, satellite campuses, and study centers. This mode holds great promise in cross-border higher education, as the providers' interest in expanding through this mode is demonstrably exceedingly high. This mode is also the most complex one. The case that two or more institutions from different countries come together to offer programs and courses while complying with regulations from as many sources and overarching international guidelines raises its trials and tribulations. Possibly, the most common criticisms with respect to this mode come from issues related to quality assurance and national autonomy. The popular trend in this mode is, of course, from developed to developing countries. The solid reputation of universities in the Anglophone developed countries combined with their financial prowess results in boundless demand in the developing countries, such as India. The incoming of foreign providers in India has been beset with regulatory complexities and policy inertia. The Foreign Education Providers Bill is a shining example of Government inaction.

Movement of natural persons: This is defined as the *temporary* movement of service providers abroad to render services. This mode essentially refers to mobility of academic professionals, such as researchers and academics across borders, as in faculty exchanges. This mobility is quite prominently observed in Indian institutions and it seems that the mobility is quite active both ways—Indian professionals going abroad and foreign academics coming to Indian institutions. The implications of this mode for international trade are relatively simple in so far as operational guidelines are concerned. According to Knight (2002), the GATS is composed of many segments such as like the general guidelines, inventories of countries' specific engagements as to the interaction between domestic sector and foreign providers, and qualifying conditions and restrictive clauses (see Table 4.1).

Altbach (2006) notes that the proponents of GATS have advocated the idea that knowledge is a commodity to be traded freely for the benefit of all the countries. Further, it has been promoted that free trade in higher education will introduce the element of competitiveness into the flow and exchange of knowledge generation and dissemination. This argument has been much criticized, both in developed and developing countries. The crux of the criticisms that are leveled at the GATS are that the policies will lead to excessive

Table 4.1
GATS Elements or Rule and Their Explanations, Applications, and Issues

GATS Element or Rule	Explanation	Application	Issues
Coverage	All internationally traded services are covered in the 12 different service sectors (e.g., education, transportation, financial, tourism, health, construction).	Applies to all services with two exceptions: i) services provided in the exercise of governmental authority ii) air traffic rights	Major debate on what the term "exercise of governmental authority" means.
Measures	All laws, regulations and practices from national, regional or local government that may affect trade.	A generic term that applies to all sectors.	
General or Unconditional obligations	Four unconditional obligations exist in GATS. • most favored nation (MFN) • transparency • dispute settlement • monopolies	They apply to all service sectors regardless of whether it is a scheduled commitment or not.	Attention needs to be given to "most favored nation."
Most favored nation (MFN) treatment	Requires equal and consistent treatment of all foreign trading partners MFN means treating one's trading partners equally. Under GATS, if a country allows foreign competition in a sector, equal opportunities in that sector should be given to service providers from all WTO members. This also applies to mutual exclusion treatment For instance, if a foreign provider establishes branch campus in Country A, then Country A must permit all WTO members the same opportunity/treatment. Or if Country A chooses to exclude Country B from providing a specific service, then all WTO members are excluded.	May apply even if the country has made no specific commitment to provide foreign access to their markets. Exemptions, for a period of 10 years, are permissible.	MFN has implications for those countries who already are engaged in trade in educational services and/or who provide access to foreign education providers. MFN is not the same as national treatment.

Conditional obligations	There are a number of conditional obligations attached to national schedules: – market access – national treatment	Only applies to commitments listed in national schedules. Degree and extent of obligation is determined by country.	GATS supporters believe that a country's national educational objectives are protected by these two obligations.
National Treatment	Requires equal treatment for foreign and domestic providers Once a foreign supplier has been allowed to supply a service in one's country there should be no discrimination in treatment between the foreign and domestic providers.	Only applies where a country has made a specific commitment Exemptions are allowed	GATS critics believe that this can put education as a 'public good' at risk.
Market Access	Means the degree to which market access is granted to foreign providers in specified sectors. Market access may be subject to one or more of six types of limitations defined by GATS agreement.	Each country determines limitations on market access for each committed sector.	
Progressive Liberalization	GATS has a built in agenda which means that with each round of negotiations there is further liberalization of trade in service. This means more sectors are covered and more trade limitations are removed.	Applies to all sectors and therefore, includes education.	
Bottom-up and Top-down approach	Bottom up approach refers to the fact that each country determines the type and extent of its commitments for each sector. Top down approach refers to the main rules and obligations as well as the progressive liberalization agenda, there will be increasing pressure to remove trade barriers.		Sceptics maintain that the top down approach will have increasing importance and impact thereby increasing pressure to liberalize.

Source: Knight (2002, pp. 7–8).

commercialization of education and that the developed countries will find ways to overpower developing countries. It follows from both criticisms that GATS can cause institutional autonomy to be jeopardized and providers of questionable integrity and merit may find opportunities to get away with providing substandard education and awarding illegitimate degrees and certificates.

India participated in the Uruguay Round, from which WTO agreements resulted and of which GATS is a segment. The Government of India's course of reasoning in participation in the Uruguay Round could be summed up thusly:

> [T]he main purpose for the creation of the General Agreement on Trade in Services (GATS) was to create a credible and reliable system of international trade rules, which ensured fair and equitable treatment of all countries on the principles of non- discrimination. It aims at stimulating trade and development by seeking to create a predictable policy environment wherein the member countries voluntarily undertake to bind their policy regimes relating to trade in services. (Government of India, n.d.)

The potential benefits from being a party to GATS are many for India. The GATS promises greater international competitiveness, innovation, employment generation, and transparency and fairness in trade operations.

As a result of economic liberalization, the commercial service export in India has continued to grow. It was US\$148,188,300,332 in 2013, according to the World Bank. The regulatory imperative to tie in the country's trade interests with international legalities must be viewed in the context of the growth in volume of imports and exports of services. A word of caution is in order. Economic liberalization, when it is held in by trade treaties, is characteristically different from when it is not. Therefore, it is advisable to analyze each of the ratified clauses in respect of its implications to India's unique realities. India's positioning in cross-border higher education with regard to GATS pivots on two key factors: India's developing country status and, more importantly, India's standing as the "sender" country of international students.

The GATS agreements hold in balance interests of signatories that, more often than not, get in each other's way. Add to this the concern that interest groups exert undue influence in the interpretation and execution of treaty clauses. If one were to look for common strains in the criticisms that are levelled at GATS by those who speak for developing countries, one would find that the criticisms are related to the broader issues of social welfare affirmative policy action and national domestic autonomy. It is often argued that a lot of service sectors, such as education, are best left to the care of governments and intermediations will do more bad than good. It is argued that the workings of international trade are better suited to some industries than others and opening up the vulnerable sectors to global networks might go against developmental goals and, even worse, might result in furthering the comparative advantage that developing countries supposedly hold. The apprehension rests on the fear that multinational companies, under the guise of politico-economic lobbies and interest groups, will coerce developing countries to privatize unjustifiably so that multinational companies can expand their market base. The criticisms typically follow the theoretical precepts of center-periphery paradigm—the hegemony of the North at the cost of the interests of the South. These criticisms commonly come from nongovernmental, public interest, and civil society organizations and academics.

Higher education has not been at the forefront of discussions on GATS. The considerations about higher education being a public good and the resultant implications have been the main reasons for this disregard. But, that order has reversed in the recent times with the prominence that cross-border higher education has acquired. Indeed, cross-border higher education has undergone phenomenal expansion in volume. Moreover, there has been something of a role reversal with respect to countries being "hosts" and "home."

The most popularly expressed concern with respect to application of GATS in India is that it is suspected to worsen the polarization in higher education, which is a concern as it is. The disparities in higher education, as has been discussed earlier, are strewn across a number of variables: regional distribution, institutional inequalities, gender-based access, and ethno-cultural divides are some of the frequently discussed disparities. It is feared that GATS will perpetuate indiscriminate privatization of higher education and eventually the multinational companies will take over, resulting in increased disparities, elitism, and indiscriminate play of market forces. On the other hand, it is widely accepted that the Government, by itself, is in no position to address the demands in access and excellence in the higher education. The private sector is positioned to bridge the gap in higher education in India, as it is in other developing countries. The real question with respect to higher education in India and GATS is whether the government has done its part in policy framing to ensure that developmental goals are not compromised at the cost of achievement of internationalization of higher education. Liberalization, inasmuch as it is a result of globalization, is an irrefutable phenomenon. The Indian Government must rise above policy paralysis to ensure that a system of checks and balances orchestrates the workings of the higher education system such that it keeps step with global advances while still meeting domestic developmental goals.

The GATS policies with respect to higher education must be viewed with caution, but also with open-mindedness. There is no one way in which the provisions of GATS will impact the practice of cross-border higher education in India; rather, the manner in which these provisions affect higher education depends on what the mode of education is. The regulations must be highly selective, and they must be customized on the basis of what the mode and mechanism are. In other words, the regulations that govern the application of the provisions of GATS in the circumstances of higher education must be differentiated. Similarly, Powar (2015) suggests that there is a need to regulate some areas stringently (joint degree and "study abroad" programs, for instance) and selectively (articulation arrangements), and to completely do away with some modes and mechanisms (franchise).

Discussions on higher education in India and GATS after the 10th WTO Ministerial Conference in Nairobi held on December 2015:

The subject of India's inclination towards GATS and higher education received much focus in media and higher education circles after the 10th WTO Ministerial Conference in Nairobi held on December 2015. According to the recent reports and commentaries in news media, the Government of India has indicated that it would debate considerations to allow international higher education providers from the 160 member countries of World Trade Organization to set up institutions and enter into collaborative ventures in India as commercial activities. It must be noted that no conclusive outcome on the Government's inclination has been made publicly available.

If the agreement comes into force, the Indian Government would be legally bound by GATS agreements to protect the interests of education providers who engage in commercial activities in India. In other words, if the Indian Government goes ahead with the agreements, through the "submission of offers" to WTO, the Indian higher education sector would be locked in with the WTO establishment.

This will have far-reaching implications. At the broadest level, it will result in "commoditization" of higher education as is so frequently opined by educationists, civil society organizations, and academics. Higher education, as with education in general, is viewed as an area important for the furtherance of "collective good." In a country that has, since Independence, claimed to champion the ideology of welfare socialism, such a proposition would run against all that the Government stands for: welfare-state-oriented values, which put egalitarianism at the heart of the state's efforts and hold the government accountable when legislation violates the spirit of positive affirmation.

The WTO-GATS "regime," as it is aptly described, stands for hard-nosed, uncompromising commercialization. It is unfortunate too that such a view mistakenly conflates privatization of higher education with commoditization. The free-market principle, on which this "regime" is founded, is singularly profit-driven and one that does not take issue with elitism and selectiveness.

In the realm of education, the "regime" would likely result in the promotion of those offerings that are demand-responsive at the cost of such pursuits as are worthy in their own right even if not coveted by the masses in the higher education cohort. Thus, classical studies, humanities, and other subject areas that are not immediately tied to job-readiness capabilities are left susceptible to suffer a hit. Perhaps, the programs that would be left the most in jeopardy would be those postgraduate programs that form the stepping stone to research, such as MPhil and PhD.

There is no gainsaying that the GATS provisions view higher education as an article of trade—a tradable service. This would make the higher education provider a trader and the student a customer, not just relationally but also legally.

Many educationists have raised their concerns that such commercialization of higher education would obviate the idea of quality assurance management, as it is traditionally understood. One of the fears is that quality in higher education, a complex and multidimensional concept, which is further compounded by the developmental challenges that India faces, might be reduced to the logic of comparative benchmarking. In other words, institutional quality would be that which is reflected in commercially oriented global rankings.

Researchers from the developing world, most notably those of the *Dependencia School*, have argued that WTO-GATS regime is a thinly disguised instrument of imperialism of the countries of the "North." This line of argument resonates in India as well. If India enters into agreements with GATS in the higher education subsector, then academic autonomy at the institutional level in India, which is precarious as it is, would probably be rendered even weaker. What is worse is that higher education, a core nation-building resource, might get disengaged from India's long-term developmental goals.

To chronicle the history of India's involvement, the Indian Government had submitted to WTO "offers" (as these are called in the official documents) for "market access" in "Higher Education Sub-Sector" as part of Doha Round Trade Negotiations in 2001 in Qatar. These have not yet become "commitments" because the trade negotiations were not conclusive.

During the Doha Negotiations, India had "offered" to make education a "tradable service," thereby allowing admittance to the 160 member-nations to enter into collaborations with Indian institution or set up their institutions as "commercial ventures." According to the GATS provisions, a country does not have to "commit" on all sectors. It would be permissible to offer a sector under a liberalized trade regime without committing it to GATS for "market access." If the "offers" are conclusively submitted to WTO in the "Higher Education Sector," these would become "commitments" on the part of the Government of India, and would not be easy to modify or withdraw.

India has a long and flourishing history of heralding international-ization of higher education. Such exchanges have traditionally taken place between nations, on a bilateral level—one country (represented in the collaborating or "sending" institution or independent student) partnering with the other.

The case with internationalization of higher education within the realm of GATS is as far apart from this practice as can be. The goal this time is not internationalization for the inherent benefits it brings in widening the students' personal and professional portfolio but the expansion of an influential and dominating trade regime, and the level is not one of the bilateral cultural exchange but supranational trade agreements.

According to the provisions, if "Higher Education Sector" is "committed" to WTO-GATS, accredited groups formed under the legal framework of WTO, Trade Policy Review Mechanism (TPRM), would undertake periodic reviews of the international trade policies of member countries and offer guidance for reform as needed. Further, armed with legal authority, TPRM members would meet the government representatives every year to ensure that the suggested reforms are implemented to the satisfaction of TPRM. This is often done by issuing recommendations to set up "independent" agencies to regulate the industry sector in question. These agencies are so designed as to enjoy relative freedom from the influence of public groups, media, and researchers, and to represent WTO-GATS interests. In effect, the above-mentioned "recommendations" by TPRM would amount to erosion of the member countries' autonomy in respect of self-governance.

The overarching power of the developed countries and their influence in the developing world, a theme discussed frequently in the book, is revealed across many dimensions, and the provisions of GATS with respect to cross-border higher education would rank at the very top of the list. In India, as in other developing countries, the two issues that are important are that it would be difficult to set down minimum standards required as qualifying criteria for the collaborating foreign institution, and it would be hard to put restrictions on the cost of tuition fees charged by foreign providers or collaborators. Another issue is the one about resolving disputes between collaborating countries not through the judiciary systems in each of the governments but through the WTO's Dispute Settlement Body.

In all likelihood, the public policy on international trade would be partially governed by WTO-GATS regime. Needless to state, the power distribution would not be equitable across the members but would be disproportionally in the favor of developed countries. It emerges that the Indian higher education system might be better served by ensuring liberalization through public policy. WTO-GATS provisions do not find favor with the Indian public opinion. The heavy criticism that is leveled against the clauses of the GATS provisions regarding higher education warrant further deliberation and debate within the public policy circles.

The discussions lead one to conclude that in light of the dynamism and competition inherent in cross-border higher education, the enthusiasm with which foreign providers are eyeing the Indian market and the lack of regulations and guidelines on the operation of foreign providers in India, the Indian government can no longer delay putting in place a reform-oriented policy structure to manage the operations of foreign institutions in the country.

References

Agarwal, P. (n.d.a). International India a turning point in educational exchange with the US. Retrieved from http://www.usief.org.in/USIHEC/Chapter%204/Internationalization%20of%20Indian%20Higher%20Education.pdf (accessed on April 6, 2016).

Altbach, P. (2006). Tiny at the top. *The Wilson Quarterly, 30*(4), 49–51.

———. (2008, July 15). Beware of the Trojan horse. *The Hindu.* Retrieved from http://www.hindu.com/2008/07/15/stories/2008071555180800.htm (accessed on April 6, 2016).

Altbach, P., & Peterson. (2007). *Higher education in the new century.* Rotterdam, Netherlands: Sense publications.

CII-AIU. (2014). *Trends in internationalization of higher education in India.* Retrieved from http://www.cii.in/PublicationDetail.aspx?enc=j+Bre1cnEnR 7Sgogrka6KohkwpLy3x9ujfczyTnGBH8Pk1aE4ly77FRtKBZo0YzFiVa GJLen1cG0O7iLKWe0szJJQOYv17/2Ud9piEIB1wUYJCzxAaL6W6H

Z0zrocFkdwNvqqO5gbqDAYy8PbqfcNF4MgwGKS4CIAGsf4gwYh
RVEQZuVQeUSm/p9oCvxp9Ll (accessed on April 6, 2016).

David, S. A., Sanyal, B. C., & Wildemeersch, D. (2006). *Engaging with cross-border higher education in India, while sustaining the best tradition of Indian values.* OECD. Retrieved from http://www.oecd.org/site/imhe2006bis/37464379.pdf (accessed on April 6, 2016).

EY-FICCI. (2012). *Higher education in India: Twelfth Five Year Plan (2012– 2017) and beyond.* Kolkata, India: Ernst & Young Pvt. Ltd.

Government of India. (n.d.). *Questions about the agreement.* Retrieved from http://commerce.nic.in/trade/faqs_gats.pdf (accessed on April 6, 2016).

Knight, J. (2002). *Higher education implications, opinions, and questions.* Paris: UNESCO.

National Institute of Educational Planning and Administration. (2004). *Internationalization of higher education issues and concerns domestic regulation.* New Delhi: NIEPA.

Powar, K. B. (2002). *Indian higher education: A conglomerate of concepts, facts and practices.* New Delhi, India: Concept Publishing Company.

———.(2015). *Changing landscape of international higher education: An Indian perspective.* Pune: DY Patil.

PwC. (n.d.). *India: Higher education sector opportunities for foreign universities.* Retrieved from www.pwc.in/en_IN/in/assets/.../India-higher-edu-sector- (251012).pdf (accessed on April 6, 2016).

Scholte, J. A. (2007). *Civil society and legitimation of global governance.* Working Paper. Coventry: University of Warwick. Centre for the Study of Globalisation and Regionalisation. Working papers (University of Warwick. Centre for the Study of Globalisation and Regionalisation) (No. 223).

Yeravdekar, V. R., & Tiwari, G. (2014). The contribution of private participants to the Indian higher education system and the impeding role of the regulatory structure. *Procedia – Journal of Social and Behavioral Sciences,157,* 330– 333. doi:10.1016/j.sbspro.2014.11.036.

The Hindu. (2013, August 24). *India is now world's third largest Internet user after U.S., China.* Retrieved from http://www.thehindu.com/sci-tech/ technology/internet/india-is-now-worlds-third-largest-internet-user-after- us-china/article5053115.ece (accessed on April 6, 2016).

5

Internationalization in a Comparative Context

International Education and the Logic of Comparative Benchmarking

Global rankings have assumed an important place as instruments of brand management exercises across the world. One learns of new rankings being added to the prevalent leading rankings such as THES, Academic Ranking of World Universities (ARWU), and QS all the time. National governments, eager not to get left behind, have joined in the trend. The National Institutional Ranking Framework (NIRF), an initiative of MHRD, is an illustrative example. It is noteworthy that NIRF has made it mandatory for institutions to participate in the competition—it is not a matter of preference at the end of institutions.

The question emerges then whether rankings and world-class universities go hand in hand. If they do, is it a fair proposition that a coterie of ranking agencies is allowed to lay down the rubric for world class universities? There is no gainsaying that the frameworks that make up the parameters related to rankings capture the institutional value-systems that are unique to just a handful of trans-Atlantic institutions. These are neither entirely relevant nor helpful to those who do not belong in the American or the British higher education system. For one, the English language alone is a great big advantage to these institutions. Research output—the singularly important parameter for global rankings—is not as inclusive as one might want to believe. To begin with, research output is limited in practice to publications in English. Moreover, the peer-reviewed journals that are touted to be the most representative of cutting-edge research are often a thinly veiled means of promotion for select institutions, which gain influence through endowments, sponsorships, and so on.

Internationalization, on the other hand, levels the playing field of institutions across the world. The concept of internationalization makes global higher education a zero-sum game by virtue of competition. It is as though each entity is pitted against the other on a global showcase. The competitiveness that the international student market exhibits in the present times is a marker of massive investments by governments and private institutions. It is the case of an ever-growing number of institutions (and governments) vying for the internationally mobile student population, which has countless means of acquiring information on institutions and stacking them in order of perceived performance and personal preference. Thus, internationalization opens many doors only to close others for institutions—the international student market is the buyers' market, not the seller's.

It is this competition indeed that creates the need to ensure positive feedback from amongst students across the entire span of the lifecycle of student-engagement—all the way from drawing students in, retaining them, and ensuring student and alumni satisfaction. It is a tall order in the face of new and emerging providers, given that technology and communication allow students and media outlets to weigh one institution against the other across infinite permutations and combinations.

In the present global higher educational landscape, the inherent competition in internationalization is expressed in institutional preoccupation with rankings. The interconnectedness that has followed on from globalization has facilitated systematization of higher education systems the world over. The coming together of institutions on an integrated platform necessitates the logic of benchmarking. It is as though to say that if all the variables that comprise institutional performance could be identified, then they could just as simply be quantified and applied to order institutions into rankings.

Global academic rankings are inextricably tied to internationalization; and the converse is true as well. The preoccupation with rankings is an expression of the ubiquity of internationalization and the far-reaching consequences of the involvement of media and publications in global higher education.

Contrariwise, internationalization (particularly, the strength of international students) is an important variable in the sum total of parameters and dimensions that are collectively utilized to assess institutional performance (and reputation). It is estimated that internationalization will grow in importance as a variable and will likely expand to include factors that add up to "internationalization at home" (in addition to the strength of international students), such as internationalization of curriculum.

Beginning with the proclamations in the "Report to the Nation" (National Knowledge Commission, 2005), the Indian Government has made rousing assertions to recast the country as "knowledge economy," purportedly, by making higher education a top national agenda item and creating world-class universities.

The government's announcements are confirmation of the value of comparative information in measuring institutional performance and its contribution to quality assurance management in higher education. One comes across laments on India's non-presence in global rankings frequently. It is held that this deficit shows that internationalization has not reached the Indian shores.

It is likely that it will be a long time before Indian institutions become a mainstay of global rankings. But that may be just as well. Global rankings have yet to embrace the more egalitarian and inclusive aspects of internationalization, those that are collectively termed under the umbrella concept of "internationalization at home." The total strength of international students in India is low, and this scenario is not likely to reverse itself any time soon.

The Anglophone institutions that are ahead in the race have enjoyed "host institution" status for decades: These are bastions of international students. Reputation begets itself, and few in the developing world can hope to compete with these strongholds for a very long time in the future.

Add to this the question about how well the concept of internationalization, as utilized in the global academic rankings and amongst the developed countries of the Anglophone world, serves us in India. We must revisit our long-held conceptions about "one size fits all" as we study internationalization and its attendant concerns such as the significance of world class universities.

The Notion of World-class Universities and Its Suitability to the Indian Higher Education System

The concept of internationalization is closely tied with the concepts of world-class universities and global rankings. Knowledge economy demands that higher education continually push the frontiers of knowledge and innovation. The question then rises: What is that frontier? And who is at the edge of that frontier? Academic rankings represent that frontier and the institutions that stand at that frontier. By the same token, the concept of world-class universities sets a benchmark to denote the standards that represent the frontier of knowledge and innovation.

The emergence of global rankings and the concept of world-class universities coincide with the precipitous growth of internationalization. The two global factors that gave form to global rankings and world-class universities—preponderance of the English language and the United Nations' espousal of bringing higher education on a global platform—have also driven internationalization of higher education forward, in general (Altbach 2008; Guruz, 2008). The fact of having institutions across the world and across many higher education systems necessitate a rubric that would lay down criteria to carry out performance evaluation in relative terms, quality-assurance management, and public- and consumer-accountability assessments. International education is relatively expensive, making it even more important that those who pay for it make their best-informed choices with respect to quality and competition (Yeravdekar & Tiwari, 2014a).

As with internationalization of higher education, rankings and the concept of world-class universities are criticized for an "elitist" approach to higher education: that they are not inclusive and lead to a culture that segregates higher education cohorts into "haves" and "have-nots." Further, it is also held that they are about symbolic attainments that stand for overly selective differentiation. Many scholars from developing countries have criticized the importance accorded to internationalization and rankings on the grounds that they divert the attention of policymakers away from the more pressing issues of access and equity.

Several Indian researchers have criticized the concept of world-class university on the grounds that it is inherently "Western" and is irrelevant to the needs of a higher education system that is nested in the realities of a developing country. Perhaps the most frequently leveled criticism from scholars of developing nations is the claim that the whole idea of world-class universities is about excellence in research and that developing nations, burdened with limited funds, would do better to invest in vocational and technical training than to invest in the luxury of internationally competitive research. Others dismiss the significance that is attached to research, which is regarded as an elitist construct, highly subjective, and designed to perpetuate Western hegemony in higher education. Those from the dependency paradigm would say that internationalization and the attendant concepts of global rankings and world-class universities are "imperialistic" instruments to deny the reality that developing countries have their own sphere of relevance and existence. These instruments, purposely, keep higher education systems of the developing world on the periphery, their quality and worth contingent on the relative distance between them and the "Western" standards of excellence. That said, there is no denying that, as with internationalization, rankings are here to stay.

In India, the government's focus on world-class universities became sharp about a decade ago:

The National Knowledge Commission (NKC) lamented that "the Shanghai University ranking of 500 world-class universities featured only 3 Indian universities" (Report to the Nation, n.d., p. 188). To fully grasp the Commission's disappointment, it is important to situate the issue in the larger context of Indian Government's proclamations to remodel the country as "knowledge economy." The Planning Commission, in the Eleventh Five Year Plan (2007–12) broadcast its intent to attract global talent through public-private partnership. At the core of this is the mandate by the Ministry of Human Resource and Development (MHRD) to set up of fourteen "innovation universities aiming at world class standards." The "innovation universities" are to be developed as "Global Centers of Innovation" in identified cities. These Centres are to be, for all intents and purposes, India's education hubs wherein higher education and other bodies will, purportedly contribute to the cause of inter-disciplinary education, entrepreneurship and, research and development in a concerted fashion. (Yeravdekar & Tiwari, 2014a, p. 66)

As with internationalization, in the discussions on world-class universities and rankings, it is frequently noted that Indian institutions and the agencies involved in higher education resort to tokenism as a substitute for real transformational reforms. The critics opine that Indian institutions are neither ready to receive internationalization and nor should internationalization be a priority item on the policy agenda. The need of the hour is the advancement of an *ecosystem* of higher education—a grassroots-oriented approach—so that all the stakeholders—be it the institutions, the students, or the faculty members—benefit to some extent. This line of argument attacks internationalization and related concepts for being "impositions from the outside" and not osmotic, enduring progressions in the system. Altbach and Jayaram (2008) suggest that the focus must be on encouraging and recognizing "meritocracy." The question that critics raise is whether investments in internationalization can result in self-generative results.

A big roadblock in bringing internationally accepted standards to Indian institutions is that a culture of academic autonomy and institutional self-governance is missing—both these properties are requirements for the type of intellectual dynamism out of which research and innovation take place. Krishnan (2005, 1,681) notes that "many [Indian] universities have not recruited faculty for years and are managing with temporary staff . . . [In India, there is] politicisation intertwined with bureaucratic control."

There are many other factors that would make it very difficult for Indian institutions, even the ones that selectively receive investments and other resources for the purpose of being launched as "world-class" universities, to achieve international competitiveness: the affiliated system of universities, high undergraduate enrolment and low postgraduate enrolment, high incidence of teaching staff members that are not research-minded, and the Indian government's selective preference in extending grants and other incentives to institutions that are not fully formed universities, such as the IITs, IIMs, AIIMS, and IISc (Yeravdekar & Tiwari, 2014a). In view of these fundamental challenges, it would seem that the Indian higher education system must devise its own vision and goals, those that serve the immediate socio-economic realities and the long-term developmental plans. The system is far from the culture (and resources) of higher education that is required to sustain world-class universities.

Comparison with Other Asian Countries

A comparison of India's performance with other Asian countries in respect of internationalization of higher education is important from the standpoint of acquiring an evaluator's perspective. How has the country fared relative to its neighbors, who are on a level playing field, at least, in a broad sense? Insofar as competition for inbound international students goes, India faces the most daunting threat from its neighbors to the East.

China: The 2013 ARWU, which is released by the Center for World-class Universities at Shanghai Jiao Tong University, has listed 28 Chinese universities and one Indian university amongst the top 500 universities across the world. China has invested heavily in creating world class universities through initiatives such as Project 985, which work at focused steps, such as boosting research productivity, hiring of research-active international staff, and collaborating with world class universities in foreign countries.

China's many successes in internationalizing its higher education system are no less impressive. This finding will serve as a representative example: A recent report by Project Atlas, a division of IIE, has revealed that China has vaulted to the top of the list of "host countries" from near insignificance (see Tables 5.1 and 5.2).

Inbound mobility of international students, both a lever and measure of internationalization of higher education, continues on a steady ascent in China. The number of international students in China in 2011 was the highest recorded figure at 292,000. (Relatedly, 3.2 percent of the inbound international students in China in 2011 were from India; Project Atlas 2014). As early as 2003, legislation

Table 5.1
Top Eight Host Countries of Globally Mobile Students in 2001

Countries	Percentage
United States	28%
United Kingdom	11%
Germany	9%
France	7%
Australia	4%
Japan	3%
Spain	2%
Belgium	2%
All others	34%

Source: Project Atlas (2014).

Table 5.2
Top Eight Host Countries of Globally Mobile Students in 2012

Countries	Percentage
United States	19%
United Kingdom	11%
China	8%
France	7%
Germany	6%
Australia	6%
Canada	5%
Japan	3%
All others	35%

Source: Project Atlas (2014).

was in place to regulate foreign collaboration. It is remarkable that China has managed to score so high on the inbound mobility aspect in spite of English not being the official medium of instruction. In 2011, US students accounted for 8 percent of the total international student population in China—an approximate 23,360. *Au contraire,* only 782 US students were enrolled in India in 2012—a paltry figure considering English is the medium of instruction in practically all Indian institutions that draw international students. The key to China's success is focused steps. The strategy of adding international competitiveness by way of "brain gain" serves as a representative example: The University of Beijing, among many others, actively draws in international researchers of Chinese origin as part of its policy on internationalization.

Lessons from China: Move from Center to Periphery

It is easy to see why China and India are judged in comparative terms in the discussion on internationalization of higher education. Although the two countries have very different higher education systems, they are both "giants" in respect of the volume of higher education demographic that they serve and the "outbound" international students that they "export" to trans-atlantic countries. Both the countries have made higher education an item of top priority on the national agenda, and this is tied to plans to recast the countries as "knowledge-economies." Both are eager to move inwards from the periphery to the center and are objects of much attention in the Western world with regard to their developmental achievements in higher education and in the global labor market place. There is much anecdotal information and impressionistic knowledge that both countries make significant contribution to the international human resource base, especially in science and technology.

At the core of the discussion on the two higher education systems is the most conspicuous difference—the public expenditure on higher education: Whereas China spends $250 billion, India spends a meagre $37.13 billion (PwC, n.d.). The matter of policy-making and implementing is just as important. The Chinese government has been more successful than the Indian one in carving out goal-oriented directives that pointedly target increase in gross enrolment ratio, international competitiveness (especially world class universities and rankings), and professional–vocational education.

With the possible exception of China's emergence as the third largest "host" country of international students (as reported by Project

Atlas 2014), the country's most sterling achievements are related to a phenomenal increase in research publications in high impact factor journals. Research represents the high point of academic excellence and is the prime criterion in global rankings. For this reason, more than any other, China has succeeded in launching itself as a formidable presence on the global higher education scene.

> [China's]...lead in research is head and shoulders ahead of India, not to say, all the BRICK countries. In 2011, India produced 45,172 research publication, and China 156,574 (Adams, Pendlebury and Stembridge, 2013). A number of initiatives have made this possible, for instance, the Knowledge Innovation Program of Chinese Academy of Sciences to launch innovation centers in fundamental and applied sciences and Project 211 in 1995 to upgrade 117 universities. (Yeravdekar & Tiwari, 2014b, p. 370)

Related to research output is the case that China has put in place policy measures to increase postgraduate enrolment, which have succeeded in yielding results. In particular, Project 211 and Project 985, which have in their jurisdiction over 150 universities, vouch for the system's commitment to quality assurance management. The 2013 ARWU global rankings listed 28 Chinese (and one Indian) amongst the top 500 universities.

On the front of internationalization, China's recent achievements have been truly extraordinary, especially viewed in light of the country's oblivion up until quite recently. In 2011, China recorded 292,000 international students, putting the country on the list of top host countries (Project Atlas, 2014; IIE 2013). An important point is that English, the unofficial medium of international education, is not nearly as prevalent in China as it is in India.

Highly goal-directed projects are the key to China's success:

> The strategy of adding international competitiveness by way of "brain gain" serves as a representative example: The University of Beijing, among many others, actively draws in international researchers of Chinese origin as part of its policy on internationalization. The Indian Diaspora, which adds up to over 25 million in 130 countries, remains an unexploited resource in the context (Kumar, Sarkar and Sharma, 2009). (Yeravdekar & Tiwari, 2014b, p. 370)

China's achievements in increasing the base of the enrolment pyramid are also impressive. In 2000, China's gross enrolment ratio in tertiary education was 7.76 percent, increasing to 24.33 percent in 2011. Interestingly, India was ahead of China in 2000, with a corresponding figure in gross enrolment ratio in tertiary education of 9.53 percent, but could not keep up with the growth in access in China and recorded 23.27 percent in 2011 (UNESCO n.d., cited in Yeravdekar & Tiwari, 2014b, p. 370).

The success of the Chinese policies rests, primarily, on the government's attempts to revive higher education along two principles, vertical and horizontal differentiations, which, in turn, have resulted in authentic shift towards "massification." In the Chinese system, differentiation has been suitably served by the tertiarization of higher education. The carving up of the mass of institutions (and divisions within institutions) along teaching, research, and vocational training has allowed the government to prioritize resources very efficiently.

Similarly, differentiation of institutions along the lines of potential has allowed the majority to serve the needs of those at the base of the pyramid, while allowing high-caliber institutions (primarily research-oriented) to deliver such quality as would not be possible otherwise. It is differentiation again that allows the system and institutions to preferentially match funds with the projected goals, thereby ensuring institutional accountability and offering institutions the opportunity to expand without compromising on specialization. An illustrative example of horizontal differentiation is the expansion of industry-based vocational education: the system serving nearly 9.6 million students in vocational training programs (Yeravdekar & Tiwari, 2014b).

The Chinese system, as with the Indian, calls to mind a pyramid with a very large base (879 regular colleges and universities, 1266 junior colleges, and 287 independent colleges), but it differs from the Indian in that it has a much larger proportion of institutions resting at the top (Ministry of Education of the People's Republic of China, n.d.).

The Chinese higher education system benefits from ample public expenditure on higher education and from policy action. Much of the success of the Chinese system follows on from authentic and comprehensive differentiation, which allows the system to make the best use of allocated funds, ensure quality management, and generate institutional accountability. China has proved that it is possible to move from the periphery to the center of international education.

Malaysia: Malaysia is deservedly noted as a prominent Asian education hub. A number of features account for its success in that respect. The country is placed at the geographic and cultural junction of many civilizations (Malay, Chinese, Indian, and colonial British). More importantly, it has reinvented itself as a knowledge economy and "network society." The English language is widely employed as the medium of instruction in higher education institutions. The institutions themselves strike balance between quality in education and advancements in infrastructure on the one hand and affordability on the other. Possibly the greatest thrust comes from the country's express drive to privatize higher education in accordance with market demands; therefore, the higher education system is heavily tilted towards technical and professional training. The curriculum is designed in keeping with the accreditation and qualifying guidelines in other countries that are targeted as prospective "sending" countries. The institutions make informed and productive attempts to draw in international students by offering collaborations with institutions abroad. The key idea is to analyze current global and regional trends in higher education and anticipate long-term trends so as to be armed with the guiding information. The Ministry of Higher Education (MOHE) is responsible for initiatives related to internationalization of higher education. There are a total of 900,000 students enrolled in higher education in 20 public universities, 33 private universities and university colleges, 4 foreign university branch campuses, 22 polytechnics, 37 community colleges, and about 500 private colleges. According to the IIE reports, there were 86,923 international students in Malaysia in 2010. The top five places of origin in 2010 were Iran, China, Indonesia, Yemen, and Nigeria. The MOHE aims to attract at least 200,000 international students to higher education institutions in the country by 2020 (Dessoff, 2012).

The Malaysian Government aims at targeting those international students who are looking for an international degree without the high costs that one incurs in Western countries. It seems that the most recent attempts at increasing internationalization of higher education are found in the circumstance of education hubs, which are set up as special zones, complete with all the imaginable amenities and conveniences. While the Malaysian Government proclaims to invest in internationalization with a view to support the knowledge economy model, in reality, it also aims to showcase Malaysia as a progressive, "networked" nodal point in South East Asia so as to draw international students from neighboring regions, especially India, China, and Indonesia and countries in the Arabic-speaking world.

According to a NAFSA report, Malaysia was the first Asian country to devise plans to launch education hubs (Although Singapore launched the first education hub, Malaysia had the first original plan; Dessoff, 2012). There are two separate plans to launch education hubs in Malaysia. The first is Kuala Lumpur Education City (KLEC), which was launched by the Malaysian Government in 2007. It was designed to be a privately managed project, with a long gestation period of 20 years. The project is to bring together domestic and international higher education institutions and schools in a 500-acre academic park. The other education hub is EduCity at Iskandar. This privately managed hub aims to launch higher education institutions that are the best in the class and supported by superior infrastructural facilities. Both the projects make claims to further internationally competitive research and academe-industry collaboration. There is no gainsaying that the investments are impressive and the internationalization projects are customized to address the market demands of international students, but the results remain to be seen.

Singapore: Singapore is credited with the first education hub in Asia, which is a clear testament to its drive to stay at the forefront of internationalization of higher education. The Singapore Economic Development Board (EDB) and the Ministry of Education are credited with launching the "Global Schoolhouse" initiative in 2004. Much like Malaysia, Singapore has also espoused internationalization of higher education mainly through education hubs.

The Global Schoolhouse was launched with the key goal of promoting EDB's industry development efforts. The main goals of the Global Schoolhouse project are as follows:

[R]ecruitment of "foreign talent," economic development through foreign investment, and attracting research and development firms as well as multinational companies specializing in the knowledge economy and service industries. (Gribble & McBurnie, 2007, cited in Knight, 2011, p. 226)

Knight lauds Singapore for being the "furthest along" amongst Asian countries in education and innovation hubs (Dessoff, 2012, p. 19). The Singapore Government, in an effort to market higher education to international students, has even come up with a brand name—Singapore Education! Among some of the big name foreign universities that have partnered with higher education institutions in Singapore to offer joint academic programs are the University of Chicago's Booth Graduate School of Business, the Technical University of Munich, Duke University's School of Medicine, Yale University, the Massachusetts Institute of Technology, and Britain's Imperial College. The key focus of academic programs is the development of "industry relevant capabilities" (Dessoff, 2012, p. 19). In 2007, Singapore had 86,000 international students (Lasanowski 2009, cited in Knight & Morshidi, 2011, p. 597) and in 2010 about 1,120 cross-border education program arrangements were operational in Singapore (Ministry of Education, 2010, cited in Knight & Morshidi, 2011, p. 597).

The Education Excellence Framework, an initiative launched by the government of Singapore in 2004 to further its goal of emerging as an international education hub, is a commendable model that holds potential for replication in India and other countries. An important part of the framework is the CASE Trust for Education (CTE), a quality assurance agency. To be able to enroll international students, all private institutions must first get a qualifying certificate from CTE. In return, these institutions receive funding to promote themselves internationally and are offered the ease and facility of having visa applications and other formalities processed for international students as a matter of priority. The extension of such concrete incentives to institutions and the joining of hands between the government and private participants is an important reason why Singapore is projected to succeed in its efforts towards internationalization (Guruz, 2011, p. 11).

Hong Kong: Internationalization of higher education in Hong Kong has an additional aspect: the goal of drawing international students in and *retaining* them (Dessoff, 2012, p. 24). Hong Kong's unique ability to attract international students derives, to a certain extent, from being a gateway to mainland China and having a very cosmopolitan culture. Similar to Malaysia and Singapore, Hong Kong also espouses internationalization of higher education systems through regional education hubs. A key feature of Hong Kong's education hub model is the interlocking system:

> [W]here [sic] the whole higher education sector is viewed as one force, with each institution fulfilling a unique role, based on its individual mission and particular strengths. Differentiation of role and international competitiveness of each institution's teaching and research strength are identified as the backbone for domestic reform and an important feature for the hub. (Knight & Morshidi, 2011, p. 598)

South Korea: Internationalization of higher education is closely integrated into the economic development strategy of South Korea. In a fashion similar to the Southeast Asian countries, South Korea has focused on launching regional hubs of higher education. In fact, two separate free economic zones have been earmarked for this purpose. The Songdo Global University Campus in the IFEZ leads the way. The "education city," when it is ready for business, will be a self-contained unit with residential and business facilities, and a research park. The government is also working to draw in ancillary industries, including IT and knowledge-based businesses to create a symbiotic ecosystem.

Although the project clearly aims to draw in international students, the key goal is to put a stop to "brain drain." South Korea's main target groups are students from China, Russia, Mongolia, and other Eurasian countries; in so doing South Korea will contend with Singapore. Songdo has succeeded in drawing in many top American universities, one of them being the State University of New York (SUNY).

In competition with Songdo is the Jeju Global Education City in the Jeju Free International City Development Center. The Jeju

Global Education City also aims at retaining domestic students, as Songdo does, but it focuses more on retaining those students who go abroad for learning the English language. Another specialized aspect of Jeju is that it targets students from non-English speaking countries, especially China, Japan, Taiwan, and Hong Kong. Jeju derives its inspiration from Dubai's "Knowledge Village," and is slated to host up to 15 higher education institutions by 2016 (Dessoff, 2012, pp. 20–24).

Sri Lanka: Internationalization of higher education is high on the list of priorities for the government of Sri Lanka, as has been made publicly known by the Ministry of Higher Education, on several occasions. Similar to other countries discussed in this section, Sri Lanka, aims to achieve internationalization by presenting itself as a knowledge-driven economy and regional education hub. This would seem to be an ambitious target, given that the country is now just beginning to recover after a three-decade-long civil war. However, the government's strong backing of the project makes it seem that the project, propelled by heavy political force, stands a good chance of achieving success (Dessoff, 2012, p. 25).

The United Arab Emirates and some Gulf countries: The past decade has witnessed the setting up of large education hubs in Gulf countries. Dubai, an emirate in the UAE, followed by Qatar, has been at the forefront of that development and in the last few years, Abu Dhabi, Saudi Arabia, and Bahrain have also joined in. A lot of participating institutions aim at attracting higher education institutions and corporate training institutions from the developed Anglophone countries such as US, UK, and Australia. Many hubs are called "education cities," which are duty-free zones that permit extraordinary latitude to foreign providers across a number of dimensions, such as, tax breaks and institutional autonomy in decision-making in respect of hiring, curriculum, and admissions. As a result of these incentives, the inflow of students is very impressive: In Dubai alone, as many as 38,000 students are enrolled in higher education programs.

The Dubai International Academic City (DIAC) is the only "free zone" that pertains to higher education. It is home to more than 30 institutions, including Hult International Business School, Herriot-Watt University Dubai, Manchester Business School, and the

French School of Fashion. Another cluster is the Dubai Knowledge Village (DKV), which boasts international collaborators and providers such as Middlesex University and Wollongong University.

Many countries in the Gulf are actively competing with Dubai to get a piece of the pie. The government of Abu Dhabi has roped in "big name" universities to collaborate with, including Paris-Sorbonne University and Massachusetts Institute of Technology (MIT). Qatar's Education City, similarly, boasts Carnegie Mellon University, Weill-Cornell Medical College, and Texas A&M University.

Saudi Arabia has invested massively in attracting foreign institutions. In a bid to offer incentives, it has plans to set up "education zones."

> Between 2010–14 [sic], Saudi Arabia will allocate 50.6 per cent of its $384bn five-year plan to education and training to support 5.3 million school students and 1.7 million university students. The most advanced project is King Abdullah Economic City (KAEC), where the education zone includes a university for 18,000 students. Medina Knowledge Economic City, due to open in 2020, will specialise in hi-tech industries, medical sciences and biotechnology. Created through private–public partnerships, the cities will generate more than $150bn a year and promote private investment in industries including education and training. (Thomas, 2010)

Bahrain is the last to get on the wagon, but it is just as ambitious as the rest of them. The government of Bahrain has made announcements to invest over a billion dollars to set up a "Higher Education City" (Thomas, 2010).

It would be fair to state that the Gulf countries display some similarities in their modes of internationalization. Pretty much all of them have focused on the setting up of urban centers that are eager to offer alluring incentives, such as tax breaks and organizational autonomy, to foreign universities. It would also be reasonable to assume that the enviable investments in these urban centers go a long way in drawing big name "parent" universities from the Anglophone world. It would seem that marketing and promotions are decisive components of this exchange. It is no surprise that the range of programs and courses is constricted to business management and administration and allied streams. Also restricted are the modes of delivery—the vast majority of initiatives are limited to "branch campuses."

The internationalization of higher education in the Gulf region reflects the region's enthusiasm to "play catch-up" with Western countries. The domestic students have long exhibited aspiration to pursue higher studies in Western countries, as a degree from a Western university is highly prized. The sweeping regard in which Western universities are held is possibly a result of the absence of a homegrown tradition of academic excellence. This void creates a falsely exalted impression of Western universities and a motiveless yearning to acquire a degree from these institutions.

Although these international branch campuses fulfill, even if partly, the domestic student's wish to own a piece of a Western university in his portfolio, the campuses cannot rest easy. The competition from Asian countries is a formidable and growing threat: "There hasn't been a rush of overseas schools aggressively entering the Middle East market . . . [sic] Most top schools are North American, and most have focused on Asia." (Naufel Vilcassim, Dubai faculty director for London Business School, cited in Thomas, 2010). The Asian countries may be unequal with respect to financial resources, but a large population in the higher education demographic tilts the competition in favor of the Asian countries. Furthermore, many Asian countries, such as India, China, and Japan, have many institutions that are ready to partner with "big name" Western countries, in the sense that these institutions have sufficient accrual of academic resources to function at par with the "home" institution; therefore, these institutions are prepared to enter into a true partnership and find their own way, without the need to import all resources from the "home" institution.

In comparing India with the Gulf countries, an additional factor emerges. India's cultural heritage contributes to a mind-set that places education on a high pedestal. The Indians are a resilient people, born into a culture that encourages philosophical self-enquiry. It is not accidental that India has managed to persevere at democracy ever since it gained independence. The Indians' sturdy reputation for being academically high-achieving, combined with their keen entrepreneurial spirit, stands them in good stead.

India certainly faces stiff competition from other Asian countries as it moves forward in its efforts to internationalize education. Although India is advantaged on account of having many institutions that are internationally competitive, it is disadvantaged on other scores as a result of weak political will. It is discouraging to compare the Indian government's initiatives with the proclamations of governments of other Asian countries. The Indian government has neither expressed willingness to offer incentives such as tax breaks and "free zones" to attract potential partners and students, and nor has it outlined specifics, such as target students, to guide its efforts on the course of internationalization. Given that the international market of crossborder students is a zero-sum game, the "weaker links in the chain" will be left behind with the passage of time.

References

Altbach, P. (2008, July 15). Beware of the Trojan horse. *The Hindu.* Retrieved from http://www.hindu.com/2008/07/15/stories/2008071555180800.htm

Altbach, P., & Jayaram, N. (2008, October 23). Towards creation of world class universities. *The Hindu.* Retrieved from http://www.hindu.com/2008/10/23/stories/2008102355501000.htm (accessed on April 6, 2016).

Dessoff, A. (2012). Asia's bourgeoning higher education hubs. *International Educator, 21*(4), 16–26. Retrieved from www.nafsa.org/_/file/_/ie_julaug12_asia.pdf (accessed on July 19, 2016).

Guruz, K. (2008). *Higher education and international student mobility in the global knowledge economy.* New York: State University of New York Press.

Institute of International Education. (2013). "Open Doors Fact Sheet: India." *Open Doors Report on International Educational Exchange.* Retrieved from http://www.iie.org/~/media/Files/Corporate/Open-Doors/Fact-Sheets-2013/Country/India-Open-Doors-2013.pdf?la=en (accessed on July 19, 2016).

————. (2015). A quick look at global mobility trends. In *New 2015 Project Atlas Trends and Global Data Fact Sheet.* Retrieved from http://www.iie.org/Research-and-Publications/Project-Atlas#.VxcaCaD6WYs (accessed on July 19, 2016).

Knight, J. (2011, March 12). *Regional education hubs: Rhetoric or reality?* Retrieved January 22, 2013, from http://ihe.britishcouncil.org/going-global/sessions/education-hubs-reality-or-rhetoric (accessed on April 6, 2016).

Knight, J., & Morshidi, S. (2011). The complexities and challenges of regional education hubs: focus on Malaysia. *Higher Education, 62*(5), 593–606.

Krishnan, R. T. (2005). Building world class universities. *Economic and Political Weekly, 40*(17), 1681–83.

Kumar, P., Sarkar, S., & Sharma, R. (2009, May 2009). *Migration and diaspora formation: Mobility of Indian students to the developed world.* IMDS Working Paper Series No. 7–9.

Ministry of Education of the People's Republic of China. (n.d.). *List of Chinese higher education institutions.* Retrieved from http://www.moe.edu.cn/publicfiles/business/htmlfiles/moe/moe_2812/200906/48836.html (accessed on April 6, 2016).

National Knowledge Commission. (2005). Report to the nation. Retrieved from http://knowledgecommissionarchive.nic.in/ (accessed on July 19, 2016).

Project Atlas. (2014). *Research and publications.* Retrieved from http://www.iie.org/Research-and-Publications/Project-Atlas (accessed on April 6, 2016).

PwC. (n.d.). *India: Higher education sector opportunities for foreign universities.* Retrieved from www.pwc.in/en_IN/in/assets/.../India-higher-edu-sector-(251012).pdf (accessed on April 6, 2016).

Thomas, K. (2010). Knowledge hubs grow in numbers. *Middle East Economic Digest.* Supplement p, 12. Retrieved from http://connection.ebscohost.com/c/articles/55572163/knowledge-hubs-grow-numbers (accessed on July 19, 2016).

UNESCO. (n.d.). *Global flow.* Retrieved from http://www.uis.unesco.org/Education/Pages/international-student-flow-viz.aspx (accessed on April 6, 2016).

Yeravdekar, V. R., & Tiwari, G. (2014a). Global rankings of higher education institutions and India's effective non-presence: Why have world-class universities eluded the Indian higher education system? And, how worthwhile is the Indian Government's captivation to launch world-class universities? *Procedia—Journal of Social and Behavioral Sciences, 157,* 63–83. http://dx.doi.org/10.1016/j.sbspro.2014.11.010.

———. (2014b). China's lead in higher education: Much to learn for India. *Procedia – Journal of Social and Behavioral Sciences, 157,* 369–72. doi:10.1016/j.sbspro.2014.11.036.

Yeravdekar, V. R., & Tiwari, G. (2014c). China's lead in higher education: Much to learn for India. Procedia – Journal of Social and Behavioral Sciences, 157, 369–372. doi:10.1016/j.sbspro.2014.11.

6

International Student Mobility: Old and New Patterns

In the Global Setting

International student mobility is on rapid ascent and previous trends carry on, at least, in broad terms. The developed anglophone countries continue to lead the way as hosts and Asian countries go on sending a very large segment of students to them (UNESCO, n.d.). For further details, see Tables 6.1 to 6.5. According to Project Atlas, IIE, the number of international students in 2014 stood at 4.5 million. The top eight "host" countries are the US (28%), the UK (11%), Germany (9%), France (7%), Australia (4%), Japan (3%), Spain (2%), and Belgium (2%); all others accounted for 34 percent.

On closer inspection, two trends emerge prominently. First, international student mobility is steadily on the ascent. Much more out of the ordinary is that China has vaulted to the top of the list of host countries from near insignificance.

As has been noted earlier, the developed Anglophone countries and some countries in the Western Europe are the top hosts to internationally mobile students, and this is true for all measures, ". . . flows of international students, franchisers of academic programs to foreign providers, international accreditors or quality guarantors, or controlling partners in 'twinning' arrangements . . ." (Varghese, 2008).

Table 6.1
International Students Worldwide

Year	International Students in Millions
1975	0.8
1980	1.1
1985	1.1
1990	1.3
1995	1.7
2000	2.1
2005	3.0
2010	4.1
2011	4.3
2012	4.3
2014	4.5

Source: Project Atlas (2014).

Table 6.2
Top Eight Host Countries of Globally Mobile Students 2001 (2.1 Million Students Worldwide)

Countries	Percentage
United States	28%
United Kingdom	11%
Germany	9%
France	7%
Australia	4%
Japan	3%
Spain	2%
Belgium	2%
All others	34%

Source: Project Atlas (2014).

Table 6.3
Top Eight Host Countries of Globally Mobile Students 2012 (4.3 Million Students Worldwide)

Countries	Percentage
United States	19%
United Kingdom	11%
China	8%
France	7%
Germany	6%
Australia	6%
Canada	5%
Japan	3%
All others	35%

Source: Project Atlas (2014).

Table 6.4
International Enrollment as a Percentage of Total Higher Education for Top Countries for 2011–12

Countries	Percentage
China	1.0%
U.S.	3.9%
Germany	11.1%
France	12.1%
UK	19.0%
Australia	26.4%

Source: Project Atlas (2014).

The students typically come from "middle-income countries" in Asia, Africa, and Latin America. The majority of these countries are not equipped with higher education systems that can meet the demands of the population demographic. It is no surprise then that the largest market in cross-border higher education is found in programs that are designed to absorb demand. It is also explainable that these programs

Table 6.5
Top Host Destinations Worldwide for 2011 and 2012

Destination	2011 Total Int'l Students	2012 Total Int'l Students
United States	764,495	819,644
United Kingdom	480,755	488,380
China	292,611	328,330
France	284,945	289,274
Germany	252,032	265,292
Australia	242,351	245,531
Canada	193,647	214,955
Japan	138,075	137,756

Source: Project Atlas (2014).

are generally short term, specialized, and elitist in the sense of being restricted in their aim at the prospective student group.

Varghese (2008), in a report by International Institute for Educational Planning (IIEP), UNESCO, had estimated that cross-border higher education will continue to increase in respects of enrollment and the size of the playing field, but not phenomenally so. There is some variance in projections related to international student mobility from several sources, as is observed by CII-AIU (2014, pp. 9–10),

> The growth trajectory suggests that the figure is likely to touch 4.5 million in 2014. Earlier estimates (Bohm, 2003) indicated that the number would to about 8 million by 2025. However, a recent OBHE Report (Lawton et al., 2013) concludes that the rate of increase of student mobility is set to decline, consistent with a projected drop in the rate of global tertiary enrollment from 5–6 per cent to 1.4 per cent annually in the developed world, decrease in the size of the 18–24 cohort, development of education in the developing world, especially the BRIC countries; and the rapid expansion of trans-national education and distance education. An important factor could also be the tightening of grant of visa.

It was projected that the US will continue to consolidate its leadership position as provider of cross-border higher education. China and India, it was estimated, will continue to send the largest share of students for the purpose of cross-border higher education. Moreover, a number of countries—Saudi Arabia, Vietnam, Mexico, and Brazil—were said to be poised to become important participants.

A distance of only a few years away, it seems IIEP, UNESCO, report was temperate in its projections. The most recently available estimates are unequivocal in heralding China and India's lead as "sending countries."

> By 2024, one in every three outbound higher education student across the globe will be from India and China. By 2024, it is expected that there will be 3.85 million outbound mobile higher education students globally, up from 3.04 million in 2011. India and China will contribute 35% of global growth during this period. While nearly 8.5 lakh Chinese students will travel abroad for higher education in 2024, Indian students will be the second highest with 3.76 lakh of them travelling to enrol in foreign universities . . . "India, by some distance, is forecast to be the fastest growing market, with an additional 12.7 million enrolments by 2024; other emerging economies with significant forecast growth in higher education enrolments between 2011 and 2024 include Indonesia (5 million), Brazil (2.6 million), Nigeria (2.3 million), China (1.9 million), Ethiopia (1.6 million), Pakistan (1.3 million), Mexico (1.0 million), Philippines (0.9 million), Colombia (0.9 million)," . . . (British Council, 2013, cited in Sinha, 2013)

The report "The future of the world's mobile students to 2024" (British Council, 2013), which is a follow-up to "The shape of things to come: higher education global trends and emerging opportunities to 2020" (British Council, 2012) makes the following forecasts:

- The major bilateral students flow in 2024, in terms of volume, will continue to be from China and India to traditional host markets. But flows between Nigeria and the UK, Saudi Arabia and the US and UK, Pakistan and the UK, and Nepal and the US will be among the top 10 fastest growing bilateral flows between 2011 and 2024.
- By 2024, India, China, Indonesia and the US will be home to over 50 percent of the world's 18–22 year old population, despite the fact that the Chinese tertiary-aged population is projected to fall by roughly 40 million in the next decade.
- Saudi Arabia, Nigeria, Nepal, Pakistan, Iraq, Brazil, Turkey, and Indonesia will emerge as important origin markets.

- The UK as a host destination will benefit from large outbound markets from India, Nigeria, Saudi Arabia, and Pakistan.
- The US as a host destination will be the major beneficiary of growth of outbound students from China and India.

Even more extraordinary is the finding that China will emerge as a prominent "host country."

According to IIE data released in 2014, China is the "third most favoured nation of international students after the US and UK" (Chhapia, 2014). An important area for future research emerges: what are the motives and considerations that guide international students in making a decision about the host higher education institution and the host country? The findings will provide valuable information to countries and institutions on both sides of international student mobility fulcrum on how to turn the tide in their favor.

It is also projected that mobility patterns will undergo a proto-typical shift as several traditional "sending" countries emerge as prominent host countries, far-fetched as that may seem at this point. In broad terms, it emerges that a window is beginning to open on to new sub-directions on the map that depicts international student mobility. This marks a movement away from the rigid one-directional movement of international students from "North" to "South." As is cited in the block quote below, CII-AIU (2014, pp. 10–11) raises three notable points in the context of the evolving patterns: South-South mobility, North-South mobility (as a result of encouragement by the governments of many countries of the North), and new destinations and emerging markets that reflect a new variable—strength of international students against total student strength, and countries that now feature prominently as both "sending" and "receiving" countries. All in all, one infers that internationalization is increasingly being considered indispensable to quality higher education, as should be.

> With the rapid development of higher education in Asian countries, especially in China, Singapore, Malaysia and India; and with the establishment of a number of educational hubs in the Gulf region and South Eastern Asia, south-south mobility is now common. An important development that may have far-reaching implication is the fact that governments in North America and Europe are now encouraging

outward mobility giving a boost to north-to-south mobility. The US under its "100,000 Strong Initiative" aims at sending 100,000 American students to China by 2014. Under the British Council's "Generation UK" programme 15,000 UK students will be offered subsidized places and internships in China. On its part China aims to bring in 500,000 students into the country by 2020. . . . To the traditional destinations of the US, the UK and Western Europe have been added Australia, New Zealand, Canada and China. Singapore and Malaysia are also emerging as destinations. . . . In terms of per cent of international students, against total student strength in higher education, Australia leads with 26.4 per cent, followed by the UK (19 per cent), France (12.1 per cent), Germany (11.1 per cent), the US (3.9 per cent), and China (1.0 per cent) (IIE, 2013). . . . What is significant is that Germany, France, the US, Russia and China figure in both lists (that is exporters and importers).

International Student Mobility in India

Inflow of International Students

As has been stated earlier, India boasts an abiding tradition of hosting international students since the ancient time. The inflow of this student group took a downturn in the medieval period, and that continued up until Independence from the British rule in 1947. The country's sovereign status and the case that several other countries in Asia and Africa gained independence at the same time certainly helped India attract international students in the period after the Independence. As can be expected, the newly independent India had many crosses to bear. The country was beset with a number of critical developmental challenges; the higher education system, as with many other realms, was in gross disrepair and required heavy reorganization and investment. This did not leave much room for initiatives with respect to internationalization. As the country began to realize its developmental potential, internationalization came to assume more of a presence in the list of higher education goals.

The data on the profile of international students in India can be traced back to the 1980s. The reliability of the data has been frequently questioned as significant variations are often present in the figures. Quite possibly, both sides have not held up their end of responsibilities. The regulatory bodies, most relevantly AIU, has yet to devise a better data collection and processing mechanism, and the higher education institutions, for their part, have not complied well in supplying data to AIU and other such bodies. The UGC, the uppermost Government of India organization responsible for regulation and coordination of the higher education system, has recently begun looking into the data on the inflow of international students; but, then again, it is not nearly enough. Indeed, it must be UGC, with the governing authority and the financial possessions that it wields, which must manage the data on inbound and, for that matter, outbound international students in India. More than being a matter of fittingness, the point is about the significance that internationalization holds in the scheme of higher education. The statistics related to international students—which should be the wellspring of policy on internation-alization of higher education—would have fallen within the purview of UGC, if internationalization was an agenda item of high priority. The fact that for all this time the highest regulatory body had little to do with recording information on international students does not bode well for internationalization. There is a separate dataset from the Foreigners Division, Ministry of Home Affairs, the Government of India, which is based on the information related to student visas that were made available to international students. The figures of international students, in this case, are far higher than those supplied by AIU. The reason for this variation is that in the former case, students on short term courses and programs are included in the total figures, and in the latter case, only those students that are enrolled in a degree program by an Indian higher education institution, are counted up.

A common discrepancy pertains to the question who is an international student? This question comprises many aspects of student mobility as part of cross-border higher education: programs that result in award of degree vis-à-vis programs that result in award of diploma or certificate, the minimum duration of program, and so on. The UNESCO Institute of Statistics (UIS) considers international students to be "those who have crossed a national or territorial border for the purpose of education and are now enrolled outside their country of origin." "The definition [UNESCO's] excludes students who are in a programme for less than a year. The Institute of International Education (IIE) in its Open Doors Reports (IIE, n.d.) does not have the one-year time restriction" (CII-AIU, 2014, p. 7).

In the context of the discussion on international students in India, a recurring dilemma presents as to whether students enrolled in distance education mode qualify as international students or not. This assumes an important dimension since Indira Gandhi National Open University (IGNOU)—an Indian higher education institution that offers programs exclusively in the distance education mode—is a big draw for international students, particularly students from the developing world. Further compounding the issue is the element of student visa.

> The ministry of human resource development (MHRD) regards all persons coming under a student visa to be international students, irrespective of whether they come for post-secondary education programmes or otherwise. The Association of Indian Universities (AIU) follows the Unesco [sic] definition while the University Grants Commission (UGC) follows the IIE one. (CII-AIU, 2014, p. 7)

Thus, the AIU, in congruence with the UNESCO [definition], considers only those foreign students "international students" who are enrolled in

> a university and colleges, for post-higher [sic] secondary programmes, of at least one academic year duration . . . Consequently, students coming for short-term certificate/diploma [sic] courses in subjects like English language and computer-literacy are not being covered, nor are students coming for "study India" programmes. Likewise, students registered with Indian open universities, but residing abroad are excluded from the latest survey. (CII-AIU, 2014, p. 19)

The UGC, in accordance with the definition of international students stated by IIE, "does includes in its data-base the categories excluded by AIU, i.e. students on short-term programmes, including 'study India' and those registered with open universities but non-resident in India" (p. 19).

The earlier figures included students enrolled in IGNOU, but the more recent figures exclude this set. Perhaps the definition of international students as recently issued by UIS, which excludes students enrolled in the distance mode and those that are enrolled in programs and courses that are less than a year, is responsible for the change in the criteria that is utilized to determine the status of international student. To muddy those waters even more, the newer statistics does not specify if students enrolled in short duration courses and programs, such as semester based programs, are included or not. An integrated definition of "international student" requires that proviso clauses leave no room for misinterpretation and ambiguity to which the definition might be liable. In a country such as India, the room for obscurity is infinitely large. Consider the point raised by CII-AIU (2014, p. 19) and the extent to which it clouds MHRD's definition of international student, which is grounded in acquisition of student visa.

> . . . the large number of "Tibetan students" listed as international students by many universities. India accepts the fact that Tibet is a part of China and, therefore, these will have to be classified as being students from China. At the same time, it is a fact that most of them are children of political refugees, born and bred in India. None of them has visited Tibet. Logically, all of them should be classified as Indian or "stateless." (CII-AIU, 2014, p. 19)

It is hoped that, as internationalization becomes more of a governmental priority, the statistics on international students will be better representative of the actual presentation. From an evaluative standpoint, it seems that the Indian policymakers' dismissal of "off-campus" education and short term offerings is one that will not go the distance. The years to come will mark a departure from what international education has entailed so far. Advances in information and communication technology, most importantly instructional technology, will help international education move from elitism to equalitarianism, so that students will cross physical borders when they must and not when that best serves.

It may well be the case that the data on international students in India is not entirely reliable, but one must not make too much of it. As has been noted earlier, student mobility is not the lone marker of cross-border higher education. More than that, student mobility is projected to growingly share space with modes that are not quite "bricks and mortar," including MOOCs. In this light, it would be well to not get caught up with UIS definition of international student and open up the discussion to cross-border higher education complete with all the various modes. Coming from this perspective, one would like to have seen students who come from other countries to pursue higher education in India classified into the three categories: students that are enrolled in "on campus" programs, students enrolled in distance education programs, and students enrolled in short-term courses and programs, such as "semester-abroad" (Yeravdekar, 2012). Were we to consider the entire gamut of students from foreign countries, we would find that the Indian higher education system has continued to draw students from other countries and that there has even been an increase in the inflow of international students.

The data on international students in India reveals that this group commonly comes from a few identifiable sources, in terms of geography, other aspects related to ethno-cultural origins, and sponsorships.

> Choudaha et al. (2013) have identified four categories of international students, based on the two dimensions of financial resources and academic preparedness:
>
> Explorers: Students with high financial resources and low academic preparedness
>
> Highfliers: Students with high financial resources and high academic preparedness
>
> Strivers: Students with low financial resources and high academic preparedness
>
> Strugglers: Students with low financial resources and low academic preparedness (CII-AIU, 2014, p. 9)

Although it would be difficult to categorize international students on the basis of points raised by Choudaha et al. (2013), Powar (2013, pp. 162–63) has stated that the international student in India is often found to be in one of the following categories in respect of sponsorship:

- Students sponsored by the Government of India
- Self-sponsored students

- Students sponsored by foreign governments or international agencies such as the World Bank, United Nations Development Program (UNDP), and Asian Development Bank
- Students sponsored by interuniversity and other bilateral agreements
- Students sponsored by Nonresident Indians and Indian expatriates

In ascending order of the total number of international students based on the sponsorship, the smallest share is that of students from developed countries; they are ordinarily self-sponsored or sponsored by foreign governments, interuniversity, bilateral, and multilateral agreements. They are often enrolled in shorter programs in liberal and performing arts.

The above group is followed by students sponsored by Nonresident Indians and Indian expatriates primarily from developed countries (mostly, the US, the UK, Canada, and Australia) and secondarily from developing countries (mostly, countries in Asia and Africa). This group is quite large and is enrolled in "demand absorbing" programs, mostly in engineering and medicine. It is also observed that they tend to be enrolled in private institutions, which are more oriented to skills development and work preparedness; they are also more expensive than public institutions. It could be that the relative affordability and ease of admission account for drawing this group to Indian institutions.

Last, the students who come from developing countries form the largest segment and count for 95 percent of the total figure. These students are enrolled in all manner of programs and institutions.

Categorizations of international students based on their nationality and residence, although quite complicated, are important and have been overlooked thus far. The author suggests the below-mentioned categories within which to place international students in India.

An international student is one who holds at least one of the following statuses:

1. Foreign passport,
2. Dual citizenship,
3. Non-resident Indian who has given his last qualifying exam (intermediate, postsecondary, or graduation) outside India and wishes to complete his higher studies in India, and

4. Persons of Indian Origin (PIO) and Overseas Citizenship of India
    (OCI).

The author suggests another categorization on the basis of the type of program of enrolment, including the following categories:

1. International students enrolled in degree programs, both under-graduate and postgraduate
2. International students coming for short-term programs, such as twinning arrangements, semester abroad, and Study India Program
3. International students coming for research-based programs, such as doctoral programs
4. International students coming to India for internships in Indian companies. (It is relatable that the number of such students has increased significantly over the last few years. These students come for duration between six months and one year. These internships are academic in their focus, but also offer opportunity to learn about the Indian corporate culture)

The Indian Diaspora, which adds up to over 25 million in 130 countries, is a very prominent group (Kumar, Sarkar, & Sharma, 2009; Ministry of Overseas Indian Affairs, 2015) and an unexploited resource in the context of internationalization. Kuznetsov (2006) has demonstrated the comparative advantage that Diaspora can add to international competitiveness by enriching its networks, such as alumni association (cited in Salmi, 2009). Salmi (2009) has illustrated the significance of diaspora by utilizing the example of University of Beijing, which actively draws in researchers of Chinese origin as part of its human resource policy.

It is also demonstrated that international students in India are drawn to certain cities and institutions. In this sense, international student presence is far from homogenous. In descending order, the cities of Pune (29.30%), Delhi (20.48%), and Manipal (12.78%) have continued to lead the way (Powar, 2013, p. 38). The distribution of students in cities is clearly tied to institutions therein. The city of Pune has dominated as steadfastly as it has because of the higher education institutions in the city. Between 2001 and 2002, the total number of international students who were enrolled in six universities in Pune was 2,057. This number grew to 3,000 in 2005–06. In the year 2011, the number doubled to 6,000. The city of Pune puts the state of Maharashtra at the top, so that the state accounted for 32.50 percent of international students, followed by Karnataka (22.37%), and New Delhi (20.48%) (UGC, 2007, as cited in Powar, 2012b, pp. 247–49).

A dataset was provided by a Government of India source in 2015, which recorded the population of international students in Indian states and union territories. This population was categorized as such on the basis of student visas issued by the Foreigners Division, the Ministry of Home Affairs, between the year 2010 and 2013. The high figures are explained on the account of application of this criterion in determining the population of international students.

The distribution of inbound international students across Indian states and union territories between the years 2010 and 2013, as provided by the dataset, is presented in Tables 6.6 to 6.9.

The data reveals that in the years 2010, 2011, 2012, and 2013, five states— Karnataka, Maharashtra, Delhi, Andhra Pradesh, and Tamil Nadu—stayed at the top in respect of hosting international students even if the states changed ranks from one year to the next.

Table 6.6
International Students in 2010 in Top 10 States and Union Territories

Number of Students	State/Union Territory
20,087	Karnataka
13,052	Delhi
8,396	Tamil Nadu
6,731	Maharashtra
6,467	Andhra Pradesh
2,536	UP
1,359	West Bengal
1,191	Kerala
860	Gujrat
721	Himachal Pradesh

Source: Personal communication, July 3, 2015.

Table 6.7
International Students in 2011 in Top 10 States and Union Territories

Number of Students	State/Union Territory
16,035	Delhi
13,521	Karnataka
9,723	Tamil Nadu
6,679	Maharashtra
3,473	Andhra Pradesh
3,096	UP
1,656	West Bengal
1,189	Kerala
773	Gujrat
642	Himachal Pradesh

Source: Personal communication, July 3, 2015.

Table 6.8
International Students in 2012 in Top 10 States and Union Territories

Number of Students	State/Union Territory
20,302	Karnataka
18,918	Delhi
10,125	Tamil Nadu
7,313	Andhra Pradesh
6,368	Maharashtra
3,764	UP
1,735	West Bengal
1,408	Kerala
1,018	Gujrat
782	Himachal Pradesh

Source: Personal communication, July 3, 2015.

Table 6.9
International Students in 2013 in Top 10 States and Union Territories

Number of Students	State/Union Territory
19,715	Delhi
19,222	Karnataka
16,162	Andhra Pradesh
14,169	Maharashtra
12,095	Tamil Nadu
3,370	UP
2,129	West Bengal
1,652	Punjab
1,379	Gujrat
1,210	Kerala

Source: Personal communication, July 3, 2015.

In the year 2010, Karnataka led by a huge margin and was followed by Delhi, Tamil Nadu, Maharashtra, and Andhra Pradesh. Between the first three states, there emerges a significant drop from one to the next.

In the year 2011, Delhi ranked first and was followed by Karnataka, Tamil Nadu, Maharashtra, and Andhra Pradesh. Similar to the previous year, a significant drop was noted in the figures for the top three states.

In the year 2012, Karnataka scored the highest figure and was followed by Delhi, Tamil Nadu, Andhra Pradesh, and Maharashtra. It is notable that between Delhi and Tamil Nadu, there was a drop of 8,793 students.

In the year 2013, Delhi stood first and was followed by Karnataka, Andhra Pradesh, Maharashtra, and Tamil Nadu.

The highest figure for all the three years hovered in the range of 20,302 and 19,715, except for the year 2011, when it was 16,035—a significant decline.

The top positioning of the Peninsular Indian states is not surprising since Maharashtra, Karnataka, and Andhra Pradesh have reigned since as far back as documented records would go. This is to be explained on account of several factors.

These states boast a strong "homegrown" tradition of excellence in higher education. The Peninsular India is a regional cluster of institutions that have a long track record of excellence in teaching and research in a wide range of disciplines and streams.

As has been discussed at length elsewhere, the Peninsular India has been at the forefront of advances in higher education. For one, this region heralded the entry of private institutions into the Indian higher education system. Moreover, this region brought in transformative progression as it introduced technical–professional education in a substantive way into the system.

It is also relatable that the peninsular states have generally enjoyed prevalence of stable political rule and law and order in the society. Tied to a relatively more progressive socio-economic landscape are high literacy rates, forward-looking cultural attitudes, and law-abiding and peaceable civic-conduct amongst citizenry. All of these have resulted in a thriving economy, which serves to supports the higher education system by providing infrastructural backing and ancillary businesses, which make cities hospitable to student populations. In particular, this region has been at the forefront of businesses and research and development in IT and communication sectors. These well-connected knowledge and career networks go a long way in sustaining the growth of institutions and drawing in students, both domestic and international.

A number of institutions have held on to their reputations as strongholds of international students. In no specific order, the University of Pune, the Symbiosis International University, Delhi University, Mysore University, Osmania University, and Manipal University, each with more than a thousand international students, feature in the discussion (Powar, 2013, p. 40).

The international student population at IGNOU has been on the increase in the recent years. It stood at 4,468 in 2007–08 (Snehi, 2012, p. 37) and grew to 5,861 in 2008–09 (Powar, 2012b, p. 246). The increase is attributable to a number of policy measures, including designing special information booklets for international students and adopting single window approach (Snehi, 2012, p. 37).

At the outset, it must be pointed out that the facts and figures on international students that are cited in this book include two sets.[1] The first set was published by AIU and contains information up until the year 2008–09. The second set was cited in CII-AIU (2014) and is sourced from a recent survey, "A fresh survey, with modifications in the format for information, was conducted recently for the academic year 2012–13" (CII-AIU, 2014, p. 23). Since it is expressly stated that the survey featured "modifications in the format for information," it would be unscientific to merge or compare the data from the first set to that from the second. For this reason, the more recent data, which includes information from 2008–09 onwards, is presented subsequently in the section.

Biennial pattern in the data on the total number of international students coming to India: The records from UGC and AIU show that, as early as 1988–89, Indian higher education institutions hosted students from 90 countries and since then the number of countries sending students to India has increased (Snehi, 2012, p. 32). The data reveals quite a lot of ups and downs that are significant enough to warrant an inquiry into why the numbers should vary so much: compare the highest figure at 21,778 in 2008–09 with the lowest at 5,323 in 1998–99. The numbers have also fluctuated significantly in consecutive readings, and this one will serve as an example: In the year 2002–03, the number stood at 7,756, and it spiked to a little short of doubling at 13,267 in 2004–05. As has been stated earlier, these figures are inclusive of student population at IGNOU; this is an important rider as international student enrolment with IGNOU is quite substantial—it was 5,861 in 2008–09 (Powar, 2012b, p. 246).

In the years between 1990 and 1995, the numbers continued to fall, although the decline was not alarming. In a sudden downturn, the next reading for the year 1996–97 recorded a halving of the international student population at 5,841. It fell some more the next year at 5,323, but things picked-up the year after and the number rose to 6,896 in 2000–01. It is welcome that the upward trend has continued thereafter. The next reading was slightly higher at 7,756 and it increased by 5,511 to stand at 13,267. The consecutive figures show that the upturn has continued steadily: 18,391 and 21,778, as noted in Table 6.10.

Table 6.10
Inflow of International Students in India

Year	1990–91	1992–93	1994–95	1996–97	1998–99
Students	12,899	12,767	11,888	5,841	5,323
Year	2000–01	2002–03	2004–05	2006–07	2008–09
Students	6,896	7,756	13,267	18,391	21,778

Source: Powar (2012b).

The AISHE reports that, in the year 2012–13, the total number of "foreign students" in the higher education system in India was 35,178; of these, there were 21,915 men students and 13,263 women students (MHRD, 2014). The AISHE report titled Higher Education Statistics at a Glance notes that, in the year 2013–14, there were 39,517 "foreign students," of these 25,565 were men students. The AISHE sources do not present additional information on international students such as information on "sending countries," "discipline-based", and "program level-based" enrollment. Further, none of the AISHE sources present data on the number of international students for the year 2014–15.

Snehi (2012, p. 34) attributes the sharp downfall in the period between 1996 and 1999 as well as the escalation after 2000 to changes in governmental policies in India and abroad:

> By the year 1996–97, the enrolment of foreign students had reached up to half. This change in trend can be attributed to two factors, firstly at this point of time the internationalization of education was occurring at a faster pace and many developed countries such as USA, UK, Australia started promoting and marketing of their higher education programmes; in this process they took initiatives to improve their universities even at national level to market their education abroad and attract more students in order to reduce their fiscal pressure. During this period of internationalization, many other countries like France, Germany, Canada, and Netherlands also emerged as educational destinations for mobile students. Impact of these initiatives resulted in increase in market-oriented delivery of higher education across borders, often by the institutions run for profit (Sanyal and Martin, 2006). During this period, India was inactive and initiatives in this regard were lacking. The profiles of sending countries reveal that the

students who were coming to Indian universities were mostly from the neighboring countries and African countries which had less developed higher education systems. These countries were the ones which had large number of Indian Diaspora. Reputation of some established Indian universities also influenced the inflow of foreign students. However, the beginning of twenty-first century witnessed a reversal in this trend and the number of foreign students started increasing since 2001–02. These changes may have occurred due to policies adopted in the wake of 10th Five Year Plan and setting up of committees like COPIEA by UGC and programme initiative called PIHEAD to promote higher education abroad in a systematic manner and targeting countries for increase in number of students. These efforts paid off and consequently the number of foreign students has increased significantly from the targeted countries during the last couple of years.

Quinquennial pattern of inflow of international students distributed on the basis of regions from which the students come: The most prominent incidence is that the vast majority of students come from the continents of Asia and Africa. The interplay between the numbers from the two continents is quite interesting. At the beginning, in 1990–91, Africa was slightly ahead (5,741 and 6,318). Five years on, and the numbers were practically alike (4,831 and 4,081). Ever since then, Asia has continued to lead, and the disparity in the two sets of figures carries on growing. At present, the difference is striking indeed (16,004 and 4,193), as noted in Tables 6.11 and 6.12.

The continent of Asia has been an abiding patron of the Indian higher education system. Between 1990 and 2001, there presented a continuous decline in the number of international students. The record for 2005–06 shows a remarkable leap of more than doubling (3,866 and 10,493). The upward trend continued and the next reading was steadily higher at 16,004 in 2008–09.

The numbers from Africa have been a cause for concern. The highest record of 6,318 was for the first reading in 1990–91, at which point, the African students counted up to almost half of the total international student population. The numbers continued to fall steadily up until the last reading in 2008–09, which is 4,193, and amounts to almost 19 percent of the total international student population.

With an eye to reversing the downward trend in student inflow from Africa, the Indian Government undertook many steps in the last

Table 6.11
Inflow of International Students Distributed on the Basis of Regions that the Students Come from, 1990–2009

Region	1990–91	1995–96	2000–01	2005–06	2008–09
Asia	5,741	4,831	3,866	10,493	16,004
Africa	6,318	4,081	2,964	2,403	4,193
North and South America	263	309	327	654	614
Europe	173	127	179	206	304
Australasia	35	40	44	71	66
Miscellaneous	369	699	405	629	597
Total	12,899	10,087	7,785	14,456	21,778

Source: Powar (2012b).

Table 6.12
Inflow of International Students Distributed on the Basis of Regions that the Students Come from, 2004–09

Region	2004–05	2005–06	2006–07	2007–08	2008–09
Asia	9,849	10,493	13,400	15,437	16,004
Africa	2,005	2,403	3,316	3,796	4,193
North and South America	593	654	776	629	614
Europe	178	206	238	309	304
Australasia	55	71	69	81	66
Miscellaneous	587	629	592	957	597
Total	13,267	14,456	18,391	21,206	21,778

Source: Powar (2012b).

two decades. These efforts were frequently promoted in the context of strengthening regional cooperation with African countries in the spirit of South-South cooperation. A few such efforts were initiated in Africa by IGNOU. These projects typically aimed at making available programs and courses in higher education in African countries through distance learning options. The Pan-African e-Network project, which was launched in 2008, merits note in the discussion. The plan is an information and communications technology project between India and the African Union. It strives to link all the 53 member states of the Union through a satellite and fiber optic network to India and to each other to enable access to and sharing of expertise between India and African nations. The distance learning is carried out through teleconferencing mode and covers programs and courses at all levels—from short term certificates to postgradu-ate degrees. The success of these programs is partly responsible for the drop in total enrollment of international students. (This again brings up the quandary about whether to include distance learners or not in determining the criteria for who qualifies as an international student. A point worthy of note is that even though the UIS definition excludes this group, AIU does not make any qualifying references in this regard.)

The setting up of the African Union, which has taken on a number of initiatives with the aim of enhancing higher education with in the Union, has succeeded in improving the quality of higher education in the region. This obviates the need for students to seek higher education abroad as the exclusive source of quality learning (Powar, 2013, pp. 194–99).

In terms of enrollment, other parts of the world are not nearly as prominent as countries in Asia and Africa. But, that must serve to impel us in our efforts in improving international enrollment. Between 1990 and 2001, the students from North and South America ranged in upper 200s and 300s. But, this figure jumped to double in the 600s in the following decade.

The student enrollment from Europe hovered in between 100 and 200 between 1990 and 2001. The number doubled to be in the range of 600 and 700 between 2005 and 2009.

Summing up some prominent features in the inflow of inter-national students, Snehi (2012, p. 36) notes:

During the last two decades, analysis of country-wise participation revealed that the number of countries participating/sending students in the Indian higher education institutions has increased from 88 in 1986–87 to 125 in 2007–08. Iran and Nepal occupy the topmost slots of sending the maximum number of students with UAE and Ethiopia following closely. The proportion of students coming from top ten countries in the last couple of years has increased to 56 per cent. Out of 125 countries in 2007–08, ten countries are contributing more than half of foreign students studying in Indian Universities.

Pattern of inflow of international students distributed on the basis of countries from which the students come

As stated earlier, countries from Asia and Africa have proved to be abiding patrons of the Indian higher education system, as noted in Tables 6.13 to 6.16. For this reason, it is important to monitor patterns of inflow from these regions closely. First and foremost, it emerges that there is a great deal of variation between countries that are in the same region, and it leads one to conjecture that political climes and diplomatic relations play important roles in determining student inflow.

Iran features high on the list of top "sending" countries. The total number of students from Iran wavered between 100s and 300s in the years from 1990 to 2003. This numbers rose to 1120 in 2004–05.

Table 6.13
Inflow of International Students Distributed on the Basis of Countries that the Students Come from, 2004–08

Countries	2004–05	2005–06	2006–07	2007–08
Iran	1,120	1,264	2,180	2,669
Nepal	1,352	1,411	1,728	1,821
United Arab Emirate	1,500	2,034	1,878	1,560
Ethiopia	226	302	1,033	1,289
Sri Lanka	582	530	466	997
Afghanistan	35	65	422	976
Saudi Arabia	419	551	771	835
Bahrain	382	481	446	600
Kenya	418	523	621	592
Oman	646	505	608	548
Total	6,680	7,666	10,153	11,887

Source: Dongaonkar and Negi (2009).

Table 6.14
Inflow of International Students Distributed on the Basis of Countries that the Students Come from, 1990–2005

Source Country	1990–91	1993–94	1998–99	2000–01	2002–03	2004–05
Iran	370	338	106	217	336	1120
	2.86%	2.46%	1.99%	3.14%	4.33%	8.44%
Ethiopia	488	685	403	301	225	226
	3.78%	4.99%	7.57%	4.36%	2.90%	1.70%
UAE	40	39	26	68	68	1,500
	0.31%	0.28%	0.48%	0.98%	0.87%	11.30%
Nepal	651	909	574	821	801	1,352
	5.01%	6.95%	10.78%	11.90%	10.32%	10.19%
Afghanistan	113	111	59	35	24	35
	0.87%	0.81%	1.11%	0.50%	0.30%	0.26%
Saudi Arabia	70	38	5	44	36	419
	0.94%	0.27%	0.09%	0.63%	0.46%	3.16%
Bahrain	16	134	34	109	59	382
	0.04%	0.97%	0.63%	1.65%	0.76%	2.87%
Sri Lanka	540	420	574	383	391	582
	4.18%	3.06%	10.78%	5.55%	5.17%	4.38%
Bhutan	149	123	115	175	227	286
	1.15%	0.88%	2.16%	2.53%	2.92%	2.15%
Kenya	3,495	4,268	403	301	521	418
	27.01%	31.13%	7.57%	4.36%	6.71%	3.15%
Oman	8	9	74	216	94	646
	0.06%	0.06%	1.39%	3.13%	1.21%	4.86%
Yemen	115	184	100	154	242	345
	0.89%	1.34%	1.88%	2.23%	3.12%	2.60%
Bangladesh	399	736	461	576	372	940
	3.41%	5.36%	7.91%	8.85%	4.79%	5.67%
Mauritius	20	296	398	546	366	527
	0.15%	2.18%	7.47%	7.91%	4.71%	3.97%
Sudan	1,521	1,294	245	381	186	140
	11.79%	9.44%	4.60%	5.52%	2.39%	1.05%

Source: Powar (2012b).

Table 6.15
Inflow of International Students Distributed on the Basis of Countries that the Students Come from, 2005–09

Source Country	2004–05	2006–07	2008–09
Iran	1,120	2,175	2,961
	8.40%	11.70%	13.60%
Ethiopia	226	1,041	1,938
	1.70%	5.60%	8.90%
UAE	1,500	1,878	1,731
	11.30%	10.10%	7.95%
Nepal	1,352	1,729	1,720
	10.20%	9.30%	7.90%
Afghanistan	35	n.a.	1,197
	0.30%	–	5.50%
Saudi Arabia	419	762	1,045
	3.20%	4.10%	4.80%
China	19	n.a.	871
	0.30%	–	4.00%
Sri lanka	582	n.a.	779
	4.40%	–	3.40%
Bhutan	286	539	774
	2.15%	2.90%	3.10%
Kuwait	305	n.a.	479
	2.30%	–	2.20%
Kenya	418	622	n.a.
	3.15%	3.35%	–
Oman	527	605	n.a.
	3.90%	3.30%	–
Yemen	150	595	n.a.
	1.05%	3.20%	–
International Students (Total)	13,267	18,594	21,778

Source: Powar (2012b).

Table 6.16
Inflow of International Students in India (Most Recent Data Based on the UIS Definition)

Country of Origin	Number of International Students
Iran	1,258
Nepal	1,252
UAE	1,110
Kenya	508
Saudi Arabia	506
Mauritius	497
United States	444
Bahrain	435
Oman	432
Sri Lanka	431
Bhutan	365
Bangladesh	345
Thailand	309
China	305
Ethiopia	290
Vietnam	263
Kuwait	235
Qatar	231
Yemen	214

Source: International Student Flow, UIS, UNESCO, August 2014, United Nations Education, Scientific and Cultural Organization.

Note: There is no qualifying info on the criteria used to determine international students, but possibly the UIS definition is utilized, given that the numbers are much lower than the latest data issued by the Association of Indian Universities (AIU).

The upturn continued; it almost doubled to 2,175 the next year and grew further to 2,961 the year after.

Ethiopia, much like Iran, had stayed still in the range of 200s and 600s from 1990 to 2005. But, in a welcome spin, it jumped to 1,041 in 2006–07 and grew to almost double at 1,938 in 2008–09.

The United Arab Emirates (UAE) also counts among countries that have recently begun to send an increased number of students to India. The number of students from the UAE was less than a hundred up until 2003, but shot to 1,500 in 2004–05, increased the next year, and continued to be in that range the year after.

The increase in student inflow from Nepal has been slow and steady. The numbers stayed in the range of 500 and 1,000 up until 2003, but increased to 1,352 in 2004–05, and rose some more to 1,700s in the next two consecutive readings.

The student inflow from Afghanistan was quiet from 1990 to 2008, the highest recording being close to 100, but it jumped to almost 2,000 in 2008–09. It would be worth our while to investigate as to what caused the change to occur and utilize that finding to determine if the Indian Government can take measures to carry on the upward trend. One of the possible reasons could be that during this time, the Indian Government, through Indian Council for Cultural Relations (ICCR), made available a large number of scholarships to students from Afghanistan.

The numbers from Saudi Arabia were less than a hundred in the years before 2004–05 but rose to 419 in that year, and have continued to increase since then.

The student inflow from Sri Lanka and Bhutan has gone up and down, but not radically so. In both cases, the student population has yet to cross the 1,000 mark.

In the case of Kenya, the student inflow pattern is worrisome. It went from being in the 3,000s and 4,000s between 1990 and 1994 to being less than 1,000 in the years thereafter.

The student inflow from Oman effectively began in 1998–99 and rose steadily after 2004–05.

Student inflow from Yemen, although small, has been on the rise steadily.

The AISHE reports that, in the year 2012–13, the top 10 "sending countries" were Nepal (4,080), Afghanistan (2,066), Iraq (1,533), Sudan (1,512), Bhutan (1,437), Iran (1,096), Malaysia (686), Rwanda (652), Sri Lanka (447), and the USA (392) (MHRD, 2014).

The previously-mentioned dataset from the Foreigners Division, Ministry of Home Affairs, the Government of India, source in 2015 recorded numbers of international students that were categorized as such on the basis of student visas issued by the Ministry of Home Affairs between the year 2010 and 2013. Table 6.17 presents the provided dataset.

The numbers of students from Africa have been increasing steadily, except for the year 2011, when there was a dip. In particular, the increase in the years 2012 and 2013 has been remarkable. Of all the African countries, Sudan not only draws the most students, but also a sizeable segment. Tanzania is next, and also a significant "sender", followed by Uganda, Eritrea, and Libya.

Compared with the number of students from Africa in the dataset provided by AIU for the years 2014–05 to 2008–09, the increase in numbers is notable. The highest figure in the data from AIU is 4,193 (2008–09), whereas the highest figure in the dataset from the Foreigners Division, Ministry of Home Affairs, is 26,816 (2013). The significant increase in numbers between the two datasets (the one from AIU and the one from the Ministry of Home Affairs) could, partly, be explained on account of the difference in criteria

Table 6.17
International Students from the Top Five African Countries (Categorized on the Basis of Student Visas Issued by the Ministry of Home Affairs Between the Years 2010 and 2013)

		Number of Foreigners Registered on Student Visa				
Sl. No.	Top five African Countries	Continent	2010	2011	2012	2013
1.	Sudan	Africa	3,830	3,050	4,759	4,869
2.	Tanzania	Africa	1,128	1,021	1,641	NA
3.	Uganda	Africa	579	434	654	753
4.	Eritrea	Africa	340	192	316	622
5.	Libya	Africa	291	225	299	458
Total Number for All African Countries			**16,139**	**13,247**	**20,888**	**26,816**

Source: Personal communication, July 3, 2015.

that is applied to the two datasets. It stands to reason that students categorized on the basis of only visa are likely to outnumber students categorized on the basis of multiple criteria that are more restrictive in nature. Nonetheless, the increase is remarkable.

As with the dataset for years 2004–05 to 2008–09 (provided by AIU), the dataset that lists figures from the Foreigners Division, Ministry of Home Affairs, demonstrates that Asia continues to be the continent to send the most students. It is notable that the data related to the Foreigners Division, Ministry of Home Affairs, shows that the numbers for each of the four years revealed that Asia sends more than double the number of students as does Africa.

The numbers of international students from Asia have been steadily increasing, except for the year 2011, when it fell. The increase in the following year, 2012, is remarkable (7,479 students) as is the one for the next year, 2013 (10,161 students). The top five "senders" in descending order are Iran, Afghanistan, Yemen, Malaysia, and Sri Lanka (see Table 6.18).

The numbers of international students from Europe have been steadily increasing, except for the year 2011 when it fell (Table 6.19). France sends the most students and also a sizeable segment within

Table 6.18
International Students from the Top Five Asian Countries (Categorized on the Basis of Student Visas Issued by the Ministry of Home Affairs Between the Years 2010 and 2013)

			Number of Foreigners Registered on Students Visa			
Sl. No.	Top Five Asian Countries	Continent	2010	2011	2012	2013
1.	Iran	Asia	5,668	4,689	5,354	7,212
2.	Afghanistan	Asia	4,092	4,345	5,214	6,559
3.	Yemen	Asia	3,439	2,009	3,192	5,440
4.	Malaysia	Asia	3,131	3,401	4,494	4,007
5.	Sri Lanka	Asia	2,616	2,121	2,547	2,551
Total Number for Asian Countries			**38,525**	**34,656**	**42,135**	**52,296**

Source: Personal communication, July 3, 2015.

Table 6.19
International Students from the Top Five European Countries (Categorized on the Basis of Student Visas Issued by the Ministry of Home Affairs Between the Years 2010 and 2013)

			Number of Foreigners Registered on Students Visa			
Sl. No.	Top Five European Countries	Continent	2010	2011	2012	2013
1.	France	Europe	1,442	1,455	1,576	1,753
2.	Austria	Europe	145	127	118	125
3.	Sweden	Europe	139	145	170	254
4.	Finland	Europe	113	69	69	93
5.	Belgium	Europe	85	78	66	98
Total Number for European Countries			**5,676**	**5,632**	**6,064**	**7,101**

Source: Personal communication, July 3, 2015.

Europe; the numbers from France have been increasing as well. The top five "senders" from Europe are France, Austria, Sweden, Finland, and Belgium. It is to be noted that the majority of students from Europe come for short-term courses; therefore, the AIU data discards this group of students, resulting in significantly lower figures as compared with the figures from the data from the Foreigner Division, Ministry of Home Affairs.

In keeping with the trends for Asia and Africa, the increase in number of students from Europe from the dataset from AIU to the one from the Foreigners Division, Ministry of Home Affairs is remarkable.

The numbers from North America have been increasing steadily, except for the year 2011, when there was slight dip. It is notable that USA sends the most students from North America. Canada ranks next, but the numbers amount to almost one-quarter of those from the USA. Mexico follows Canada, but there is a significant decrease in the numbers. The numbers from Cuba and Trinidad and Tobago are not significantly high (see Table 6.20).

The numbers from South America have been increasing too, except for the year 2012, when they fell substantially, but rose to more than double the next year, 2013 (Table 6.21). The only country

Table 6.20
International Students from the Top Five North American Countries (Categorized on the Basis of Student Visas Issued by the Ministry of Home Affairs Between the Years 2010 and 2013)

Sl. No.	Top Five N American Countries	Continent	Number of Foreigners Registered on Students Visa			
			2010	2011	2012	2013
1.	USA	North America	4,707	4,630	4,752	5,646
2.	Canada	North America	930	770	781	939
3.	Mexico	North America	86	82	103	160
4.	Cuba	North America	34	5	5	5
5.	Trinidad & Tobago	North America	28	34	37	42
Total Number for North American countries			**1,130**	**953**	**988**	**1,237**

Source: Personal communication, July 3, 2015.

that sends significant numbers from South America is Brazil, and it is encouraging that the numbers from there have been steadily increasing during the years in question.

The numbers of international students from Oceania have been increasingly steadily, except for the year 2011, when there was small decrease (Table 6.22). Fiji is, by far, the largest "sender" of all the Oceania countries.

The numbers from Australia peaked in 2011 at 592, and have hovered around 300 for the other years (Table 6.23).

Russia, the only country in Eurasia, recorded the highest figure of international students—655—in 2012 (see Table 6.24).

It is important to note that one of the reasons that explain why the numbers from developed countries are so low is that these students typically come for short-term courses and, on this account, they do not qualify to count towards the figures of international students that are issued by AIU. On the other hand, the numbers from developing countries are as high as they are due to the fact of their being enrolled in degree programs. One hopes that, with the new image of India that

Table 6.21
International Students from the Top Five South American Countries (Categorized on the Basis of Student Visas Issued by the Ministry of Home Affairs Between the Years 2010 and 2013)

			Number of Foreigners Registered on Students Visa			
Sl. No.	Top Five S American Countries	Continent	2010	2011	2012	2013
1.	Brazil	South America	146	169	185	227
2.	Suriname	South America	55	46	6	5
3.	Colombia	South America	50	58	81	90
4.	Chile	South America	41	39	35	43
5.	Argentina	South America	30	37	44	68
Total Number for South American Countries			**414**	**447**	**282**	**575**

Source: Personal communication, July 3, 2015.

is being promoted by Hon'ble Prime Minister Mr Narendra Modi, the numbers from developed countries will rise. Students from these countries come to India for many reasons; an important one of which is their interest in and willingness to learn about the Indian culture.

Distribution of inbound international students in India on the basis of gross national income (GNI) per capita of the "sending" countries: The AIU (2009) study cited in Snehi (2012, p. 35–36) notes that of the 10 countries that were included, four were in the "high income" category. Amongst them, only Saudi Arabia recorded a consistent increase. The other three, UAE, Bahrain, and Oman did not show significant increase or decrease. The two "lower-middle income" countries (Iran and Sri Lanka) and the three "low-income" countries (Nepal, Ethiopia, and Afghanistan) have recorded a steady increase.

Table 6.22
International Students from the Top Five Oceania Countries (Categorized on the Basis of Student Visas Issued by the Ministry of Home Affairs Between the Years 2010 and 2013)

		Number of Foreigners Registered on Students Visa				
Sl. No.	Top Five Oceania Countries	Continent	2010	2011	2012	2013
1.	Fiji	Oceania	106	105	150	178
2.	New Zealand	Oceania	67	65	73	88
3.	Papua New Guinea	Oceania	6	1	12	12
4.	Samoa (West) Togolese	Oceania	2	2	2	–
5.	Vanuatu	Oceania	1	2	1	1
	Total Number for Oceania countries		**182**	**176**	**248**	**316**

Source: Personal communication, July 3, 2015.

Table 6.23
International Students from Australia (Categorized on the Basis of Student Visas Issued by the Ministry of Home Affairs Between the Years 2010 and 2013)

		Number of Foreigners Registered on Students Visa				
Sl. No.	Country	Continent	2010	2011	2012	2013
1	Australia	Australia	275	592	304	306

Source: Personal communication, July 3, 2015.

Table 6.24
International Students from Eurasia (Categorized on the Basis of Student Visas Issued by the Ministry of Home Affairs Between the Years 2010 and 2013)

		Number of Foreigners Registered on Students Visa				
Sl. No.	Country	Continent	2010	2011	2012	2013
1	Russia	Eurasia	527	635	655	613

Source: Personal communication, July 3, 2015.

Snehi (2012, p. 35–36) notes that in the year 2007–08, 65 percent international students came from low and lower middle income group countries, as shown in Table 6.25. Approximately, a quarter of the students came from high income countries and only six percent came from upper-middle income countries. A total of six, of the top 10 sending countries, fall in the low and lower-middle income group and the remaining four in the high income group. The six low and lower-middle income countries account for 40 percent of the total international student population. The SAARC member countries Nepal, Sri Lanka, Afghanistan, Bhutan, Bangladesh, Maldives, Myanmar, and Pakistan accounted for one-fourth of the student

Table 6.25
Inflow of International Students in India Distributed on the Basis of Gross National Income (GNI) of the "Sending" Countries

Countries	Income Group	2004–05	2005–06	2006–07	2007–08
Iran	Lower-middle	1,120	1,264	2,180	2,669
Nepal	Low	1,352	1,411	1,728	1,821
United Arab Emirate	High	1,500	2,034	1,878	1,560
Ethiopia	Low	226	302	1,033	1,289
Sri Lanka	Lower-middle	582	530	466	997
Afghanistan	Low	35	65	422	976
Saudi Arabia	High	419	551	771	835
Bahrain	High	382	481	446	600
Kenya	Low	418	523	621	592
Oman	High	646	505	608	548
Total		**6,680**	**7,666**	**10,153**	**11,887**
Total no. of foreign students in the year		**13,267**	**14,456**	**18,391**	**21,206**
% share of top ten countries		**50**	**53**	**55**	**56**

Source: Snehi (2013).

strength. Approximately, 45 percent students came from one of the University Mobility in the Indian Ocean Region (UMIOR) member countries: Iran, United Arab Emirate, Sri Lanka, Kenya, Oman, Yemen, Thailand, Mauritius, Bangladesh, Tanzania, Malaysia, Singapore, Indonesia, South Africa, Mozambique, Australia, Seychelles, and Madagascar.

Distribution of inbound international students in India on the basis of stream and discipline that the students are enrolled in: A study carried out by UGC and Information and Statistics Bureau in 2007, which was cited in Snehi (2012, pp. 38–39), demonstrates that the three streams Arts, Science, and Commerce and Management, account for the vast majority of international student enrollment in Indian higher education institutions. Student enrollment in Arts has been steady; it has increased over the years, but not remarkably so. On the other hand, the numbers in science have substantially decreased. Commerce and Management have continued to waver around 25 percent. The categories Engineering and Technology, and Medical Sciences have also continued to draw international students, although the enrollments have stayed quiet in the range of 7 percent and 13 percent. Other streams and disciplines draw smaller share of international students. For a better understanding, see Table 6.26.

The previously mentioned source notes that the total share of women in the international student group has shown an upward movement. Between 2002 and 2006, it rose from 34.59 percent to 39.3 percent. Also of note is that all disciplines, except veterinary sciences, have recorded an increase in the number of women students. Education has emerged as the most preferred discipline for women: more than 85 percent of students enrolled in it were women in 2005–06. Similarly, medical sciences recorded high enrollment of women. On the other hand, women enrollment in engineering and technology has been low. It was found to be in the neighborhood of 20 percent. If we add to this the finding that overall enrollment in engineering and technology is low in itself—close to 10 percent—then the numbers for women in the discipline would be marginal indeed.

Table 6.26
Distribution of Inbound International Students in India on the Basis of Stream and Discipline that the Students are Enrolled in (%)

Sl. No	Faculty	2002–03	2003–04	2004–05	2005–06
1.	Arts	20.01	20.8	25.47	25.05
2.	Science	27.29	20.8	16.32	13.84
3.	Commerce and Management	25.78	27.92	25.57	29.24
4.	Education	1.60	1.94	3.17	2.80
5.	Engineering and Technology	8.91	7.21	10.33	9.53
6.	Medical Sciences	9.74	11.4	12.13	12.49
7.	Agricultural Sciences	0.83	0.63	1.35	1.21
8.	Veterinary Sciences	0.11	0.08	0.20	0.19
9.	Law	2.41	2.03	2.31	2.26
10.	Others	3.33	3.59	3.15	3.39

Source: Snehi (2013).

The same study also elaborates on the distribution of international students on the basis of the level of the degree program that they were enrolled in. It emerged that undergraduate degree programs recorded the highest enrollment. Postgraduate programs lag far behind and recorded only one-quarter of the total share of international student enrollment. MPhil programs, which are a stepping stone to doctoral programs, enlisted the least number of students. On a positive note, it is observed that enrollment in MPhil programs is picking up. Enrollment in doctoral programs, unsurprisingly, is also low. In the year 2005–06, it was observed that short duration programs, including certificate and diploma programs, drew around eight percent of the total number of students from foreign countries. (It is to be noted that students enrolled in such programs do not qualify as international students, going by the UIS definition.)

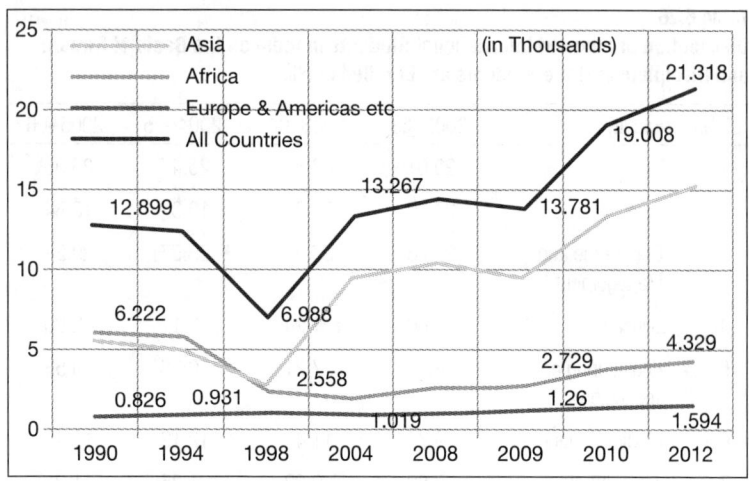

Figure 6.1 Number of Inbound International Students (in Thousands)

Source: AIU and UGC (adapted from Powar and Bhalla, 2014).

Figure 6.1 is information on international students from the year 2008–09 onwards, cited from CII-AIU (2014). As can be seen, the numbers for previous years in the following text are inconsistent with those noted earlier in the section; this variance presents on account of difference in the criteria that was utilized to identify international students by the source agencies. Please note that in some of the illustrations, the year for which the data is presented has not been noted CII-AIU (2014).

Salient features of the demographic profile of international students in Pune: Findings and Recommendation from a report on the data of international students in the city of Pune

Introduction to the Policy Context

Higher education is a pillar of the city of Pune's social and economic development. This is especially relatable within the context of knowledge economy, as investment in learning becomes a critical variable in the growth equation. Learning, at all levels, produces a workforce qualified to meet the demands of a growing economy, fosters advances in knowledge, generates financial revenues amongst local ancillary businesses and services, and adds to the socio-cultural ethos and the reputation of the city (and the region) that contributes to higher education processes and institutions. This serves a larger function—increases productivity, generates economic growth, and promotes India's international competitiveness.

As a key strategy to achieve the above goals, it is critical that education, especially education at the postsecondary level serve the requirements of the learners and prioritize its policies such that they succeed in meeting the higher education and career goals of learners.

At an entirely different level—of the institutions that participate in higher education—it is vital to ensure that learners are offered ready access to higher education opportunities. It is also critical that they continue successfully to graduation and are prepared to undertake whatever their aspiration might be—further education, work–study arrangements, or the career.

All of this assumes more complex "shadings and proportions" when applied to, not the general population of students, but a segment therein. It is important to bear in mind that such categorizations, whether they run along the lines of "disadvantaged" groups or not, are crucial because the demographic profiles, learning goals and outcomes, long-term aspirations, and many other such variables vary across student segments by a long way.

The student segment that is denoted as "international students" is one such special group. In the present times, the subject of international students has assumed importance, following many policy statements[2] and reports of working groups.[3]

Of note is the consideration that the majority of published literature, sourced from both academic and governmental bodies, tends to overlook aspects related to the demographic profile of international students. Some recent reports (Snehi, 2012) have outlined data and other information related to international students, but these are very few and cover the facts and figures at the national and not regional level.

At the issue is the point that an understanding of the spatial distribution of international students is an important matter because this distribution is not uniformly spread out over the length and breadth of the country, but concentrated in regional pockets. It is also demonstrated that international students in India are drawn to certain cities and institutions. In this sense, international student presence is far from homogenous. In descending order, the cities of Pune (29.30%), Delhi (20.48%), and Manipal (12.78%) have continued to lead the way (Powar, 2013, p. 38). The distribution of students in cities is clearly tied to institutions therein.

The city of Pune puts the state of Maharashtra at the top, so that the state accounted for 32.50 percent of international students, followed by Karnataka (22.37%), and New Delhi (20.48%; UGC, 2007, cited in Powar, 2012b, pp. 247–49). The city of Pune has dominated as steadfastly as it has because of two higher education institutions—the University of Pune and the Symbiosis International University. Between 2001 and 2002, the total number of international students who were enrolled in six universities in Pune was 2,057. This number grew to 3,000 in 2005–06. In the year 2011, the number doubled to 6,000. Patil (2014) notes that, in the year 2014, the population of international students in Pune stood at 10,166. This figure includes the figure released by AIU—7,290—which reflects the official enrolment in higher education institution at the graduate and postgraduate levels (cited in Powar, 2015, p. 161).

The universities, colleges, and other higher education institutions, which are many in number and cover practically all streams and levels, have a long-standing culture of excellence. There are also many research centers and laboratories that frequently work collaboratively with higher education institutions. The large network of multinational companies and enterprises add to the cosmopolitan culture of the city and offer career opportunities to graduates. The city has evolved over many decades, some might say a hundred years or more, and has been nourished by a culture that is not only conducive to higher education institutions, industry, and research and development, but also hospitable to international students.

The city of Pune presents a model for policymakers and researchers as they study demographic profiles of international students and their unique requirements and aspirations. This model has the potential to be of much value in grooming other Indian cities into centers of excellence in international education. Although favorable public policy and effective executive structure are necessary, an educational eco system that is not prepped and primed from the grounds up cannot sustainably support a sizeable international student population.

Overview of the Study

The Symbiosis Centre for International Education, a constituent division of the Symbiosis International University, in collaboration with the Foreign Registration Office, Pune Police, Pune, undertook an extensive research study to examine some salient features of the demographic profile of international students who were enrolled in programs and courses in postsecondary degree, diploma, and certificate in institutions of postsecondary education in the city of Pune between the years 2009 and 2014.

The purpose of the study was to ascertain certain key characteristics of international students with the view to gain more insights into the postsecondary education choices of this group. The larger guiding goal of the study is the Center's aim to deliver outcomes that may contribute to attainment of higher scores on the variables that are utilized in determining student satisfaction and engagement of those international students who are enrolled in institutions of postsecondary education in the city of Pune.

Outcomes of the Study

Key Findings and Recommendations

The data for the study was provided by the Foreign Registration Office, Pune Police, Pune, Maharashtra, India. The data included information of a large population of international students—21,541 students.

Of the respondents whose data included information about gender, the vast majority were males (78%). This trend is in keeping with findings from several previous published sources—male students routinely account for the vast majority of international enrolments.

The overwhelming majority of the students came from Asia (83%), followed by Africa (12%). Students from North America

(2.5%), Europe (2%), South America (0.1%) recorded miniscule representation. In this, the findings are consistent with the records at the level of the country, as supplied by AIU. The decline in students from Africa is a cause for concern at the national level too.

The top 10 "sending" countries in Asia are as follows:

Afghanistan	5,105
Iran	4,770
Yemen	1,885
Bahrain	1,150
Iraq	977
Korea	961
Bangladesh	256
Saudi Arabia	251
Oman	246
Turkmenistan	238

Similarly, the top 10 "sending" countries in Africa are as follows:

Sudan	556
Eritrea	258
Nigeria	221
Congo DCR	174
Tanzania	169
Libya	154
Uganda	93
Ethiopia	92
Kenya	84
Ghana	79

Several items in the questionnaire asked students to state the nature of their institutions and programs. Of the respondents who supplied information related to the management and ownership of their institutions, the majority stated that they were enrolled in public universities (60.5%). Furthermore, of the respondents who supplied information related to their program or course, the majority stated that they were enrolled in bachelors level programs (55%), followed by diploma or certificate program (32%), and masters (13%); the enrollment in doctoral programs was negligible.

As for the discipline and stream of enrollment, management (18%), recorded the highest enrolment, followed by arts (14%), commerce (12%), and engineering (6%); the category "other," which included the subjects that could not be categorized in any of the main groupings, recorded a little less than half the enrolment (46%). In a separate item, students were also invited to report whether their program of study fell in the "general" category or "professional." In response, almost three-quarters stated that their program was "professional." The broad trends in outcome related to institutions and programs in this survey are not inconsistent with those that emerged from a research study conducted by NUEPA in 2013, even if the figures for each of the categories vary.

The recommendations that follow from the findings are similar to recommendations that are presented across the book. First, efforts should be made to draw in more women students. Second, targeted schemes must be undertaken to increase enrollment of students from Africa. Furthermore, it is of concern that postgraduate programs continue to record less enrollment than undergraduate programs; doctoral programs, in particular, are grossly neglected by inbound international students. High enrollment at the postgraduate level is indicative of quality in higher education because postgraduate programs are the stepping stone to meaningful research. It is established that research in Indian institutions is substandard, if not entirely absent; therefore, it would not be far-fetched to hypothesize that this could be related to low enrolment in postgraduate programs.

Outflow of International Students in India

The outbound mobility of international students in India is a conspicuous phenomenon, not just at the national level but also at the global level. India sends the second largest number of international students, next only to China. Table 6.27 provides the figures related to outbound mobility of Indian students; Tables 6.28 and 6.29 provide

Table 6.27
Increase in the Number of Indian Students Going Abroad

Year	Total Number of Indian Students Abroad	Annual Growth Rate
1998	8,003	
1999	47,305	491
2000	53,266	13
2001	58,683	10
2002	91,189	55
2003	110,716	21
2004	125,881	14
2005	138,072	10
2006	136,238	−1
2007	154,116	13
2008	176,454	14
2009	190,781	8

Source: Snehi (2013).

the leading destination countries, and Table 6.30 shows the leading destination regions for outbound Indian students.

The outbound mobility has gathered force in the last decade or so. The number of Indian students in foreign universities has grown from 53,266 to 190,781 during the period 2000–09, reflecting 258 percent growth. Moreover, the annual growth rates have remained over eight percent, except for the year 2005–06 (UNESCO, cited in Snehi, 2012, p. 26).

The regional distribution of students from India enrolled in foreign universities is heavily jagged. North America and Western Europe account for not only the largest share, but the overwhelming majority. Further, the numbers have continued to grow steadily over the years, except for the year 2006, at which point, there was a slight dip.

East Asia and the Pacific region follow. These regions have also shown increased inflow of Indian students. The only remarkable variation was the year 2001, when the numbers fell, but, in an upturn, they spiked the following year.

Table 6.28
Major Destinations of Indian Students

Country	1999	2000	2001	2002	2003	2004	2005	2006	2007	2008	2009
United States of America	34,504	39,084	47,411	66,836	74,603	79,736	84,044	79,219	85,687	94,664	101,563
Australia	3,697	4,578	–	9,539	12,384	15,742	20,515	22,357	24,523	26,520	26,573
UK and Northern Ireland	3,922	3,962	4,302	6,016	10,422	14,625	16,685	19,204	23,833	25,901	34,065
China	–	–	–	–	–	–	–	–	–	7,234	–
Singapore	–	–	–	–	–	–	–	–	–	6,700	–
Russian Federation	–	–	–	–	–	–	–	–	–	4,314	4,286
New Zealand	73	201	355	952	1,205	1,698	1,563	–	2,452	4,094	5,710
Canada	804	969	1,314	1,830	2,472	2,724	2,829	1,812	3,219	3,501	–
Germany	1,004	1,282	1,412	2,196	3,429	4,237	4,339	3,585	3,421	3,257	3,273
Ukraine	–	–	–	–	–	–	957	1,170	1,466	1,785	2,180
Malaysia	91	714	497	965	930	844	–	813	897	1,065	1,152

Source: Snehi (2013).

Table 6.29
Outflow of Indian Students

Country of Destination	Number of International Students
United States	103,968
United Kingdom	38,205
Australia	20,429
New Zealand	6,650
Canada	4,617
Russian Federation	4,286
Germany	3,867
Ukraine	2,413
Sweden	1,596
Cyprus	1,506
France	1,444
Ireland	1,396
Malaysia	1,152
Japan	576

Source: International Student Flow, UIS, UNESCO, August 2014, United Nations Education,
Scientific and Cultural Organization.

Distribution of the data on the basis of countries shows that the US is ahead by head and shoulders. The numbers have continued to increase, except for the years 2004 and 2005 in which period there was a fall.

Australia, and UK and Northern Ireland (the last two countries form a singular category) have shown continued growth in numbers. Although Australia has drawn more students from India in some years, the UK and Northern Ireland have led in others.

Of note is the incidence of increase in the number of countries that host students from India—amongst these, New Zealand, Canada, Germany, and Malaysia are very prominent.

The data provided in Table 6.31 and Figure 6.2 on outbound international students from India is sourced from Project Atlas, IIE, report published in 2013 and cited in CII-AIU (2014). The difference in numbers is quite significant, and reflects the difference in criteria utilized for identifying outbound international students.

Table 6.30
Region-wise Distribution of Indian Students in the Period 1998–2009

Region	1999	2000	2001	2002	2003	2004	2005	2006	2007	2008	2009
Arab States	230	4	11	11	350	347	389	367	365	957	1,023
Central and Eastern Europe	486	352	623	631	589	875	2,287	2,375	2,781	7,343	7,315
Central Asia	666	682	1,054	226	985	1,313	1,624	1,990	1,628	2,260	1,637
East Asia and the Pacific	4,236	5,726	1,260	1,1931	15,069	19,333	23,172	24,282	29,089	33,263	34,781
Latin America and the Caribbean	21	25	19	24	5	18	3	12	17	62	200
North America and Western Europe	41,609	46,473	55,687	78,362	93,713	103,930	110,548	107,152	120,209	132,557	145,814
South and West Asia	0	0	0	0	0	56	45	48	25	10	2
Sub Saharan Africa	57	4	29	4	5	9	4	12	2	2	9
Total	47,305	53,266	58,683	91,189	110,716	125,881	138,072	136,238	154,116	176,454	190,781

Source: Snehi (2013).

Table 6.31
Top Destination of Indian Students

Year	USA	UK	Australia	Canada	NZ	China	Germany	Total
2012	96,754	31,595	12,629	28,929	11,349	10,237	5,745	197,238
2011	100,270	29,900	15,395	23,601	12,301	9,370	4,825	228,774
2010	103,895	39,09	21,932	17,549	11,616	9,014	3,821	253,743
2009	104,897	38,500	28,020	9,561	9,252	8,468	3,236	247,631
2008	103,260	34,065	28,411	8,325	6,348	8,145	3,217	216,516
2007	94,563	25,905	27,078	7,304	3,855	7,190	3,431	205,852
2006	83,833	19,228	25,497	6,927	2,599	3,245	3,583	158,215
2005	76,503	16,872	22,529	6,688	N/A	N/A	3,807	N/A

Source: CII-AIU (2014).

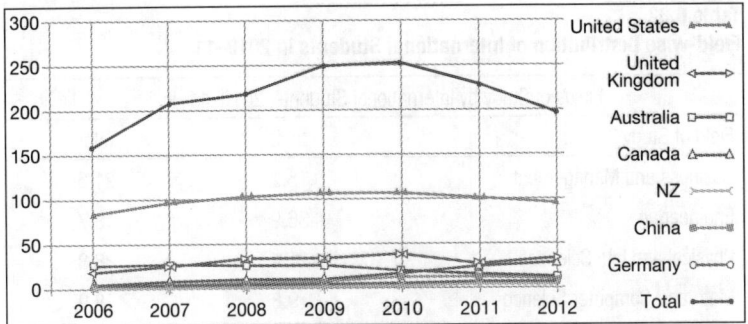

Figure 6.2 Top Destinations of Indian Students and Outflow of Indian Students to Different Destinations

Source: CII-AIU (2014).

Distribution of Outbound Students in India on the Basis of Field of Study

The data for the year 2010–11 reveals that STEM disciplines (Science, Technology, Engineering, and Medicine) are clearly the favored choices. In that year, engineering scored the highest (36.9%), followed by math and computer sciences (19.8%), business and management (15.2%), and physical and life sciences (11.4%). For more details, see Table 6.32.

This is certainly a departure from the top choices that the students in India are shown to make in selecting streams and disciplines within the Indian higher education system. As stated previously, in the year 2010–11, the arts made up the largest share (36.3%), followed by science (18.4%), commerce and management (17.11%), and engineering and technology (16.86%). This finding is a call to policymakers to wade into the waters of quality improvement in the teaching and learning of STEM disciplines.

Report on a Survey of Perceptions of International Students

The Symbiosis Center for International Education (SCIE), a constituent institute of Symbiosis International University (SIU),

Table 6.32
Field-wise Distribution of International Students in 2010–11

Fields of Study by International Students, 2010–11, in %		
Field of Study	India	Total
Business and Management	15.2	21.5
Engineering	36.9	18.7
Physical and Life Sciences	11.4	8.8
Math and Computer Science	19.8	8.9
Social Sciences	3.0	8.8
Fine and Applied Arts	1.3	5.1
Health Professions	4.9	4.5
Intensive English Language	0.7	4.5
Education	1.0	2.3
Humanities	0.6	2.2
Agriculture	–	1.4
Other Fields of Study	4.7	10.5
Undeclared	0.5	2.8
Total	100	100

Source: Snehi (2013).

Pune, India, presented a research study based on the findings and recommendations that emerged from a survey that was conducted amongst international students (Yeravdekar & Tiwari, 2012).

The guiding idea was to determine several aspects of the international student experience in Pune. The overall level of student satisfaction and engagement is one of the key benchmarks of quality-assurance management and the lack of matrices to evaluate this presents challenge to educationists and policymakers alike. Institutional research must be the bedrock of public policy on higher education, but it is observed that such is not the case in India.

The survey was designed to capture, in a scientific manner, an overview of the demographic profile and perceptions of international students and their engagement with the host institution and the country. The findings that emerged from the survey were utilized to extrapolate the characteristics of international students in Pune and also the nature of internationalization in India. In other words, the survey report was designed to answer the question, "What sets internationalization in India apart?" The salient characteristics of international student mobility and other aspects of internationalization vary from country to country, and it is important to identify and determine these defining characteristics.

The survey revealed that the overwhelming majority of international student population in Pune is young—the vast majority being in their mid-twenties. The gender distribution was shown to be skewed significantly in the favor of male students. There were three times as many male students as female. These two trends are in keeping with the national trends that were noted in other research studies. It could be that these are results of factors related to the Indian higher education system or those related to higher education systems in sending countries. The vast majority of students were reportedly single—not a surprising finding considering that a similar proportion of students were young.

The survey yielded interesting outcomes related to nationality, ethnicity, and first language. The country to top the list was Afghanistan, and Iran stood second. Amongst the first languages, Arabic stood first, followed by Dari, Persian, Pashto, English, and Nepali. (Dari is spoken in Afghanistan and Iran, and Pashto in Afghanistan.) The ethnicities that garnered the most responses were Afghan, Pashtan, Hazara, and Arab. The information related to languages and ethnicities is particularly valuable because it is not generally found in published data.

The outcomes related to regional distribution were very consistent with those in research studies at the national level. It emerged that the neighboring countries to the west of India send more students than those to the east. Apart from Nepal, none of the countries to the east are strong markets. Not surprisingly, all of the student respondents stated that they were in India on student visa.

The information related to the highest level of education attained is important to determining and predicting student success and retention. Somewhat less than one-third of the students had attained postsecondary education before coming to India. Equal numbers of students had completed secondary and graduate degrees; these were followed by the group that marked undergraduate degrees. The group that had attained postgraduate degrees was the smallest. Consistent with this was the outcome that the overwhelming majority of students were registered in undergraduate degree level programs; the postgraduate degrees recorded very low enrolment and the doctoral programs none.

Amongst the reasons for exploring higher education alternatives outside home country, the popular results were "quality of education" (ranked first) followed by "political instability," "income constraints," "personal/professional growth," and "social issues."

Of the top three choices of countries for higher education, the US ranked first followed by the UK, Canada, and Australia. It is notable that these are all English speaking countries.

Amongst the factors that helped students select India, "the quality of education" emerged as the top response, followed by financial issues such as "cost of living," "availability of scholarship," and "culture."

In stating their top three preferred Indian cities as destinations for higher education, the students favored Pune followed by Delhi, and Bangalore. The University of Pune, the Symbiosis International University, and the University of Delhi ranked as the top preferences for higher education institutions in India.

Amongst the sources responsible for the student's awareness of their institutions, the vast majority reported that they learned about their institution "from friends," and a small percentage said it was "advertisements and the University website."

The top factors that led students to select their institution were quality of education, reputation, and infrastructure. The "quality of education" in Indian institutions was also the top reason why international students explored higher education alternatives outside their home country and selected India.

Responses to miscellaneous administrative factors such as "student visa processing," "laws," "safety," and "infrastructure" were temperate. Responses to socio-economic parameters such as "cost of living" and "language barrier," and "level of acceptance" were also middling. The students reported that their perception of institutional resources such as "infrastructure," "admissions procedure," "campus accommodation," "specializations of course offerings," and "student support services" was passable.

On the whole, more than three-fourths reported that they would recommend India. It could be inferred that strengthening networks with embassies and other diplomatic offices would offer useful outlets for the purpose of enhancing student services and student relations.

To questions related to the awareness of and integration with the socio-cultural landscape of the country, the majority of students responded in the affirmative but almost half stated that they found the "transition to life as an international student" difficult. The biggest challenges were "the language barrier," "encounters with the law and order authorities for the purpose of registration," and "accommodation."

The students' perception of India with respect to the cost of living was temperate. About half of them stated that India was more expensive than their country. The top two source of funding were "parents or guardians" and "scholarships." The majority of respondents stated that their monthly expenditure was in the range of ₹10,000 to ₹15,000. Further, the top three areas of expenditure incurrence were housing, food, and transportation.

The survey revealed that the international student population in Pune is not different from that at the national level in respect of the demographic profile. The results with respect to student awareness, perception, and attitudes with respect to socio-cultural administrative aspects were middling, as were those regarding satisfaction and engagement with the institution. An important finding is that this student group is "walking a tight rope" in terms of finances and would greatly benefit from assistance on this front.

Outflow of International Students from India to the US

At present, India sends the second largest number of international students to the US. At a broad level, there has been a growing trend in the yearly data of outflow of students from India to the US, even

Table 6.33
Top Three Sending Countries' Share of International Students in the US (2006–13)

Year	China	India	South Korea
2006	11%	14%	9%
2007	12%	14%	9%
2008	13%	15%	11%
2009	–	15%	11%
2010	18%	15%	10%
2011	22%	14%	10%
2012	25%	13%	9%
2013	29%	12%	9%

Source: Institution of International Education.
Note: Adapted from *A closer look at US enrolment growth,* ICEF Monitor (2013).

if the numbers have dipped in a few instances. The other remarkable pattern is that India is falling farther behind in comparison to China as the top "sender" of international students to the US. Table 6.33 notes the numbers of students from the top three sending countries enrolled in the US between 2006 and 2013.

The number of Indian students in the US in 2011–12 dropped 3.5 percent compared to the previous year, marking two consecutive years of decline. India had been the leading place of origin for international students in the US from 2001–02 through 2008–09. In 2000–01, there was a surge in enrollments from India, with an increase of 30 percent followed by two more years of strong growth (12 percent in 2002–03 and 7 percent in 2003–04). The increases tapered off in 2004–05 and then decreased slightly in 2005–06 before resuming much larger increases in 2006–07 and for the next two years. In 2009–10, the increases leveled off, and China became the top sender and remains in that position. Students from India make up approximately 13.1 percent of the total foreign student population in United States (IIE, n.d.a).

According to the Institute of international Education, the majority of international students from India in the US are enrolled in graduate programs. In the year 2011–12, only 13 percent were enrolled in undergraduate programs, whereas 58.9 percent were enrolled in graduate programs, 1.5 percent in the category "other and 26.7 percent in "Optional Practical Training." According to Open Doors 2010, the top three fields of study for Indian students were engineering, math and computer science, and business and management (IIE, n.d.b)

The Office of US–India Higher Education Cooperation (USIHEC) is an important channel through which academic exchanges come about between higher education institutions in the US and India in areas of collaborative research, study abroad programs, faculty exchanges and seminars for higher education administrators. The USIHEC also administers the Indo-US 21st Century Knowledge Initiative (formerly known as the Obama–Singh 21st Century Knowledge Initiative) awards and maintains a database of Indo–US Educational Collaborations. Some of its more recent activities are as follows:

1. *Fulbright–Nehru International Education Administrators Grants*: This includes organization of capacity building seminars for American and Indian higher education administrators.
2. *Study Abroad Capacity Assessment Projects*: These are collaborative projects between IIE, Forum on Education Abroad, and American Association of Community Colleges that are funded by the US Department of State's Bureau of Educational and Cultural Affairs.
3. *Transforming Boundaries: Community College Development in India*: This project was a result of US Department of State grant to Montgomery College. The aim was to help build capacity in vocational and technical education in India. The project resulted in the development of successful community college models for India. The program focused specifically on faculty development and training, student affairs and support systems, aligning training programs with local and emerging industry, and organizing an online symposium on topics related to the growth of community colleges in India.
4. *Association of US Academic Programs in India (AUSAPI) Annual Conference*: USIHEC hosts the annual conference for AUSAPI. As a part of the conference activities, resident directors from US study abroad programs based in India as well as administrators from American and Indian academic institutions are invited to share best practices.

The Obama–Singh 21st Century Knowledge Initiative (US–India Institutional Partnership Grants)

The United States–India Educational Foundation (USIEF) administers an open competition for the support of projects through the Obama–Singh 21st Century Knowledge Initiative (OSI). The OSI aims to strengthen collaboration between American and Indian institutions of higher education, facilitate educational reforms, and foster economic development. The activities that are undertaken include curriculum design, research collaboration, team teaching, focused series of exchanges, and seminars. Typically, project proposals are invited in the fields of energy, climate change and environmental studies, education and educational reform, public health, and sustainable development and community development.

Popular Vehicles of Academic Mobility Within Cross-border Higher Education in India

Academic mobility of cross-border higher education refers to mobility across countries that occurs within the purview of academic exchanges. It might be more useful to understand this in a reductionist manner as mobility that excludes nonacademic exchanges, such as the ones concerned with corporate training, deployment of experts, feasibility studies, edutourism, and developmental assistance. Thus, academic mobility is marked-out by the nature of content of exchange, and not on the grounds if it takes place between institutions of higher education or not.

Student mobility is clearly the most popular form of academic mobility. A large number of students travel across countries, sponsored and supported by programs and schemes, some of which are instituted by global bodies (such as the UN) others are the results of multilateral or bilateral arrangements (such as Erasmus Mundus and ICCR scholarships). The following are *representative* examples of popular instruments of student mobility. (Please also see the section on internationalization of higher education and "soft power" for additional programs and activities.)

1. *Erasmus Mundus program*: Erasmus Mundus program is frequently confused with the Erasmus program. The former is really a division within the latter. The Erasmus Mundus program is open to non-Europeans, whereas the Erasmus program is for European nationals only.

   The Erasmus program (European Community Action Scheme for the Mobility of University Students) is an initiative of the European Union student exchange program established in 1987. The Erasmus Mundus Program runs parallel to the Erasmus program and is geared towards globalizing European education. Erasmus Mundus composed of three divisions: joint programs, partnerships, and attractiveness projects.

   (i) Joint programs: These include master and doctorate degrees that are operated by consortia of higher education institutions from the EU and elsewhere. These programs offer integrated courses and joint diplomas in award of study or research at two or more higher education institutions.

   (ii) Partnerships: Partnership projects bring together higher education institutions from Europe and from a designated region in the world. The partnerships regulate academic mobility between Europe and the region for a range of exchanges.

   (iii) Attractiveness projects: These projects serve to enhance the attractiveness and visibility of European higher education in foreign countries. Frequently, the projects focus on a region or a stream.

   The Erasmus Mundus is a popular instrument of outbound mobility for Indian students. Scholarship schemes commonly availed by Indian students include Erasmus Mundus India to Europe scholarship program, India4EU, India4EU II, Interdisciplinary Bridges for Indo–European Studies, and HERITAGE.

2. *Deutscher Akademischer Austauschdienst (DAAD)*: The German Academic Exchange Service supports international exchange of students and scholars. Since it was founded in 1925, it has funded more than 1.5 million scholars in Germany and abroad. It receives monetary support from the German Federal Foreign Office, the European Union, and other agencies.

   The DAAD has an extensive operation network in India. Its regional office was established in 1960. It promotes academic exchange between Germany and India, Bangladesh, Bhutan, Nepal, and

Sri Lanka. It disseminates information on the education in Germany, grants scholarships, promotes academic exchanges between South Asian countries and Germany, and supports bilateral research projects.

The DAAD Regional Office, New Delhi, has close ties with DST, Department of Education, MHRD, UGC, CSIR, ICCR, IIT, and IIM.

3. *Study India Program (SIP)*: An exemplary model of international education is the Study India Program. The program aims to further international students' personal and professional portfolio by opening up the Indian culture to them. The project was initiated by the Symbiosis International University in India. In light of its rewarding outcome, the program was adopted by other Indian universities and formally instituted by the Ministry of Overseas Indian Affairs (the Government of India) as an instrument of promoting awareness and interest in Indian culture through higher education in foreign countries. The program comprises of short courses that offer insight into the Indian culture in a manner that is engaging and informative. The courses frequently utilize instructional excursions, which help students to absorb course content effectively. The students are selected on grounds of merit alone, and they are supported financially and offered assistance to ensure that their sojourn is productive, even if it is brief. Powar (2015, p. 188) notes that the number of students currently coming to India through SIP stands at about 1,000.

It would be fair to hold that the program has proved its worth. It has been administered skillfully, and has gained popularity in the short period that it has been in effect.

A number of organizations and institutions are working towards promoting SIP and study abroad programs for Indian institutions, such as IIE, New York; United States–India Educational Foundation, New Delhi; American Institute of Indian Studies, Chicago; Council of International Educational Exchange, Hyderabad; Nordic Centre in India; MHRD; Symbiosis International University, Pune; Jawaharlal Nehru University, New Delhi; Ministry of Overseas Indian Affairs; University of Hyderabad, Hyderabad; University of Goa, Goa; and Lovely Professional University, Jalandhar (Powar, 2015).

A listing in IIE Passport indicates that many American universities collaborate with Indian institutions and organizations to offer study abroad programs and SIP in India. Some of them are Brown University, Duke University, Emory University, Michigan State

University, Temple University, University of Iowa, and University of Virginia are some of them.

Powar (2015) lists some private organizations that offer SIP in India to foreign students. These organizations frequently operate out of rented premises, hire part-time staff, and make use of home-stay arrangements for the visiting students. Some examples are IES Abroad, Delhi; SIT Study Abroad, Jaipur, Delhi, and Leh; Alliance for Global Education, Pune; South India Term Abroad, Madurai; University Studies Abroad Consortium, Bengaluru; BCA Study Abroad, Pondicherry and Chennai; and International Partnership for Service–Learning, Kolkata (p. 194).

4. *Study Abroad Programs*: Study Abroad Programs (SAP), although not being specific to India, have served to bring very many international students to India. It is notable that these programs have successfully brought students from North America and Europe and, in doing so, they have fared far better than other modes. Powar (2015) opines that SAPs have been very successful and recommends that there is potential for more. These programs are aimed at improving cross-cultural competencies of students so that they become more appreciative of other cultures and more at home outside their country.

These programs were conceived and introduced to the world by American educationists. It was opined by many of them that American undergraduates lacked exposure to international experience, especially cross-cultural communication skills, and knowledge of foreign languages. In fact, the American Council on Education, 1995, came out with a report that detailed the American students' failings in this regard and the need for steps to push these students out of their comfort zone. A similar sentiment was expressed two decades later by Goodman and Berden (2014).

The SAPs vary quite a lot in duration: three to six weeks; one semester (12–14 weeks); or an academic year (9–10 months). According to Open Doors (IIE, 2013), 59 percent of students opt for short-term programs (less than eight weeks); 38 percent for a semester; and 3 percent for an academic year.

The top three preferred streams are social sciences (22%), management (21%), and humanities (11%).

In the discussion on SAPs in the context of India, Chow and Cho (2011, cited in Powar 2015) point out that mission statements related to these programs could be categorized in the following groups:

1. Programs that cover knowledge about India, especially the socio-political-cultural aspect
2. Programs related to community or project research, awareness, and placement
3. Programs that are service centerd and related to socio-humanitarian issues, such as poverty alleviation, public health, or public education
4. Programs oriented to the development of leadership and management skills or sensitization to the concept of global citizenship

Powar (2015) mentions that many American universities were discouraged by Indian universities' unenthusiastic approach towards partnership and decided to conduct SAPs all on their own or in collaboration with private enterprises. This resulted in taking away any level of academic rigor from the programs and turning them into "grand tour" models of international education (p. 194).

There is no consensus on the number of students who come to India for these programs. Figures released by IIE are much higher than those by UGC or any other Government of India agencies. Again, this could be explained by the variation in the criteria that is used to judge who qualifies as a Study Abroad student and who does not. There is another gray zone. Often times, orientation programs such as "Connect with India" are wrongly categorized as Study Abroad programs. It is important to lay down the specific conditions that must be met before a program is declared to be Study Abroad. For all this to materialize successfully, a centralized supervisory body must be constituted in partnership with one of the Government of India agencies related to higher education: UGC, AIU, or NUEPA.

Emerging Avenues in Distance Education

Distance education is a gift of technological advancements in communication. It is an area of immense expansion, in terms of both enrollment and the number of modes of instructional delivery that are utilized. Distance education, as the name implies, refers to that form of teaching–learning in which the student and the instructor are not present with in the physical confines of the classroom. Distance education heralded a new era in pedagogy, marking a shift away from the traditional classroom instructions.

It has its limitations and is considered a peripheral form of higher education by many traditionalists. Frequently, the sphere of distance education is not included in studies that examine the state of higher education in India and other countries. That being said, this area is set for more growth and for commanding more space in the mainstream higher education system.

Conventional distance education, which utilizes print and audio–video material, is well-suited to "general education." More recently, distance education delivery mechanisms have added online portals, which are better suited to meet the requirements of professional–vocational streams and disciplines. Online portals have greatly enhanced the opportunities in distance education because students who aspire to attain education in nonconventional areas, such as continuing education, independent studies, and personal enrichment programs, see distance education mode as the more suitable option for them. Add to this the case that professionals and people who are outside the "higher education demographic" bracket seek higher education with the view to either add to their professional or academic repertoire or to increase their personal capabilities. Distance mode allows these students to pursue their higher education goals without disrupting other commitments. The last few years have witnessed two developments in the realm of distance education—the advent of Open Education Resources (OER) and MOOCs.

It is no surprise that distance education is important in the discussion on the internationalization. This mode, especially the Internet-based delivery systems within distance education, does not require additional investments in order to expand reaches across borders. Powar (2015) cites the example of the Commonwealth of Learning, Vancouver, Canada, which has utilized the distance education mode to acquire a transnational character. Powar and Bhalla (2014) noted that, in the year 2008–09, AIU reported that 5,861 overseas students were enrolled in Indian institutions in distance education programs. These figures are very low compared with equivalent figures for the same year for UK (112,000) and Australia (16,000) (as cited in Powar, 2015, p. 87).

It is to be noted that distance education, as part of trade in cross-border higher education, has not been an object of critical attacks by those who fear that GATS could spell commoditization of higher education and exploitation of developing countries. This is so because distance education involves program mobility, with people and physical resources playing subordinate roles.

Virtual universities merit note in the discussion on internationalization. In the developed countries, these are mainly privately managed and in developing publicly managed. In India, BITS Virtual University at Pilani, which is privately managed, is a prominent example. The University offers a whole range of web courses to students, many of whom are spread across borders (Powar, 2015).

India's undertakings in this area are of note in light of their contributory role in the neighboring countries in Asia and Africa. Three factors, that explain why it is that way, are to be borne in mind. These are India's generally strong reputation as provider of quality higher education, Indian Diaspora's inclination to the Indian higher education system, especially distance education, and India's lead in technology related innovations.

India's achievements are quite impressive. India has 14 open universities and more than 200 distance education centers in dual mode universities. Of the 14 open universities, six are mega universities (they record more than one million enrolments; Powar, 2015, p. 91). These institutions cater to catchment areas and groups of international students that are no different from areas and groups that "send" international students to traditional institutions.

It is relatable that IGNOU is the largest open or distance learning institution in the world and boasts centers all over the world and enrolls 6,000 overseas students. In light of its past success, it has ambitious plans to expand its reach in West Asia and Africa. Under the Pan-African e-Network Project, IGNOU plans to connect 53 countries in Africa. Further, IGNOU has signed memorandums of understanding with 16 African countries to offer tele-education at all levels: diploma/certificate, under graduate, postgraduate, and doctoral level. The thrust of these programs is professional education, especially management education (Nanda, 2011, as cited in Powar, 2015, p. 92).

Some cautionary words are in order. Although it is indisputable that technological advancements are bound to render higher education more of an "individual-oriented" and less of an "institution-oriented" experience, distance education for offshore students is beset with complexities. First, Indian institutions must be aware of the level of technology that is available to overseas students in each of the countries that provides students. It is not enough that Indian institution have sufficiently high level of instructional–technological delivery methods. In other words, free accessibility and affordability are just as important as availability.

Open Education Resources (OER): UNESCO-COL (2011) defines OERs as follows:

> teaching learning, and research materials in any medium that lie in the public domain, or have been released under an open licence, that permit their free use, and in some instances, re-proposing by others . . . Open educational resources can include full courses, course materials, modules, text books research articles, videos, tests, software, and any other tools, materials, or techniques used to support access to knowledge. (As cited in Powar, 2015, p. 94)

The key idea is that these resources are not only open in their availability, but also freely available.

The most prominent exponent and propagator of OER is Massachusetts Institute of Technology (MIT)—MIT-OCW (MIT OpenCourseWare). Two international organizations—Commonwealth of Learning and UNESCO—have further propelled the concept of OER in the last few years.

Taking cues from the success of OER in developed countries, India has taken some steps in this direction as well: the National Programme on Technology Enhanced Learning (NPTEL), which is a joint venture of five IITs and IISc; the Virtual Academy for the Semi-Arid Tropics (VASAT), a division of the International Crops Research Institute of the Semi-Arid Tropics (ICRISAT); and FlexiLearn, a division of IGNOU (Powar, 2015).

The MOOCs refer to the making available to the masses online courses freely and openly. The credit of the genesis of MOOCs, as with OER, goes to MIT.

India is uniquely suited to MOOCs. A very large higher education demographic, extensive technological advancement in telecom, and a very high regard for higher education systems in developed countries make for some compelling factors in favor of expansion of MOOCs in India.

The MHRD has launched a MOOCs program—Study Webs of Active-learning for Young Aspiring Minds (SWAYAM)—in 2014. The program brings together IITs, IIMs, and central universities to offer free online courses through a web platform.

It is also notable that edX, a major MOOCs provider, has partnered with IIT Mumbai to offer courses. Similarly, Powar (2015, p. 108) notes that a survey conducted by Coursera, another major MOOCs provider, revealed that Indians constitute the second largest student segment.

Although MOOCs are all set to transform the higher education system in developed countries, especially the US, it is still too early to know to what extent they will impact the Indian higher education system.

Notes

1. A brief mention of the total number of international students and a gender-based splitting of the figure for the years 2012–13 and 2013–14 is provided by AISHE, as is noted later in the text.
2. The Twelfth Five Year Plan and the National Knowledge Commission's Report to the Nation.
3. The Amritsar Statement (2002) and the Mysore Statement (2001; AIU).

References

Agarwal, P. (n.d.a). International India a turning point in educational exchange with the US. Retrieved from http://www.usief.org.in/USIHEC/Chapter%204/Internationalization%20of%20Indian%20Higher%20Education.pdf (accessed on January 13, 2013).

Agarwal, P. (n.d.b). Privatization and internationalization of higher education in the countries of South Asia: An empirical analysis. New Delhi, India: Indian Council for Research on International Economic Relations (ICRIER).

British Council. (2012). *The shape of things to come: Higher education global trends and emerging opportunities to 2020*. Retrieved from https://www. britishcouncil.org/sites/default/files/the_shape_of_things_to_come_-_ higher_education_global_trends_and_emerging_opportunities_to_2020. pdf (accessed on July 20, 2016).

————. (2013). *The future of the world's mobile students to 2024*. Retrieved from https://ei.britishcouncil.org/educationintelligence/future-world-mobile-students-2024 (accessed on July 20, 2016).

Chhapia, H. (2014, February 23). Brain drain in reverse: China now world's no. 3 education hub. *The Times of India*. Retrieved from http://timesofindia. indiatimes.com/home/education/news/Brain-drain-in-reverse-China-now-worlds-No-3-education-hub/articleshow/30811833.cms (accessed on April 6, 2016).

CII-AIU. (2014). *Trends in Internationalization of Higher Education in India*. Retrieved from http://www.cii.in/PublicationDetail.aspx?enc=j+Bre1cn EnR7Sgogrka6KohkwpLy3x9ujfczyTnGBH8Pk1aE4ly77FRtKBZo0Yz FiVaGJLen1cG0O7iLKWe0szJJQOYv17/2Ud9piEIB1wUYJCzxAaL6 W6HZ0zrocFkdwNvqqO5gbqDAYy8PbqfcNF4MgwGKS4CIAGsf4gw YhRVEQZuVQeUSm/p9oCvxp9Ll (accessed on April 6, 2016).

Dongaonkar, D., & Negi, U. R. (2009). *International students in Indian universities 2007–08*. New Delhi: Association of Indian Universities.

ICEF Monitor. (2013). *A closer look at US enrolment growth*. Retrieved from http://monitor.icef.com/2013/11/a-closer-look-at-us-enrolment-growth/ (accessed on April 6, 2016).

IIE. (n.d.a). *India open doors*. Retrieved from www.iie.org/~/media/Files/ Corporate/.../India-Open-Doors-2013.ashx (accessed on April 6, 2016).

————. (n.d.b). *Open doors*. Retrieved from http://www.iie.org/Research-and-Publications/Open-Doors (accessed on April 6, 2016).

Kumar, P., Sarkar, S., & Sharma, R. (2009, May). *Migration and diaspora formation: Mobility of Indian students to the developed world* (IMDS Working Paper Series Nos. 7–9). New Delhi: Jawaharlal Nehru University

Ministry of Human Resource Development (MHRD). (2014). *Educational statistics at a glance*. Retrieved from http://mhrd.gov.in/sites/upload_files/ mhrd/files/statistics/EAG2014.pdf (accessed on April 6, 2016).

Ministry of Overseas Indian Affairs. (2015). *Population of overseas Indians*. Retrieved from http://moia.gov.in/accessories.aspx?aid=10 (accessed on April 6, 2016).

Powar, K. B. (2012a). *Indian higher education revisited*. NOIDA, India: Vikas Publishing.

————. (2012b). *Expanding domains in Indian higher education*. New Delhi, India: Association of Indian Universities Publications.

————. (2013). *Understanding internationalization of higher education*. Pune: DY Patil.

Powar, K. B. (2015). *Changing landscape of international higher education: An Indian perspective*. Pune: DY Patil.

Powar K. B. and Bhalla, V. (2014). International students in Indian universities: Source countries, gender ratio, levels of education, and choice of disciplines. *AIU Occasional Papers 2014/1*. New Delhi: AIU.

Salmi, J. (2009). *The challenge of establishing world-class universities*. Washington D.C., US: The World Bank.

Sinha, K. (2013, December 15). By 2024, 1 in 3 foreign pupils will be from China or India. *The Times of India*. Retrieved from http://timesofindia.indiatimes.com/home/education/news/By-2024-1-in-3-foreign-pupils-will-be-from-China-or-India/articleshow/27384158.cms (accessed on April 6, 2016).

Snehi, N. (2012). *Student mobility at tertiary level in India status, prospects and challenges*. Delhi: NUEPA.

Snehi, N. (2013). *Student Mobility at Tertiary Level in India: Status, Prospects and Challenges* (p. 36). New Delhi: NUEPA.

UNESCO. (n.d.). *Global flow*. Retrieved from http://www.uis.unesco.org/Education/Pages/international-student-flow-viz.aspx (accessed on April 6, 2016).

Varghese, N. V. (2008). *Globalization of higher education and cross-border student mobility*. Paris, France: International Institute for Educational Planning (UNESCO) Printshop.

Yeravdekar, V. R., & Tiwari, G. (2012). *Higher education institutions in India: Perceptions of international students*. SSRN. Retrieved from http://ssrn.com/abstract=2156800 (accessed on April 6, 2016).

Yeravdekar, V. R. (2012). *Internationalization of higher education in India* (Unpublished doctoral dissertation). Pune, India: Symbiosis International University.

7

India's "Soft Power" and Internationalization

Internationalization of higher education is an indomitable instrument of "soft power," a consideration that drives home the point that internationalization is not merely, as is frequently misperceived to be, the enrolment of international students but that it also refers to the capability to influence other's behavior through the employment of noncoercive factors. In referring to noncoercive factors, one refers to all those processes and institutions that are related to sociocultural, entrepreneurial, behavioral, intellectual, and educational outcomes. The concept of "soft power" has been applied to the study of diplomacy and international relations by many academics (Nye, 2005). In the context of national foreign policy, "soft power" refers to those resources that alter a country's ability to influence another country's decision-making processes through persuasion, inducement, and enticement. This definition marks a distinction from what might be construed as "hard power," which refers to the capability to influence through the use of coercive force that may be exercised by means such as military establishments and trade sanctions. It is self-evident that the two offer means of influence that vary greatly in respect of objectives, resources that are employed in the service of goals, impact on the receiving entity, and the risk of loss and unexpected outcomes.

It would be a long list that catalogs all the possible indicators of a country's "soft power" resources, but the following items may serve to give the reader an impression of the nature of these resources: the number of international patents, popular tourist sites and attractions, participation in international sports competition, presence in global rankings of universities, number of international students in institutions, number of internationally renowned academicians and researchers, number of people who speak English, and number of Internet users.

All the above-denoted resources have in common an element of international prominence, which suggests that they are factors of globalization. Higher education features extensively in writings on the subject (Nye, 2004). A country's higher education system's visibility on and the involvement with the global higher education scene is one of the important markers of its "soft power." Although India has inadvertently been privileged on that front, it has not done enough to harness that resource, as can be gathered from previous discussions. However, the Indian Government has recently undertaken many initiatives that mark a welcome shift. What follows is by no means a directory of such efforts; rather, it is a compilation of some representative examples.

The Indian Higher Education System's Contribution to Capacity-building in Neighboring Countries

India's contribution to capacity-building through higher education, especially in neighboring countries, greatly influences India's soft power. The importance of this contribution lies in that it is superior to financial aid, the traditional mode of assistance. Higher education enhances the human capital base, which is self-generative and sets into motion a range of developmental cycles that are inexhaustible. This explains why capacity-building through higher education is encouraged by the United Nations and amongst countries of the "South." The underlying idea is that the expansion of the knowledge base, the human resource, takes place primarily through higher education.

Developing countries, in general, suffer from major lapses in their higher education systems. Although the Indian higher education system is ridden with problems of its own, there are ways in which it can contribute to building knowledge and innovation bases in neighboring countries. In fact, India has been doing this since ancient times, as discussed earlier. This was interrupted in the Middle Ages and during the British Rule, but the trend was revived after Independence.

As has always been the case, majority of students who come to India are from the neighboring countries. Powar (2012, p. 243) notes that these students form the overwhelming majority (95%). These countries are struggling on many fronts, and along with economic challenges come gaps in higher education. Probably, the worst of it is that the higher education system does not serve the (goal of) knowledge economy. Streams that are directly skill enhancing and career oriented, such as engineering, management, and medicine, are the worst afflicted.

Although the Indian system has been able to overcome this challenge to some extent and is on its way to greater resolution in the future, thanks mainly to private institutions, such is not the case with the systems in developing countries that are India's neighbors. In developing countries, it would be very difficult, not merely prohibitively expensive, to build higher education capacity from the grounds up. Cross-border higher education offers a healthy compromise; it can allow these countries to expand their skill base and promote global career competencies in the workforce without taking precious investment away from other fundamental developmental areas (Lane 2011, cited in Lane & Kinser, 2011b).

In India, the inbound mobility of students from neighboring countries is diverse in respect of student profiles. In addition to students who come to India on their own, there are those who are supported by their governments, frequently contractually bound to return to the home country and to work on predetermined projects. As discussed elsewhere, scholarships given by the Indian Government, as the host country, and those by the sending countries are also aimed at encouraging students to undertake education in subjects that are of importance from the developmental standpoint.

India's strong reputation as a provider of quality higher education and the presence of the Indian diaspora continue to strengthen the trend. The Indian Government, cognizant of the opportunities herein, has recently undertaken several initiatives to increase India's role in enhancing skill base in neighboring countries, examples include the COPIE by the MHRD (Powar, 2002, 22) and the Ministry of Overseas Indian Affairs' "Scholarship Programme for Diaspora Children" (Know India, 2012, cited by the Ministry of Overseas Indian Affairs) and scholarships offered by the ICCR (Powar, 2013, 22).

Awareness about India as a host country also derives from the success that the alumni community brings back with it to the sending country. Education from an Indian institution is held in high esteem in many countries by both higher education institutions and employers. Many countries in Asia and Africa have track records of leaders in government, academe, and businesses who completed their higher education in India—this greatly favors the reputation of the Indian higher education system.

Yeravdekar and Tiwari (2014, p. 377) cite a report on international students who successfully completed undergraduate or postgraduate degree from a higher education institution in Pune. The report demonstrates that these students are, statistically speaking, likely to emerge as high-achieving members of the workforce and as entrepreneurs back in their respective home countries. Many of them hold leadership positions in their area of work (S. Mandore, personal communication, October 14, 2013).

> It is common knowledge that a number of heads of states and political leaders in Asia and Africa completed higher education in India, for instance Aung San Suu Kyi, (Vijetha, 2012) and Hamid Karzai (Kanwar, 2003). It would be reasonable to square the success of these students as leaders and members of the workforce with the employability and value-addition aspects of their higher education. (cited in Yeravdekar & Tiwari, 2014, p. 377)

Whereas the benefits in the sphere of knowledge base and career competencies are more observable, those that are related to socio-political attitudes and institutions are less so. Iniguez (2011, cited in Yeravdekar and Tiwari 2014c) has discussed the role that international education can play in fostering progressive outlooks. India boasts solid democratic and secular processes and institutions, which can be brought over to the source countries through international education (Agarwal, n.d.a; Gaur, 2006, cited in Yeravdekar & Tiwari, 2014, p. 377).

The Government's policy on promoting India as a host country is inspired by philanthropic and representational motivations, but most important of all, it is

> related to its overall diplomatic and ambassadorial status (Sharma, 2008; Tharoor, 2012). The notion of "soft power" (cf. Nye, 2005) and its application to the Indian context by Tharoor (2012) upholds the case about the possibility of improving higher education networks that strengthen India's brand standing, especially in the "South Asian Region" as provider of cross-border higher education and leader in knowledge creation and dissemination. (cf. Whitaker, 2004, cited in Yeravdekar & Tiwari, 2014, p. 377)

Whereas inbound mobility of international students is a more prominent mode of student mobility, more recently, Indian branch campuses in Asian countries have grown in terms of both reputation and enrolment, as has been discussed in detail in this book. Further, it is remarkable that almost all of them are managed and owned privately. It would be fair to maintain that Indian institutions, especially those in the private sector, are poised to increasingly contribute to the growth of human capital base in neighboring countries, and to India's "soft power."

The Ministry of External Affairs, Government of India, and the Indira Gandhi National Open University: Winning Contributors to "South-South" Cooperation

The MEA, Government of India, is entrusted with the responsibility of planning and executing many initiatives related to "South–South cooperation" in the realm of higher education. India's development partnerships have come to acquire a central position in the country's foreign diplomacy, as is the case with most developing nations. It has been pointed out that the MEA's efforts do not take place in sufficient conjunction with MHRD, particularly the UGC, and that this disjunction takes away from the optimization of the fruits of the partnership. The MEA brings about development activities mainly through bilateral and multilateral partnerships. The contributions of the Indian Technical and Economic Cooperation (ITEC) merit note in the discussion. The ITEC was instituted in 1964 as a program of bilateral assistance in trade and finance, capacity-building in health and education, public–private partnerships, private sector, culture, and media. More recently, the MEA added Development Partnership Administration, a new division, to streamline India's projects that are related to bilateral and multilateral collaborations. This development is significant because the need for the South–South cooperation has been voiced with renewed energy in international forums such as the United Nations—the United Nations Development Program (UNDP), in particular, is a case in point. Indeed, regional cooperation is a crucial instrument in achieving the Millennium Development Goals (MDG), and India is increasingly being recognized as occupying a position of headship in development projects. The emergence of developing economies and the reduction in official development assistance (ODA) from developed countries mark the beginning of a new paradigm in the South–South cooperation.

The Pan African E-network Project: A "shining example" of initiatives related to the "South–South cooperation" is the Pan African e-network project, which links Indian universities (and hospitals) with their counterparts in 11 African countries. The project was conceived by then President Dr A. P. J. Kalam, formally announced in 2004, and approved by the Union Cabinet in July 2007. These 11 African countries are Ethiopia, Senegal, Seychelles, Benin, Gabon, The Gambia, Mauritius, Nigeria, Rwanda, Ghana, and Burkina Faso. These countries are part of the first phase of the project, which is likely to be expanded to interlink the offices of the heads of state of all the 53 African countries. India has also made a gift of a satellite for e-connectivity in the sub-Saharan region to help bridge the digital divide. The seven Indian institutions that were initially associated with the project are Indian Institute of Science, Amity University, University of Madras, (IGNOU), Birla Institute of Technology and Science, University of Delhi, and IIT Kanpur. For more details, see Box 7.1.

Box 7.1   Tele-education as part of the Pan African e-Network Project

India, in collaboration with the African Union, launched tele-education as part of the Pan African e-network project in 2004. This project is funded by the Government of India with an approved budgeted cost of ₹5.429 billion (USD 117 million), and managed by the MEA. The project provides tele-education services to 53 African countries for a period of five years. It makes provision to cover the costs of supply, installation, testing and commissioning of hardware and software, end-to-end connectivity, satellite bandwidth, and operations and maintenance support.

The tele-education connectivity enables five African "regional leading universities" to be connected to the hub in Africa through 53 "remote virtual classes" distributed in all the 53 countries. At India's end, five universities are connected to the hub. India hosts a tele-education Learning Management System portal, which comprises the university tele-education delivery system software that incorporates e-Learning, content management KMS (knowledge management system), and digital library solutions for each university as an integrated package. The content management software is flexible, scalable, and configurable. The African universities are able to configure and generate their own local content designed for local need. Each regional university has the ability to host its own local content on its own servers. The tele-education systems can integrate with different modes of learning within the African universities. The e-learning platform is able to source for e-learning content in other areas based on requirement.

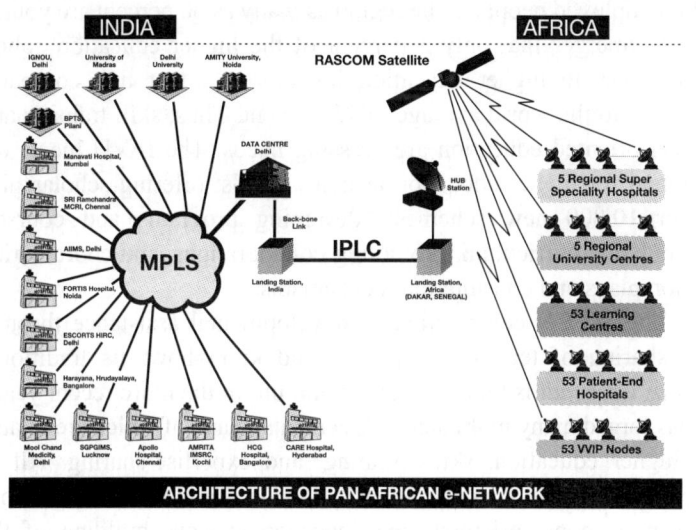

Source: http://www.tcil-india.com/new/success_stories1.php

India–Africa Virtual University (IAVU) Project: The Indian Government has engaged IGNOU to forge many partnerships in the spirit of the "South–South cooperation." The IGNOU would seem a fair choice as the leading publicly funded distance education Indian university. The IGNOU was engaged to implement the IAVU Project in May 2010. The proposal to establish the IAVU, born out of the encouraging success of the Pan African e-project, was initiated by the MEA, and IGNOU was invited to draft the blueprint and the implementation rubric. The guiding idea in all this was to strengthen Indo-African relations through higher education. In order to ensure that maximal yield could be harvested from the resources, the virtual university targeted programs in areas of developmental relevance, such as health sciences, vocational training, food and nutrition, security, and gender empowerment.

The initial cost of this project was estimated to be around USD3.5 million and the annual cost was not much less than the initial. An investment of this magnitude might be the minimal requirement after all, given how mammoth the challenge is: Africa has 7–10 million young people in the job market demographic, and of the total strength of unemployed people in the region as many as 60 percent are young.

It emerges that only 5 percent of the higher education cohort has access to higher education institution, a fact that compares pitifully to the world average of 25 percent. Thus, skill training and career-oriented education are pressing needs. The IAVU meets the demand for higher education at many levels: offering scholarships (over 10,000 new schemes), designing programs and courses, formulating curriculum, promoting collaborations, and coordinating action plans and consultation mechanisms.

The ITEC's contribution to developmental assistance through the sharing of technical expertise and know-how: Its traditional *modus operandi* is bilateral agreement, but in the more recent years, it has forged many multilateral agreements, many of which are related to higher education, skills-training, and expertise-sharing. All of the initiatives that are undertaken by the ITEC are directive, demand-driven, response-oriented, and focus on capacity-building of the partnering developing nation. The ITEC, along with the Special Commonwealth Assistance for Africa Programme, its accompanying initiative, covers 158 countries across Asia, Africa, Latin America, Central and Eastern Europe, and several Pacific and Caribbean nations. Since its inception, the program has spent over USD 2 billion, with an average annual expenditure of over USD 100 million in recent years. A big part of ITEC's work pertains to offering training courses that empower the recipients with professional skills that are not available in their own country, thereby bringing global advances to their doorsteps. The ITEC has its service at 47 empanelled institutions that conduct 280 courses of varying durations throughout the year. Some of the popular subjects include accounts, banking, finance, audits, telecommunication, English, rural development, environment, and renewable energy resources.

For the civilian training program, 8,280 slots have been allocated to ITEC/SCAAP partner countries in 2013–14. Similarly, many training programs have been undertaken for defense personnel from ITEC's partner countries in specialized areas such as security and strategic studies, defense management, marine and aeronautical engineering, and logistics management. The majority of these programs are undertaken at National Defence College and Defence Service Staff College.

Some additional characteristics of the projects include the following:

1. Project-related cooperation: India assists ITEC's partner countries through many mutually agreed projects, such as feasibility studies and consultancy services, in areas as wide ranging as from archaeological restoration to IT.

2. Deputation of Indian experts: Indian subject experts are routinely deputed to ITEC's partner countries to lend their expertise on subjects related to developmental capacity-building. Popular subjects include the teaching of the English language, telecommunications, financial management, agriculture, and IT.

3. Study tours: Several study tours are organized at the request of ITEC's partner countries. Once the subject is identified, a program of 2–3 weeks is organized, during which the delegates are taken to important institutions, training centers, and places of interest in India.

The ICCR and its Contribution to Inbound International Student Mobility The ICCR was founded in 1950 by Maulana Abul Kalam Azad, India's first education minister. It was set up by way of a centralized agency to formulate and implement policies and programs pertaining to

> India's external cultural relations; to foster and strengthen cultural relations and mutual understanding between India and other countries; to promote cultural exchanges with other countries and people; and to develop relations with national and international organizations in the field of culture. (ICCR, n.d.)

In order to promote awareness of India's cultural heritage abroad, the Council has 35 Indian cultural centers in different parts of the world. These centers function under the administrative control of the Council and the respective Indian missions abroad.

The ICCR's chief lever of promotion of internationalization is disbursement of scholarships to international students. The ICCR annually offers about 3,365 scholarships under 24 scholarship schemes. Of these scholarships, 1,000 are exclusively for the students of Afghanistan and 900 for students from African countries. International students in India, who benefit from these scholarship schemes, come from about 135 countries. Most of the scholarship holders come from developing countries such as Asia, Africa, and South and Central America. However, there are quite a few students from developed countries as well. The ICCR scholarship holders form a big chunk of the total population of about 4,750 international students who are supported by scholarships.

In addition to scholarships, the ICCR partners with developing countries through academic collaborations and helps in

> establishing and maintaining chairs and professorships for Indian studies abroad; presentation of books, audio-visual material, art objects and musical instruments; annual organisation of the Maulana Azad Memorial Lecture and Maulana Azad Essay Competition; and organisation of other programmes on behalf of the MEA. In addition, the ICCR has several publications, organises and participates in international seminars and symposia, and does other such activities. (CII-AIU, 2014, p. 48)

References

CII-AIU. (2014). *Trends in internationalization of higher education of India.* Retrieved from http://www.cii.in/PublicationDetail.aspx?enc=j+Bre1cnEnR 7Sgogrka6KohkwpLy3x9ujfczyTnGBH8Pk1aE4ly77FRtKBZo0YzFi VaGJLen1cG0O7iLKWe0szJJQOYv17//p9oCvxp9Ll (accessed on April 6, 2016).

ICCR. (n.d.). *Welcome to our universe of education.* Retrieved from http://www. iccrindia.net/students.html (accessed on April 6, 2016).

Lane, J., & Kinser, K. (2011a). *Multinational colleges and universities: Leading, governing, and managing international branch campuses.* San Francisco: Wiley Publications.

————. (2011b). The cross-border education policy context: Educational hubs, trade liberalization, and national sovereignty. *Multinational colleges and universities: Leading, governing, and managing international branch campuses. 2011*(155), 79–85, doi: 10.1002/he.446.

Nye, J. (2005). *Soft power: The means to success in world politics.* New York: Public Affairs.

Powar, K. B. (2002). *Indian higher education: A conglomerate of concepts, facts and practices.* New Delhi, India: Concept Publishing Company.

————. (2012). *Expanding domains in Indian higher education.* New Delhi, India: Association of Indian Universities Publications.

————. (2013). *Understanding internationalization of higher education.* Pune: DY Patil.

Telecommunications Consultants India Limited. (2015). Pan African e-Network Project. Retrieved from http://www.tcil-india.com/new/success_stories1. php (accessed on July 19, 2016).

Whitaker, A. M. (2004). *The Internationalization of higher education: A US perspective.* Retrieved January 17, 2013 from http://scholar.lib.vt.edu/ theses/available/etd-06202004-192329/unrestricted/WhitakerMP.pdf

Yeravdekar, V. R., & Tiwari, G. (2014). Internationalization of higher education in India: Contribution to regional capacity building in neighbouring countries. *Procedia – Journal of Social and Behavioral Sciences, 157*, 373–380. doi:10.1016/j.sbspro.2014.11.042

8

Internationalization of Higher Education in India: The Way Forward

Powar (2015, pp. 206–08) points out that the Indian Government's chief approach to improving internationalization has been to increase inbound mobility. If we were to put this consideration at the center of the discussion, then we would be presented with the abject failure of the Indian Government to achieve internationalization.

The Indian higher education system has grown phenomenally. The number of universities has increased from 266 in 2000–01 to 762 at the end of 2014. Similarly, the number of students has increased from 8.4 million to about 23.76 million (UGC, n.d.).

During this period, the number of international students across the globe has increased from 2.1 million in 2001 to 4.5 million in 2014.

The increase in figures for inbound international students in India is discouraging: from 7000 in 2000–01 (Powar, 2003) to 30,000 in 2012–13 (AISHE, 2015). In India, international students comprise only 0.1 percent of the total number of students in the Indian higher education system. The corresponding figure is 1.0 percent for China, 3.7 percent for the US, 19.0 percent for the UK, and 21.4 for Australia. Furthermore, the ratio of inbound to outbound mobility is 1:10 (Powar, 2015, p. 207)

The present pace of "massification" of higher education forces institutions of higher learning as well as governments and supranational

agencies to circumscribe the core concepts of excellence and differentiation at the global level, and no less. To fall short would result in
the threat of unsustainability and irrelevance in the long run. Sadlak
and Cai (2009, p. 14) cite a report by OECD (2008), which suggests
that virtually every country that wishes to "retain its competitive
edge" must implement policies and economic incentives to facilitate
"acquisition of such 'knowledge workers'." This translates into a
"global competition for talent and universities." The authors note
that there is another realm where international competitiveness in
higher education is increasingly exerting significance: "top level
intellectuals, entrepreneurs, researchers and artists are important
players on the global stage, in that they represent tremendous 'soft
power' sectors active in the practice of globally interdependent
relations" (p.15). Thus, international competitiveness is a goal that is
worthy on many counts. It makes possible excellence in academics
and research, it prepares a world-class "workforce," and it enhances
the country's "soft power."

All maturing knowledge economies show evidence of efforts
to produce higher education institutions that are internationally
competitive. Japan's "Twenty-first Century of Excellence Programme"
and "World Premier International Research Centre Initiative,"
China's "Project 985," South Korea's "Brain Korea 21," Malaysia's
"Accelerated Programme for Excellence (APEX)," Germany's
"Excellence Initiative," and France's "Super Campus" are cases in
point (Sadlak and Cai, p. 16).

The picture that presents internationalization of higher education
in India is not bright. The recent advances in respect of internationalization are a gift of the entrepreneurial spirit of the private sector.
These forward leaps in the private sector are not mirrored in public
institutions and are not a function of the public policy on higher
education. The achievements are unchanneled, disengaged from the
Indian Government's interests, and one might even go so far as to
say that the former have occurred in spite of the obstructionism
posed by the latter.

The Indian Government, eventually waking up to the development
in neighboring countries, did make some efforts in the pursuit of
world-class universities. The Planning Commission, in the Eleventh

Five Year Plan (2007–12)[1] broadcast its intent to attract global talent through public–private partnership.[2] At the core of this is the mandate by MHRD to set up 14 "innovation universities[3] aiming at world class standards."[4] The "innovation universities" are to be developed as "Global Centers of Innovation" in identified cities.[5] These centers are to be, for all intents and purposes, India's education hubs wherein higher education and other bodies will, purportedly contribute to the cause of interdisciplinary education, entrepreneurship, and research and development in a concerted fashion (Government of India, n.d.).[6]

The MHRD's world-class universities project has been the object of scathing criticism. The higher education system in India is grounded in an ecosystem that cannot sustain world-class universities, not at least in the near future, even if the IITs figure on the list now and again. If one were to consider a scenario where world class universities are a reality, one could not be certain of the universities' longevity and the extent to which they would successfully serve the developmental needs of the country. The Indian higher education system is overburdened and overregulated—its challenges are rooted in the ongoing crisis of belonging in a developing country and in bearing the burden of a long colonial past.

What, then, is the way forward? India's unique realities are such as to necessitate uncommon solutions—merely copying the world-class university template from the Western countries will not serve. The top-ranking global universities are essentially research universities—research is central to their idea of benchmarking and performance. The Indian higher education system serves an entirely different set of wants. Its goal of access, equity, and excellence is based on exigencies that bear no resemblance to the requirements in the developed countries. Salmi (2009, cited in Sadlak and Cai, 2009, p. 28) divides all the complementary factors that go into building academic excellence in higher education institutions, "a high concentration of talent (faculty and students)," "abundant resources," and "favourable governance." These categories should be seen for what they are—broad generalizations that can take in specific recommendations suited to meet the challenges of a higher education system. If one were to tease apart the broad causes of the challenges with respect to international competitiveness in the Indian higher education system along Salmi's (n.d., cited in Sadlak and Cai, 2009, p. 28) three categories, one would be inclined to weigh in the following.

Far too often, internationalization is about the "bricks and mortar" and not enough about the life force of academe, the professoriate. A university that claims to meet international standards must have internationally competitive professoriate. Among the factors that allow an institution to draw internationally competitive faculty members, compensation features prominently. The challenges in this regard are daunting, as has been discussed at length elsewhere in the book.

Specific Ways to Improve Inbound Mobility of International Students

At the risk of belaboring the point, it must be emphasized that inbound mobility of international students in India is beneficial on many counts. International students bring with them certain unique advantages in respect of multicultural perspective and regional sensibilities.

> [International students are] one of the most important elements of the international knowledge system . . . They are the carriers of knowledge across orders . . . They are the embodiment of the cosmopolitan culture. . . . (and they) are one of the most visible and important parts of the worldwide exchange of knowledge. (Altbach, 1989, p. 126, cited in CII-AIU, 2014, p. 8)

These advantages open the window onto a world of opportunities that enhance the higher education institution's profile with respect to skill-based education, brand's global marketability, and institutional revenue model.

Although the task of bringing in internationalization to any higher education system is massive, pervading across every conceivable aspect of the system, the specific goal of achieving improved inbound mobility is more workable. There are identifiable ways that help draw in international students in a targeted fashion. These factors are no different from those that contribute to international competitiveness; rather, these factors home in on attracting international students more pointedly.

Institutional Approaches: In light of the consideration that much of what was recommended by UGC and AIU to promote inbound international mobility in India has not generated positive outcome, one is encouraged to look to other pathways.

One of the failed approaches has been to focus on degree programs. The Indian Government must shift the focus to short-term certificate programs, especially in streams such as the English language and computer applications. Similarly, study abroad programs and Study in India programs must be promoted preferentially.

Powar (2015, pp. 207–08) points that the noninclusion of international student mobility for learning as a government priority, as indicated in the paper on "National Priorities" submitted to the International Education Summit 2012, has been a major disincentive in respect of the efforts to improve inflow of international students into India.

Infrastructural resources rank high on the international students' checklist. Infrastructure support covers a wide range of amenities, facilities, and services: campus premises, classrooms, laboratories, library, sports and extracurricular resources.

Student-friendly administrative services go a long way in attracting international students. The key is to streamline the many administrative hoops that students, especially international students, need to jump during the length of their stay in India. The administrative system that overlooks student services in Indian institutions is encumbered with endless red tape and slow-moving bureaucratic machinery. As has been discussed earlier, many such shortfalls are a result of India's long colonial heritage. The colonists governed the country by the means of an extensive and hierarchical latticework of bureaucratic office-bearers, who established a "rule of bureaucracy" in the interest of self-preservation. The challenges with respect to the bureaucratic nature of administrative services in Indian institutions are really remnants from the past. It hurts us because all over the world, including many Asian countries to our east and southeast, institutions have made big strides in modernizing administrative services.

Centralized admission processes that are routed from an admission office are helpful to international students. Online processing of admissions is also very helpful. These are really the mainstay in the developed countries, but India is just beginning to waken to them.

On the subject of admission, it would be relevant to point out that Indian institutions, both public and private, must increase the number of reserved seats for international students. A very large chunk of our international students are from low and lower middle income countries. While a sizeable segment of this group is aided by scholarships, many international students make do on their own. Higher education institutions and the Indian Government must offer more by way of waiver of or cut back on tuition fees to attract international students.

Bringing in internationalization to the academic component of higher education is complex but important. It is about time Indian institutions incorporated modern advances in pedagogical practices. The Indian curriculum is frequently criticized for being too centered on the Indian side of things and for not keeping step with the newer finding and approaches to curriculum content as well as to teaching–learning processes. Indian universities must also restructure their academic programs to incorporate choice-based credit system along with the provision for the transfer of credits. Instructional technology is also an area of neglect in Indian institutions, for instance, online classroom portals and webinars are employed as a matter of course in developed countries, but Indian institutions that utilize these methods are not in the majority in doing so. A judicious balance of classroom teaching and modern education delivery methods is the way to go. It is important to point out that streams in "professional education," such as computer applications, management education, media and communication, and engineering, are in even greater need for revision to bring them up-to-date with all that is internationally competitive.

There is no way to achieve internationalization without collaborating with foreign institutions. Academic exchanges are a great way to collaborate with foreign institutions, as are partnering through memorandums of understanding, guest lectures, and joint programs. There is something to be said for in-person exchanges with academics from foreign countries. In the absence of such collaborations, meaningful internationalization is not a possibility. Academics, both students and teaching staff, from foreign countries bring with them their perspectives and experiences, which go a long way in internationalizing the ethos of an institution.

Powar (2015) points out that many Indian institutions of international standing were set up through massive financial and academic assistance by foreign institutions: institutions in the US assisted in the establishment of IIT Kanpur in 1959; G. B. Pant University of Agriculture and Technology in 1960; IIM Calcutta in 1961; and IIM Ahmadabad in 1962. Similarly, institutions in erstwhile the USSR helped set up IIT Bombay in 1958 and IIT Kharagpur in 1961. Institutions in the UK assisted in the setting up of IIT Delhi in 1963. Institutions in erstwhile West Germany helped set up IIT (Madras) in 1959. BITS (Pilani) was developed in association with MIT (US) and received assistance from the Ford Foundation Grant. The Indian School of Business (Hyderabad) was set up in 2005 in partnership with the Kellogg School, the Wharton School, and the London School of Business.

At present, international collaboration in Indian institutions takes place mainly through articulation arrangements that involve study on two campuses—the majority of the period being spent in the institution in India and the remaining in the institution abroad. Typically, the Indian institution provides the core infrastructural and faculty-related support and the foreign institution provides miscellaneous support, such as equipment for laboratory and hands-on training. The majority of these programs do not have full statutory backing in either India or the home country; therefore, articulation programs frequently take the form of transfer of credits from the Indian to the foreign institution.

Powar (2015) lists several noteworthy programs that facilitate international collaborations with Indian institutions: Erasmus Mundus (EU), UKIERI (UK), and OSKI (US).

The USIEF (US) administers many programs including the Fulbright–Nehru Fellowships, the Hubert H. Humphrey Fellowships, Ford Foundation International Fellowships, New Century Scholar program, and Indo–American Environmental Leadership program.

The Indo–US Science and Technology Forum (IUSSTF) promotes Indo–American bilateral collaborations in research in science and technology.

The Indo–US Collaboration for Engineering Education (IUCEF) promotes engineering education through learning-centered teaching, excellence in research, outcomes-based quality, and innovation and entrepreneurship.

The International Academic Partnership Program (IAPP), funded by the US Department of Education, implemented through the Center for International Partnerships in Higher Education (CIPHE) of IIE, funds and assists American institutions in establishing joint programs, student exchanges, and faculty mobility for collaborative research and teaching (Powar, 2015, pp. 210–12).

Powar (2015, p. 208) points out that faculty mobility in India is primarily an institutional and individualistic initiative, but it is promoted extensively by international programs. Some of these are Fulbright program (US), UKIERI, the Erasmus Mundus program (EU), and the Obama–Singh Knowledge Initiative.

Similarly, collaboration in research has been undertaken mostly through individual initiative. In recent years, institutional collaboration in research has gained some prominence. Research and innovation are particularly significant for a developing country like India. To state the obvious, the collaborator in the developed country shoulders most of the weight of investments and other resources. It is also observed that the institution in the developed country takes the lead in framing and organizing the research project, and the institution in the developing country follows the lead.

A number of Memoranda of Understanding have been signed between Indian institutions and foreign institutions in the last few years. The majority of these institutions are located in the US, the UK, Germany, Australia, Korea, Japan, Taiwan, and Singapore. A very large percentage of these memoranda have been initiated through the Fulbright–Nehru Research Fellowships, Erasmus Mundus program, and UKIERI.

The Indian Government has signed on many agreements that are categorized as cultural exchanges in order to facilitate and coordinate exchange of scholars. Many such exchanges are mediated through ICCR, Indian Council for Social Science Research (ICSSR), and UGC.

The teaching of the English language is an integral function of a higher education institution that is international. English is undoubtedly the reigning medium of instruction in international education. The English language has continued to grow in significance and usage, and this trend is here to stay. This necessitates that training in the English language be offered to those international students who need it.

The majority of international students who come to India are from countries where English is not the first language. This poses obvious challenge as English is the medium of instruction in most, if not all, institutions that draw international students to India. Many international students do not do well in their coursework on account of lack of proficiency in English. Many prospective international students are discouraged to apply to Indian institutions for the fear of not being able to cope with the relatively high level of fluency in the English language prevalent amongst the students and teaching staff in Indian institutions.

Higher education institutions, both public and private, are encouraged to avail many opportunities related to scholarships, fellowships, and chairs. A large number of these opportunities are made available through ICCR. During the year 2014, ICCR gave 6,252 scholarships to international students at 146 universities. It also distributes "junior-level" fellowships (to scholars undertaking doctoral studies) and "senior-level" fellowships (to eminent scholars) to scholars who pursue academic interests in the Indian culture and related subjects. In 2014, four fellowships were awarded in either of the two categories. The ICCR has set up 100 chairs for Indian studies in various foreign universities. Moreover, the Indian Government hosts 10 UNESCO chairs (Powar, 2015, pp. 208–09).

Distance Education is another area of neglect. Countries that boast substantial population of the Indian Diaspora must be targeted for expansion of distance education. Many open universities and others that follow dual-mode education have expanded by setting up centers in East Africa, the Gulf region, and SAARC countries. The IGNOU, which has set up 300 study centers, presents some exemplary practices. The Pan-African tele-education project has been discussed earlier. Nanda (2011) points out that a Pan-SAARC e-network project is also in the offing (cited in Powar, 2015, p. 210). The setting up of branch campuses is an area for exploration, although, as has been suggested earlier, it is one that requires much caution and preparation. The closing of many branch campuses of Indian home institutions must be borne in mind as forewarning of possible outcomes as a result of overly enthusiastic goals that were not supported by sufficient groundwork. Also true is that many branch campuses have done well and generated both profit and brand standing. It goes without saying that the presence of home institution abroad brings copious prestige and adds to the international competitiveness. The International Academic City, Dubai, hosts Amity University, BITS Pilani, J. S. Education Foundation, Manipal University, S. P. Institute, and Welingkar Institute. Ras al Khaimah hosts Madurai Kamraj University and Mahatma Gandhi University. By the way, Mahatma Gandhi University has branch campuses in Qatar, Bahrain, Kuwait, and Oman. Furthermore, BITS Mesra operates in Oman, Manipal University in Nepal, Malaysia, and Antigua in West Indies, and Amity University in US, UK, China, and Singapore (Powar, 2015, p. 213).

The significance of extracurricular activities cannot be overstated in promoting internationalization. Some instances of successful initiatives in this regard are the Association of Indian Universities' International Youth Festivals for SAARC countries and the Symbiosis International Universities' International Students Day.

Public Policy Oriented Approaches

The countries that have succeeded, even if partially, in bringing internationalization to their higher education systems exhibit a keen willingness on the part of their respective governments to undertake internationalization of higher education as a matter of high priority public policy. As has been discussed earlier, most of the countries from the Anglophone world advocate and practise internationalization of higher education through clearly defined channels of public policy. The goals and guidelines to undertake are public statements that are shared and discussed with all participating higher education institutions. The UK, Australia, Canada, New Zealand, and many other countries—English speaking and otherwise—promote internationalization through expressly stated mandates. CII-AIU (2014, p. 12) cites some examples,

> The "100,000 initiatives" of the US, and the British Council's "Generation UK" programme covering 15,000 students (both of which target China), are excellent examples. According to statistics released by the European Commission in 2012–13, a record of 270,000 students received Erasmus Grants for study abroad, with the most popular destinations being Spain, Germany and France. Erasmus+, launched in 2014 with a budget of Euro 15 billion will provide, over the next seven years until 2020, grants to 4 million people including 2 million higher education students and 300,000 staff (European Commission, 2014). Brazil and Saudi Arabia have programmes supporting the mobility of thousands of students while a few other countries have less ambitious programmes. These government-sponsored programmes, though they form only a small part of the total flow of international students, are important (Altbach & Engberg, 2014), because they send out a message of support.

On the whole, there is a trend of liberalization of policies in the spirit of inclusiveness and positive affirmation all across the world. Many countries in North America and Western Europe go as far as to make it easy for international students to apply and process immigration formalities (CII-AIU, 2014, p. 12). International students go through a trying ordeal with respect to securing the visa and completing other travel and registration formalities. There is a glaring need to simplify these processes. The Indian Government must collaborate with foreign embassies and aim for a close-knitted and more harmonious interplay between MHRD, Ministry of External Affairs, Ministry of Overseas Indian Affairs, UGC, AIU, higher education institutions, and the law and order officials to ensure that all the processes and activities with respect to international students are orchestrated smoothly and efficiently. An important point is that, in many countries that have successfully implemented public policy on internationalization, it is noted that the ministry of commerce (or whatever the stand-in might be) is brought into the sphere of activities pertaining to internationalization of higher education. This is not the case in

India. It has been stressed previously in the book that international students bring many gains to the economy, both at the national and regional lev ⸻ ɔ this in many ways. As opposed to what is commonly ⸺ ʋ, the most important contribution of international students t⸺ economy is not that they pay higher tuition fees than their domestic counterpart, but it is that they help generate ancillary businesses around their institution. These students participate with gusto in the activities related to the student life and the financial aspects of doing so. Further, the Indian tourism industry is certain to benefit from international students too.

Higher education, in the context of globalization, is increasingly being subject to the influence of brand management and promotion. Institutions have no choice but to embrace this reality. Thus, it becomes imperative that institutions work on increasing awareness about their services and offer that which is asked for. This, in turn, necessitates investment in feasibility studies to explore and evaluate potentially new avenues. As has been discussed previously, the present is an exciting time for those who want to discover and seize unchartered territories. Indian institutions have much to gain from surveying possibilities in the more recent modes of cross-border higher education, such as offshore branch centers, distance education, and MOOCs. It emerges that private institutions have taken the lead on this front in India—it would be more accurate to hold that such initiatives have come exclusively from private institutions, the lone exception being IGNOU's contributions to distance education in Africa. It is easy to explain why it should be that way. Private institutions are not as burdened with the stifling rigidity that is the affliction of public institutions, especially state universities, which make up the vast majority of degree-granting institutions. As has been noted earlier, the affiliating structure of state universities makes it exceedingly difficult to incorporate dynamism and innovativeness into the workings of institutions. It takes a mammoth effort to bring about the most trivial reforms into the system. These institutions are so overwhelmingly consumed with inertia and indifference that the fulfilment of rudimentary duties is all that can be expected of them—internationalization is a goal too far afield.

Concluding Thoughts: India in the Global Context

Internationalization of higher education is a definite reality of the present day globalized world. In order for any higher education system or institution to remain relevant and meaningful, it must embrace internationalization. The inextricable relationship between higher education and internationalization has been referenced all through the book; however, it would still be useful to cite Altbach and Peterson (2007, p. 111), who list the three broad ways in which this relationship is likely to not only continue but grow stronger.

> First, there is an increasingly unmet demand for higher education in the world. Second, the number and types of new providers are proliferating. With the exception of countries like the United States where there has always been a combination of public universities and private (not-for-profit) universities, public universities have been the dominant factor in most countries. But an increasing number of private and for-profit universities are entering the higher education arena at the national level (as, for instance, in Latin America), but increasingly on an international scale. Third, all kinds of innovative delivery methods of higher education are developing: e-learning, franchise operations abroad, satellite or branch campuses abroad, and joint degree programs. New terms are also evolving with this new field as, for example, transnational education and cross-border education. While the cross-border movement was primarily of people, now programs and institutions are also moving cross-border.

The above-mentioned three factors resonate with the three key themes that are interspersed across the discussion on internationalization of higher education in India in this book, namely, the urgency of "massification" of higher education in India, the emergence and lead of private participants in the higher education system in India, and the introduction of newer delivery modes of cross-border higher education in India.

It is the fact of the matter that the "economic rationale" has come to acquire the center stage in the scheme of internationalization of higher education. We can make of it what we will, but it remains that internationalization has clearly moved towards the "competitive model" (Reinalda & Kuiesza, 2005; Schapper & Mayson, 2005;

Tuinamuana, 2005, cited in Altbach & Peterson, 2007, p. 112). With this in mind, it would be wise to embrace the "economic rationale" while still holding out for the "cooperation" model, which derives from the more traditional view of higher education as a "greater good." Thus, we must find a way to weave into the fabric of internationalization the concept of what Altbach and Peterson (2007, p. 112) term as "social cohesion."

Nowhere does this idea hold more befittingly than in the case of developing countries, such as India. The ground realities of India are such as to necessitate a model that first serves the teeming masses at the broad base of the pyramid that is the higher education system. The MHRD has rightly captured the challenges and the solutions thereto in the slogan "access, equity, and excellence."

It has been discussed that the scale of the Indian government's failure in respect of "access, equity, and excellence" suggests that solution be sought outside the government's sphere of initiative.

The private sector is lauded for stepping in and rising to the challenge. Private institutions are also credited with bringing internationalization into the Indian higher education system with an unparalleled vigor and creativity. Although the private sector's contributions to internationalization are without doubt significant, this partaking rests within the subset of all round powerful engagement with the higher education system. Private institutions have their finger on the pulse of the higher education demographic in India. In comparison with their public counterparts, private institutions are more abreast with global advances in pedagogy and curriculum, are equipped with technologically more sophisticated instructional delivery methods, infrastructural facilities, and extracurricular amenities, and are more responsive to the career-preparedness aspect of higher education, which is increasingly becoming central to the value and purpose of higher education.

Private institutions are relatively free from the bindings that are imposed by the affiliating structure on public universities in India, especially, the state universities, which account for the overwhelming majority of degree-granting institutions in India. The relatively greater degree of autonomy and self-determination lend private institutions considerable latitude in engineering innovative and resourceful ways out of the deep-seated pervasive challenges that plague public institutions.

The recent forward leaps in internationalization in the private sector are not mirrored in public institutions. It would be more accurate to view this development as an aggregate of individual successes amassed from private institutions all over the country rather than a function of the public policy on higher education. The growth is largely self-directed and unchanneled, disengaged from the Indian Government's field of action. Yet, to attribute the success of private participants to the corresponding failure of the public sector, and not much else, would be highly reductive.

It is noteworthy that the make-up of public and private ownerships in higher education all over the world has undergone a paradigm shifts. It is about time that educationalists in India acknowledge and integrate this transformation into the regulatory approach. The realities of "massification" of higher education, decline in public funding, and increased competition for enrolment have created a "quasi-market situation within and between the public and private sectors" (Slaughter & Leslie, 1997; Teixeira, Dill, Jongbloed, & Amaral, 2004, cited in Altbach & Peterson, 2007, p. 79). Put otherwise, it means that the distinctions that separated public from private institutions do not hold as much as they did in the past.

In no realm of higher education in India is this transition more needed than in internationalization. Internationalization, by definition, is a protean phenomenon. It brings with it the need to respond to a large number of highly changeable variables. The regulatory structure in the Indian higher education system must overcome its reactive and unyielding stance in dealing with private institutions, which are increasingly moving inwards from the periphery to the mainstream. It is very much required that as India takes on internationalization, the regulatory bodies work by joining hands with private participants. Given that the scale of engagement in internationalization is increasingly tipping in favor of private institutions, issues in quality assurance, accreditation, and evaluation in international collaborations and international student mobility cannot be worked through without bringing private interests into the heart of the public policy on higher education.

Internationalization of higher education holds the key to much more than putting India on the global map of higher education. It is also a powerful lever of "soft power," especially with respect to India's relations with many developing countries in the Asian and African continents. The Ministry of External Affairs' recent initiatives with respect to internationalization are commendable. The South-South cooperation has been infused with new life in the recent years and India's headship role, especially in the South Asian Region, must be borne in mind as the Indian Government undertakes collaborative initiatives in higher education.

Notes

1. The discussion on India's trajectory onto knowledge economy brings into the picture the Planning Commission, an apex Government of India body, responsible for drawing up the "Five Year Plan," which is a set of objectives that guides economic planning for the subsequent five years. The Plan serves as a rubric for the direction that the national economy is to take in the succeeding years.

2. Public–Private Partnership which is defined by the Ministry of Finance thusly, partnership between a public sector entity (sponsoring authority) and a private sector entity (a legal entity in which 51% or more of equity is with the private partner/s) for the creation and/or management of infrastructure for public purpose for a specified period of time (concession period) on commercial terms and in which the private partner has been procured through a transparent and open procurement system (Urban India, 2007, p. vii).

3. Later renamed as "Innovation Universities" aiming at world class standards (http://mhrd.gov.in/schemes_he_B).

4. New Initiatives in Higher Education (http://mhrd.gov.in/schemes_he_B).

5. "Bhubaneswar in Orissa, Kochi in Kerala, Amritsar in Punjab, Greater Noida in Uttar Pradesh, Patna in Bihar, Guwahati in Assam, Kolkata in West Bengal, Bhopal in Madhya Pradesh, Gandhinagar in Gujarat, Coimbatore in Tamil Nadu, Mysore in Karnataka, Pune in Maharashtra, Visakhapatnam in Andhra Pradesh, and Jaipur in Rajasthan" (http://www.business-standard.com/article/economy-policy/setting-up-of-14-world-class-universities-gets-approval-110111100038_1.html).

6. New Initiatives in Higher Education (http://mhrd.gov.in/schemes_he_B).

References

AISHE. (2015). All India Survey on Higher Education. Government of India Ministry of Human Resource Development Department of Higher Education: New Delhi. Retrieved from http://aishe.nic.in/aishe/view Document.action;jsessionid=BB09950308D48FB94B559A9B4FDE0FF7? documentId=197 (accessed on April 6, 2016).

Altbach, P. & Peterson. (2007). *Higher education in the new century.* Rotterdam, Netherlands: Sense publications.

CII-AIU. (2014). *Trends in Internationalization of Higher Education in India.* Retrieved from http://www.cii.in/PublicationDetail.aspx?enc=j+Bre1cnEnR 7Sgogrka6KohkwpLy3x9ujfczyTnGBH8Pk1aE4ly77FRtKBZo0YzFiVaG JLen1cG0O7iLKWe0szJJQOYv17/2Ud9piEIB1wUYJCzxAaL6W6HZ0z rocFkdwNvqqO5gbqDAYy8PbqfcNF4MgwGKS4CIAGsf4gwYhRVEQ ZuVQeUSm/p9oCvxp9Ll (accessed on April 6, 2016).

Government of India. (n.d.). *Eleventh five year plan.* Retrieved from http://planningcommission.nic.in/plans/planrel/fiveyr/11th/11_v2/11th_vol2.pdf (accessed on April 6, 2016).

Powar, K. B. (2003). *Internationalisation of higher education: Focus on India.* New Delhi: Amity Press.

———. (2015). *Changing landscape of international higher education: An Indian perspective.* Pune: DY Patil.

Sadlak, J. & Cai, L.N. (2009). *The world-class university as part of a new higher education paradigm: From institutional qualities to systemic excellence.* Bucharest: UNESCO-CEPES.

University Grants Commission. (n.d.). *60th Annual report 2013-14.* New Delhi: University Grants Commission. Retrieved from http://www.ugc.ac.in/pdf news/7938259_Annual-Report-2013-14.pdf (accessed on July 20, 2016).

Urban India. (2007). *Urban India.* Retrieved from http://urbanindia.nic.in/ programme/uwss/Guideline_Scheme_IIPDF.pdf (accessed on January 23, 2013).

Index

About the Authors

Vidya Rajiv Yeravdekar, PhD, is the Principal Director of Symbiosis Society, which encompasses the Symbiosis schools and the institutions under the Symbiosis International University. A dream of her father, Padma Bhushan Dr S. B. Mujumdar, of creating 'a home away from home' for international students, Symbiosis today, has transformed itself into a multidisciplinary, multinational, multicultural International University having students from all states of India and international students from 85 different countries. The University has institutes under seven faculties viz. Management, Law, Humanities and Social Sciences, Health and Biomedical Sciences, Computer Studies, Engineering, Media Communication and Design.

Dr Yeravdekar holds a postgraduate degree in Medicine, a degree in Law, and a PhD in "Internationalization of Higher Education in India." To promote international understanding through quality education, she has brought in innovative approaches at Symbiosis International University through international collaborations with some of the top universities in the world.

Dr Yeravdekar has successfully influenced policy regulations for promoting innovative approaches to higher education in India through her appointments on various governmental bodies. She has been a member of University Grants Commission (UGC), Central Advisory Board of Education (CABE) and Indian Council for Cultural Relations (ICCR). She is also a member of the governing boards of several organizations such as Indian Institute of Mass Communication, Indian Institute of Corporate Affairs, Swarnim Gujarat Sports University, Yashwantrao Chavan Maharashtra Open University. Apart from being a member of the State Knowledge Advisory Board of Higher Education, Government of Andhra Pradesh, and the Task Team of Arts Management Strategy for Karnataka, she is also a member of many corporate bodies such as Mahratta Chamber of Commerce and Industries, Federation of Indian Chambers of Commerce and Industry (FICCI), Confederation of India Industry (CII), and not-for-profit organizations such as HK Firodiya Foundation, India International Centre (IIC), Pune International Centre (PIC), and Pune Citizens Police Foundation.

Dr Vidya has been appointed as Director on the Board of RITES Limited under Ministry of Railways, Government of India.

She has presented papers at various National and International Conferences and has numerous research publications to her credit. Dr Vidya's hard work has won her numerous awards and accolades and she is now focussed on making Symbiosis International University benchmarked amongst one of the best Universities in Asia.

Gauri Tiwari is Research Associate at Symbiosis Society, Pune. She got her Bachelor's degree from Lady Shri Ram College and her Master's degree from the University of Essex, UK. She received training in applied writing from University of California, Berkeley, and was appointed the Project Manager for the Ontario College Student Engagement Survey by the Canadian Government's Ontario Ministry of Training, Colleges, and Universities. She has taught at many community colleges in the US, including those within the Eastern Iowa Community College District, Iowa, and the Black Hawk College, Illinois. She has also worked at the Adult Education Program, which was funded by the State of Illinois in the US.